Accounting 10/12   Part II
**Accounting Systems
and Procedures**

Accounting 10/12 Part II
Accounting Systems and Procedures

M. Herbert Freeman, Ph. D.
Chairman, Business Education Department
Montclair State College
Montclair, New Jersey

J Marshall Hanna, Ed. D.
Professor of Education
The Ohio State University
Columbus, Ohio

Gilbert Kahn, Ed. D.
Professor, Business Education Department
Montclair State College
Montclair, New Jersey

GREGG DIVISION
McGraw-Hill Book Company

New York | St. Louis | Dallas | San Francisco | Toronto | London | Sydney

Accounting 10/12   Part II
Accounting Systems and Procedures

ISBN 07-022022-0   3 4 5 6 7 8 9 DODO 7 6 5 4 3 2

This book is set in Fotosetter Laurel. Chapter titles are in Standard Medium.

DESIGN: BARBARA BERT

Preface

Accounting 10/12 employs a bold new approach to traditional bookkeeping instruction to prepare students for careers in modern business. The business world is undergoing a revolution sparked by the impact of automation and the techniques of systems analysis. Manual procedures for processing data are now being supplemented or displaced by the use of machines, punched-card and punched-tape equipment, and computers. Thus emphasis must be shifted from mastering manual techniques to mastering concepts that apply to all techniques, whether data is processed by hand, machine, or computer.

The student who plans a career in business must understand concepts rather than mere mechanics, *Accounting 10/12* has been developed to meet the varying needs and objectives of business students. This is reflected in the selection and treatment of concepts, in the controlled reading level, and in the detailed explanations and the carefully constructed and numerous illustrations, which explain, reinforce, and elaborate upon the concepts taught in the textbook.

A SYSTEMS APPROACH

To ensure that students will readily grasp the accounting concepts presented, the authors have used a systems approach, which traces the flow of data in a continuous sequence from its origin to its ultimate use. The student learns that no business activity is an isolated event. He sees its significance in the sequence of events that makes up the system. This systems approach characterizes each part of the *Accounting 10/12* program.

Part One (Elements of Financial Records) takes the student through the steps of the complete accounting cycle.

Part Two (Accounting Systems and Procedures) examines systems for handling cash receipts, cash payments, purchases, and sales.

Part Three (Special Accounting Procedures) covers procedures for handling payroll, notes, depreciation, bad debts, accruals, and deferrals. The combination journal and journalless and ledgerless bookkeeping are also covered in this part.

Part Four (Business Data Processing Fundamentals) covers the four basic techniques of processing data—manual, mechanical, punched-card, and electronic.

FLEXIBLE COMPONENTS

Accounting 10/12 has a bold new format that provides a flexible arrangement for the components of the program.

Two Text Editions *Accounting 10/12* is available in a single hard-bound volume and in four soft-cover parts. As a result of this flexibility, the teacher is now able to select those components needed to meet the objectives of his course.

Two Types of Workbooks To enhance the flexibility of the program, the authors have devised two types of workbooks. Two *basic* workbooks are available: one for Parts One and Two and one for Parts Three and Four. These have study guides and the working papers for the text problems. For those who also want enrichment problems, there are four *comprehensive* workbooks, correlated with the four parts of the program.

A Four-Part Testing Program Four sets of tests (one accompanying each part) are provided free of charge to all teachers who adopt *Accounting 10/12*. Additional tests are included in the source book.

Four Practice Sets Four practice sets have been developed to provide an effective culminating activity for each part.

A Special Payroll Unit A text-workbook on payroll is available for use in those courses where Part Three is not covered.

Visual Aids Instructional transparencies, wall charts, and filmstrips enrich the presentation of principles and procedures.

Source Book and Keys *The Source Book and Key for Accounting 10/12* provides extensive teaching aids. It suggests what materials should be selected in terms of students' objectives and how to present these in the time available. Keys are available for the text questions and cases, the workbooks, the tests, and the practice sets. They have been prepared so that teachers who wish to project any part of a key can easily make transparencies.

APPLICATION MATERIALS

The application materials, varied in length, content, and emphasis, provide the student with maximum opportunity to develop skill and judgment.

Study Guides After reading each topic in the text, the student should first complete the related study guide, which is available either in the basic workbook or in the comprehensive workbook.

Topic Problems The student should then do the topic problems, short and graduated in difficulty, which permit him to demonstrate his mastery of the text.

End-of-Chapter Activities At the end of each chapter there is a vocabulary review as well as a series of questions that are based on all the topics in the chapter.

Management Cases At the end of each chapter are *management cases,* which require the student to analyze and interpret financial data and then make a critical decision. The cases are sufficiently detailed so that answers will usually vary, just as they would in actual business situations. These cases dramatize the way management uses accounting to direct and control a business.

Project A special project permits the student to make an integrated application of the procedures he has mastered.

Practice Set The *Judd Paint Company* practice set represents the ideal cul-minating activity in the entire sequence of application materials. By handling realistic business papers, the student bridges the gap between the classroom and the business world.

SPECIAL FEATURES

Accounting 10/12 Part II: Accounting Systems and Procedures is further distinguished by a variety of special features.

Modern Accounting Practices In addition to the emphasis on a systems approach to accounting, the text reflects modern accounting practices—for example, using a separate schedule of cost of goods sold, a separate statement of owner's equity, a simpler and more effective way to complete the worksheet, and a new technique for adjusting merchandise inventory.

Accounting Cycle The accounting cycle for a merchandising business is covered.

Flowcharts Flowcharts are used throughout to illustrate sequences of procedures and to provide students with an authentic grasp of the systems approach.

Marginal Notes Marginal notes included in the text provide brief definitions and summarize review procedures.

ACKNOWLEDGEMENTS

A program of the size and complexity of *Accounting 10/12* could not have been produced without the help of a great many people. We wish to express our thanks in particular to a special committee of accountants and teachers from government, educational institutions, and business, who provided invaluable assistance in the preliminary planning stages. We are especially indebted to the many teachers and professional accountants who applauded this new approach to accounting instruction and gave us the courage to innovate.

M. Herbert Freeman
J Marshall Hanna
Gilbert Kahn

The Accounting 10/12 Program

COMPLETE TEXT EDITION

SEPARATE SOFT-COVER TEXT EDITIONS

PART I: Elements of Financial Records	PART II: Accounting Systems and Procedures	PART III: Special Accounting Procedures	PART IV: Business Data Processing Fundamentals

STUDY GUIDES AND WORKING PAPERS

COMPREHENSIVE PROBLEMS, STUDY GUIDES, AND WORKING PAPERS

PRACTICE SETS

PAYROLL TEXT-WORKBOOK

(In lieu of Part III text, workbooks and practice set)

TRANSPARENCIES

FILMSTRIPS

WALL CHARTS

TESTS

SOURCE BOOK AND KEY

Contents

Part Two
Accounting Systems and Procedures

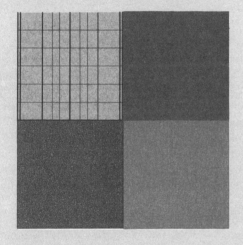

Chapter 1
Processing Cash Receipts

The basic principles of accounting are reflected in the steps of the accounting cycle: (1) journalizing the transactions, (2) posting the data about these transactions to the ledger accounts, (3) preparing a trial balance, (4) preparing an income statement and a balance sheet, (5) closing the ledger accounts, (6) balancing and ruling the accounts, and (7) preparing a postclosing trial balance. These steps are repeated within each accounting period so that at the end of the period the owners and managers of the business will know what it has accomplished during the period and will be better able to decide what actions the business should take in the future.

Accounting system: procedures and forms designed to prepare input and to process data through steps of accounting cycle.

An *accounting system,* however, includes more than the forms and procedures used in processing data *through* the steps of the accounting cycle. The accounting system for a business also includes the forms and procedures used in *preparing the data* for processing through the cycle. This phase of the system is referred to as *preparing the input* for the accounting cycle.

Although the basic principles of accounting remain unchanged, it is a necessity that accounting systems vary, depending on the size of the business, the nature of its operations, and the need it has for particular information. No one accounting system is appropriate for every business. The forms and procedures that are used should be tailored by the accountant to provide a regular flow of the needed financial information as quickly, accurately, and efficiently as possible. The following chapters will explore some of the different systems that have been established to meet the varying needs of business for financial information and financial control.

TOPIC 1 ■ A SYSTEM FOR THE CONTROL OF CASH RECEIPTS

In a very small business, one person (often the owner himself) maintains all the accounting records. However, in a larger business, it is impossible for just one person to keep all the records; thus additional people must be employed to help with the job.

Establishing Controls in an Accounting System

An accounting system must contain adequate controls to ensure accuracy, honesty, efficiency, and speed.

Accuracy   You are already familiar with a number of ways in which records may be checked for accuracy at various stages of the accounting cycle. For example, the trial balance and the postclosing trial balance are used to prove that the total of the debit balances agrees with the total of the credit balances in the ledger. The use of a bank reconciliation statement serves to check the accuracy of the balance shown on the bank statement against the balance shown in the checkbook. Later in this topic some additional ways in which to ensure accuracy in the handling of cash receipts will be presented.

Honesty   When a number of people have access to the cash or other assets of a business, effective controls are needed to prevent mishandling, theft, or the temptation to steal. The object of cash control is not only to safeguard the assets themselves but also to relieve honest employees from the fear of suspicion in the event an asset is missing. One form of control to ensure honesty involves a simple division of responsibility so that one employee's work can be checked against another's. Typically, the person who handles the asset itself should not be the person who keeps the records of the asset. Moreover, special procedures for storing cash and other assets may be required to minimize temptations to dishonesty.

Efficiency and Speed   When several people are required to process the accounting data for a business, it is essential that the records be designed so that more than one person can work on the records at the same time. One solution to the problem exists in the form of *special journals*. Special journals are so called because each one is designed to accumulate data about only one kind of business transaction. For example, a special journal may be set up to record only cash receipts. Another special journal may be used to record only cash payments. Typically, a business sets up a special journal whenever it has enough transactions of a special nature to justify a separate book of original entry.

In an ordinary business, most of the transactions fall into one of four categories. Hence four special journals are usually used.

Special Journal	*Used to Record*
Cash Receipts Journal	Receipt of cash from all sources.
Cash Payments Journal	All payments of cash.
Purchases Journal	All purchases on credit of merchandise.
Sales Journal	All sales of merchandise or service on credit.

In addition to these four special journals, a general journal is used to record all transactions that do not belong in any of the special journals. With five books of original entry established, as many as five accounting clerks can be employed at one time, each assigned to

Controls to ensure:
Accuracy
Honesty
Efficiency and speed.

Special journal: special record designed to accumulate data about only one kind of business transaction.

maintain one of the journals and to journalize only those transactions that fall within his area of responsibility. The procedures for using each of these special journals will be explained in detail in later topics.

Principles for the Control of Cash Receipts

Cash is involved in more transactions than any other asset. Yet cash is the asset most susceptible to mishandling and theft. Therefore, every business needs a good accounting system that not only provides accurate records of cash receipts but also minimizes the opportunity for mishandling and theft. Here are the basic principles for effectively controlling cash receipts.

Create Source Documents   As soon as any cash item is received, the business should immediately prepare a document that indicates (1) how much cash was received, (2) the date on which it was received, (3) why the cash was received, and (4) in some cases, who made the payment. This document then becomes the source of the data that will be entered into the accounting system. The source documents most commonly used are (1) cash register tapes, (2) prenumbered sales slips, and (3) prenumbered remittance slips.

Cash Register Tapes. A cash register is typically used to record the amount of cash received when goods or services are sold over the counter. As the prices of the items are entered and then totaled in the register, the amounts are displayed at the top of the machine. This gives the customer an opportunity to check the amounts being entered for computation and to verify that the amount requested by the clerk agrees with the total shown on the register. As a further check on accuracy, the amount of each item and the total amount of the sale are imprinted on the tape at the same time they appear at the top of the register. Two copies of the tape are created: one copy is ejected from the register and is given to the customer as a receipt, the other copy remains locked inside the register until it is removed for use as a source document. Thus the cash register tape provides the customer with proof of his payment and provides the business with an automatic record of the amount of cash received.

Sales Slips. Prenumbered sales slips may be used instead of a cash register to record the receipt of cash. An original and one or more copies of the sales slip are prepared. One copy is given to the customer as a receipt, and another is given to the accounting department as a source document describing the transaction. A third copy of the sales slip, if prepared, is retained in the sales book as the salesperson's record of all transactions which he handled personally. The pre-numbering of the sales slips provides an effective control over the transactions recorded on these slips. Once a slip has been filled out, it is impossible to conceal the fact that a transaction occurred; a sales clerk must account for any slips missing from the numbered sequence.

Since the cash register tape does not provide a record of the customer's name and address, the sales slip or some other receipt

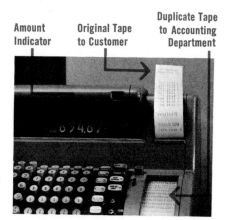

Amount Indicator   Original Tape to Customer   Duplicate Tape to Accounting Department

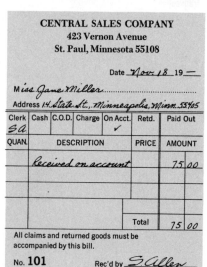

CENTRAL SALES COMPANY
423 Vernon Avenue
St. Paul, Minnesota 55108

Date *Nov. 18* 19 —

Miss *Jane Miller*

Address *14 State St., Minneapolis, Minn. 55405*

Clerk *S.A.*	Cash	C.O.D.	Charge	On Acct. ✓	Retd.	Paid Out
QUAN.	DESCRIPTION				PRICE	AMOUNT
	Received on account					75 00
				Total		75 00

All claims and returned goods must be accompanied by this bill.

No. **101**   Rec'd by *S. Allen*

must be used whenever it is desirable to have a record of such data. For example, cash received from a customer as payment on account would be rung up on the cash register as a cash transaction, and a sales slip would also be completed to identify the account to which the amount should be credited. The sales slip is marked to identify this transaction as a cash receipt rather than as a sale.

In some accounting systems, the prenumbered sales slips are contained in a *forms register* rather than in a sales book. When a forms register is used, the sales slip is also prepared in at least two copies: one copy is ejected from the register and given to the customer, and the other copy remains locked inside the register until removed. Registers are available with or without cash drawers.

Remittance Slips. When checks and money orders are received by mail, the employee who opens the mail prepares a source document known as a *remittance slip* to record the amount of cash received. For control purposes, these remittance slips are also prenumbered. The remittance slip is prepared in two copies: one copy is sent to the accounting department as a source document describing the transaction; the other copy is retained with the cash so that the amounts itemized on the remittance slips can be checked against the amounts of cash actually on hand.

Prepare a Cash Proof The amount of cash received should be verified frequently, typically at the end of each day. Ideally, a supervisor (rather than the person who prepared the source documents) should verify that the actual amount of cash taken in during the day agrees with the total amount of the cash receipts recorded on the source documents.

Cash Register Tapes. When a cash register is used, the amount of cash that is in the cash drawer at the end of the day should equal (1) the amount of the *change fund* (that is, the amount of cash that was put in the drawer at the beginning of the day for the sole purpose of making change), plus (2) the total of the cash sales recorded on the tape, plus (3) the total of the amount received on account (if any) from customers. Typically, no cash is taken out of the drawer except the amount needed to give customers the correct change. However, if a customer returns goods he has bought and wants a refund, the clerk must record on the tape the sum of money taken from the cash drawer for this payment.

The cash proof on page 140 shows how the receipts, payments, and change fund would be verified. The tape for November 2 indicates that total receipts from daily cash sales (TCa) amounted to $172.73 and that the total amount received on account from customers (TRe) amounted to $75. The total cash receipts (TCr) for November 2, therefore, is $247.73. However, the tape also indicates that $2 was paid out (TPd) in the course of the day. Thus this amount must be subtracted to show the net cash receipts for the day ($245.73). The supervisor must then count the actual cash in the drawer ($270.73). When he subtracts the amount of the change fund ($25),

Standard Register Co.

Forms Register with Cash Drawer

CENTRAL SALES COMPANY		
Remittance Slip		No. **RS-301**
Name *Smith & Adams*		
Amount	Check Number	Check Date
300.00	182	11/20/-
Explanation		
	Received on Account	
Date *11/25/-*	Received By	*N.H.*

Change fund: amount of cash put in drawer for making change.

he arrives at a balance of $245.73, which checks against the total shown on the tape.

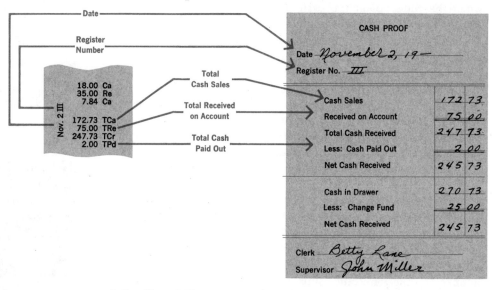

Cash proof form:

CASH PROOF

Date *November 2, 19—*

Register No. *III*

Cash Sales	172	73
Received on Account	75	00
Total Cash Received	247	73
Less: Cash Paid Out	2	00
Net Cash Received	245	73
Cash in Drawer	270	73
Less: Change Fund	25	00
Net Cash Received	245	73

Clerk *Betty Lane*
Supervisor *John Miller*

Tape detail (Nov. 2 III):
18.00 Ca
35.00 Re
7.84 Ca
172.73 TCa
75.00 TRe
247.73 TCr
2.00 TPd

Labels: Date; Register Number; Total Cash Sales; Total Received on Account; Total Cash Paid Out

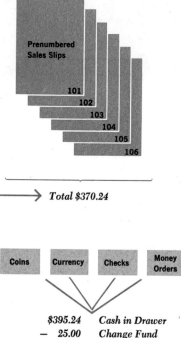

Prenumbered Sales Slips
101
102
103
104
105
106

Total $370.24

Coins   Currency   Checks   Money Orders

$395.24   *Cash in Drawer*
− 25.00   *Change Fund*
$370.24

Sales Slips. When prenumbered sales slips are used to record the receipt of cash, the cash proof is prepared as follows. The supervisor first arranges the sales slips in numerical order and then totals the amounts shown on the slips. At the same time, he scans the numbers on the slips to make sure that none are missing. (A missing slip would automatically suggest some mishandling of a cash receipt unless the sales clerk had a good explanation.) The supervisor then totals the amount of cash actually in the drawer and subtracts the amount of the change fund. The net amount of cash in the drawer should thus be equal to the amount of cash receipts recorded on the sales slips.

Remittance Slips. When remittance slips are used to record the receipt of cash through the mail, the cash proof consists of comparing the total amount recorded on the slips against the total amount of cash in the drawer. No change fund is necessary. With the use of prenumbered slips it is easy to determine whether any slip is missing.

Divide the Responsibility   Ideally, the person who prepares the source documents to record the cash receipts should not be the same person who makes the cash proof (comparing actual cash on hand with the records themselves). Moreover, the actual cash receipts should be prepared for deposit by someone other than the person who prepared the source document. Finally, the person who records the cash transactions in the journal should work from the source documents and have no contact with the actual cash receipts. When these functions are handled by different people, a business has the best opportunity of obtaining an accurate and honest accounting of its cash receipts. The most important principle of cash control is to separate the function of handling the cash receipts from the function of recording the cash receipts.

Deposit All Cash Receipts Intact   If all cash receipts are deposited intact in the bank, the business will gain one more check on the accuracy of its procedure; for total bank deposits should always equal cash receipts. If the business pays all bills by writing checks against deposits (rather than using some of its cash receipts as a means of payment), it can trace all payments to the checkbook.

In summary, the various principles just discussed—creating source documents to record cash receipts, making frequent cash proofs, dividing the responsibility for handling and recording cash, and depositing all cash receipts intact—all serve to control the accuracy with which cash receipts are processed in an accounting system.

Control of
cash receipts:

1. Create source
   documents.
2. Prepare cash proofs.
3. Divide responsibility.
4. Deposit all cash
   receipts intact.

TOPIC 1 ■ PROBLEMS

1   From the data given below, determine whether the correct amount of cash is on hand at the end of the day. Explain the difference, if any.

Cash Register Tape Totals

```
-87  346.28  Ca ←Cash Sales
-88   61.05  Re ←Received on Account
-89  407.33  Tl ←Daily Total
```

Money in Cash Register Drawer
(Change fund amounts to $10.)

Currency	Coins	Checks
10 twenty-dollar bills	30 quarters	$15
14 ten-dollar bills	28 dimes	$10
7 five-dollar bills	15 nickels	
6 one-dollar bills	28 pennies	

2   From the data given below, determine whether the correct amount of cash is on hand at the end of the day. If there is a difference, what could have caused it?

Cash Register Tape Totals

```
-244  517.83  Ca ←Cash Sales
-245   72.08  Re ←Received on Account
-246  589.91  Tl ←Daily Total
```

Money in Cash Register Drawer
(Change fund amounts to $20.)

Currency	Coins	Checks
8 twenty-dollar bills	41 quarters	$50
21 ten-dollar bills	52 dimes	$40
11 five-dollar bills	23 nickels	$30
47 one-dollar bills	31 pennies	

3   From the data given below, determine whether the correct amount of cash is on hand at the end of the day. Explain the difference, if any.

Prenumbered Sales Slips

No. 251 $23.80	No. 257 $71.18	No. 254 $30.00
No. 252 $18.65	No. 260 $62.43	No. 262 $42.71
No. 255 $29.31	No. 253 $9.24	No. 261 $60.00
No. 259 $40.90	No. 263 $11.70	No. 256 $12.45

Money in Cash Register Drawer
(Change fund amounts to $25.)

Currency	Coins	Checks
9 twenty-dollar bills	14 quarters	$10
8 ten-dollar bills	21 dimes	$24
12 five-dollar bills	14 nickels	$12
34 one-dollar bills	27 pennies	$45

4 From the data given below, determine whether the correct amount of cash is on hand at the end of the day. Explain the difference, if any.

Prenumbered Sales Slips

No. 68B ✓ $36.45	No. 75B ✓ $12.00	No. 70B ✓ $84.60
No. 74B ✓ $21.08	No. 72B ✓ $18.40	No. 69B ✓ $27.10
No. 71B ✓ $40.00	No. 73B ✓ $ 7.75	No. 77B ✓ $43.20
No. 76B ✓ $46.00	No. 78B ✓ $21.00	No. 79B ✓ $ 9.40

Money in Cash Register Drawer
(Change fund amounts to $30.)

Currency	Coins	Checks
5 twenty-dollar bills	21 quarters	$20
13 ten-dollar bills	18 dimes	$13
15 five-dollar bills	16 nickels	$ 5
47 one-dollar bills	13 pennies	

TOPIC 2 ■ THE CASH RECEIPTS JOURNAL

CENTRAL SALES COMPANY
CHART OF ACCOUNTS

ASSETS

101   *Cash*
111   *Accts. Rec./Jane Miller*
112   *Accts. Rec./Smith & Adams*
113   *Accts. Rec./Wilsons' Radio Center*
121   *Office Equipment*
122   *Store Equipment*

LIABILITIES

201   *Accts. Pay./Dixon & Hicks*
202   *Accts. Pay./Todd Electronics*
203   *Accts. Pay./Vista Corporation*
204   *Accts. Pay./George Young*
221   *Loans Payable*

OWNER'S EQUITY

301   *John Hall, Capital*

INCOME

401   *Sales*

EXPENSES

511   *Cash Short and Over*
512   *Insurance Expense*
513   *Miscellaneous Expense*
514   *Rent Expense*
515   *Salaries Expense*
516   *Supplies Expense*
517   *Utilities Expense*

Every business enters into transactions that involve the receipt of cash. The number of transactions and the amount of cash involved vary, depending upon the type and size of the business. A grocery store, for example, has many cash transactions for the sale of goods, but each sale is generally under $30. A new car dealer, on the other hand, might have only one cash transaction a day, but this sale could involve $3,000 or more.

In general, cash is received from three major sources: (1) from customers paying cash for goods or services they have bought, (2) from debtors paying amounts they owe, and (3) from owners making additional investments in their business. When cash is received, a source document is prepared to record the date, the amount, an explanation, and, in some cases, the payer. This source document provides the data needed to record the transaction in the journal.

Journalizing Cash Receipts

When transactions involving cash receipts are recorded into a journal, the Cash account is debited for the amount of cash received. The account credited depends upon the source from which cash was received; for example, the Sales account is credited to record cash sales.

When cash receipts are recorded in a simple two-column journal, each entry requires at least two lines; if an explanation is included, the entry requires at least three lines. Therefore, if a business has ten transactions involving cash receipts in one day, the entries would require at least twenty to thirty lines in the journal. Moreover, when these ten transactions are posted, ten separate entries in the Cash account must be made. In order to reduce the amount of space used in the journal and ledger accounts and to permit more than one person to work on the records at one time, a special journal is frequently used to record all transactions involving cash receipts. This cash receipts journal further increases efficiency because all the cash debits to the Cash account are made in one posting instead of ten.

In order to illustrate how special journals and various control systems are used in business, we will examine the accounting system of the Central Sales Company. The Central Sales Company (owned by John Hall) is a distributor of small electrical appliances.

Under the accounting system used by the Central Sales Company, all transactions involving cash receipts must be recorded on a cash register. John Hall deposits the cash daily, but because of the limited number of cash sales the business has each day, he totals the cash register only once a week. Thus the total deposit for any week must equal the total shown on the cash register tape, which is the total cash receipts recorded in the journal for that week.

During the month of November, the Central Sales Company received $7,475 from various sources. If each of these cash transactions were journalized in a two-column journal, the journal entries would appear as follows:

							GENERAL JOURNAL			Page 2	

DATE	ACCOUNT TITLE AND EXPLANATION	POST. REF.	DEBIT	CREDIT
19—				
Nov. 2	Cash..................................	101	5,000 00	
	John Hall, Capital.....................	301		5,000 00
	Additional investment.			
5	Cash..................................	101	400 00	
	Sales.................................	401		400 00
	Cash sales for week.			
9	Cash..................................	101	200 00	
	Accts. Rec./Wilson's Radio Center.........	113		200 00
	Received on account.			
12	Cash..................................	101	350 00	
	Sales.................................	401		350 00
	Cash sales for week.			
16	Cash..................................	101	75 00	
	Accts. Rec./Jane Miller.................	111		75 00
	Received on account.			
19	Cash..................................	101	750 00	
	Sales.................................	401		750 00
	Cash sales for week.			
25	Cash..................................	101	300 00	
	Accts. Rec./Smith & Adams.............	112		300 00
	Received on account.			
26	Cash..................................	101	400 00	
	Sales.................................	401		400 00
	Cash sales for week.			

Cash   101

5,000
400
200
350
75
750
300
400

In this form of journal, the debit entry to "Cash" must be repeated for each transaction. Thus Cash is debited eight times to record the November transactions. Moreover, eight lines are required in the Cash account in order to post these entries separately.

The following illustration compares how the November 2 transaction in which Mr. Hall increases his investment by $5,000 would be journalized in a two-column general journal to how it would be journalized in a special cash receipts journal.

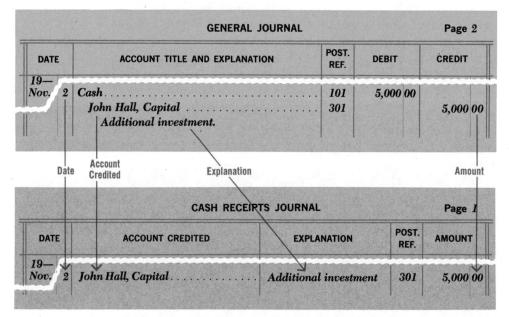

For every credit entry in the cash receipts journal, it is understood that there will be a debit entry to the Cash account.

As you can see, when the cash receipts journal is used, the date, the account to be credited, the explanation, and the amount received are all recorded on one line. Only the credit entry needs to be written; the account title "Cash" and the amount to be debited are not written because it is understood that there will be a debit entry to the Cash account that will be the total of all the credit entries in the cash receipts journal. Since the amount is written only once, time is saved and the possibility of making an error is reduced.

The use of a special journal such as the cash receipts journal does not, however, eliminate the need for a *general journal*. The general journal is the record that contains all those entries that cannot be recorded in any special journal.

The illustration at the top of page 145 shows how the November entries for the Central Sales Company's cash receipts would appear when entered in a cash receipts journal.

Note that the cash balance for November 1 is recorded on the first line. It is common practice to record in this journal the balance of the Cash account at the beginning of each month. The advantage of this practice will be explained in the next chapter when the cash payments journal is discussed. The cash balance entry is a *memorandum entry—*

Memorandum entry: entry not to be posted.

CASH RECEIPTS JOURNAL				Page 1
DATE	**ACCOUNT CREDITED**	**EXPLANATION**	**POST. REF.**	**AMOUNT**
19—				
Nov. 1	Cash Balance...............	$9,440.............	—	
2	John Hall, Capital.............	Additional investment.		5,000 00
5	Sales.....................	Cash sales for week...		400 00
9	Accts. Rec./Wilson's Radio Center.	Received on account..		200 00
12	Sales.....................	Cash sales for week...		350 00
16	Accts. Rec./Jane Miller.........	Received on account..		75 00
19	Sales.....................	Cash sales for week...		750 00
25	Accts. Rec./Smith & Adams......	Received on account..		300 00
26	Sales.....................	Cash sales for week...		400 00

an entry that is not to be posted. Therefore, the balance is written in the Explanation column instead of the Amount column, and a dash is made in the Posting Reference column.

Posting from the Cash Receipts Journal

Posting the entries from the cash receipts journal to the ledger varies slightly from the procedure that is used for posting from the general journal. Each credit entry in the cash receipts journal is posted individually to the various ledger accounts. The credit postings are made at frequent intervals during the month. The account numbers placed in the Posting Reference column of the cash receipts journal indicate those accounts that have been posted. The debits to the Cash account are posted only when the journal is ruled at the end of the month. At that time only one debit amount is posted for the total cash received during the month.

Posting the Credit Entries In the Posting Reference column of the ledger account, the letters CR are used to indicate that the amount has been posted from the cash receipts journal. In the following illustration of the John Hall, Capital account, the posting reference CR 1 indicates that the $5,000 credit to the account was journalized on page 1 of the cash receipts journal, not the general journal.

Credits: posted individually during month.

Debit to cash: posted at end of month.

CASH RECEIPTS JOURNAL		Page 1	
DATE	ACCOUNT CREDITED	POST. REF.	AMOUNT
19—			
Nov. 2	John Hall, Capital.....	301	5,000 00

John Hall, Capital							Account No. 301		
DATE	**EXPLANATION**	**POST. REF.**	**DEBIT**	**DATE**	**EXPLANATION**	**POST. REF.**	**CREDIT**		
				19—					
				Nov. 1	Opening Entry	J1	18,740 00		
				2		CR1	5,000 00		

CR: cash receipts journal.

Totaling the Cash Receipts Journal   In order to determine the amount that must be posted from the cash receipts journal to the Cash account at the end of the month, the cash receipts journal should be totaled and ruled as follows:

1   Draw a single rule under the last figure in the Amount column.
2   Write the last date of the month in the Date column.
3   Write "Cash Debit" in the Account Credited column.
4   Write "Total receipts" in the Explanation column.
5   Add the amounts in the Amount column and pencil-foot the column. After proving the addition, write the total in ink beneath the single rule.
6   Draw a double rule under the Date, Posting Reference, and Amount columns to show that the journal is completed for the month.

CASH RECEIPTS JOURNAL   Page *1*

DATE		ACCOUNT CREDITED	EXPLANATION	POST. REF.	AMOUNT
19—					
Nov.	1	Cash Balance...............	$9,440.............	—	
	2	John Hall, Capital.............	Additional investment..	301	5,000 00
	5	Sales........................	Cash sales for week....	401	400 00
	9	Accts. Rec./Wilson's Radio Center.	Received on account...	113	200 00
	12	Sales........................	Cash sales for week....	401	350 00
	16	Accts. Rec./Jane Miller..........	Received on account...	111	75 00
	19	Sales........................	Cash sales for week....	401	750 00
	25	Accts. Rec./Smith & Adams......	Received on account...	112	300 00
	26	Sales........................	Cash sales for week....	401	400 00
					7,475 00
	30	Cash Debit.............	Total receipts.........		7,475 00

Before new credits are entered in the journal for the next month, the balance in the Cash account as of December 1 should be recorded as a memorandum entry on the first line of the journal for December.

Posting the Debit to Cash   After the journal is totaled and ruled, the total amount of cash received is posted to the debit side of the Cash account. The number of the Cash account is then written in the Posting Reference column of the cash receipts journal.

CASH RECEIPTS JOURNAL   Page *1*

DATE		ACCOUNT CREDITED	EXPLANATION	POST. REF.	AMOUNT
19—					
Nov.	30	Cash Debit.................	Total receipts.........	101	7,475 00
					7,475 00

After all entries for November have been posted for the Central Sales Company, the Cash account will show only one debit—$7,475 for the month's total cash receipts. The total credits posted from the cash receipts journal to the various accounts in the ledger also equals $7,475. Thus the total debits posted equals the total credits posted.

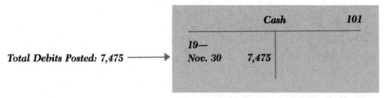

Total Debits Posted: 7,475 ——————→

Cash		101
19—		
Nov. 30	7,475	

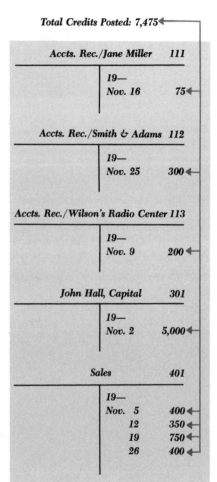

Total Credits Posted: 7,475◄—————

Accts. Rec./Jane Miller		111
19—		
Nov. 16		75◄

Accts. Rec./Smith & Adams		112
19—		
Nov. 25		300◄

Accts. Rec./Wilson's Radio Center		113
19—		
Nov. 9		200◄

John Hall, Capital		301
19—		
Nov. 2		5,000◄

Sales		401
19—		
Nov. 5		400◄
12		350◄
19		750◄
26		400◄

Suppose that a trial balance were prepared during the month. The ledger would then appear to be out of balance because only the credit entries for cash receipts would be posted. The debit to the Cash account is not posted until the journal is ruled at the end of the month. Thus, to prepare a trial balance during the month, you must examine the cash receipts journal to determine the debits to Cash.

Obviously, if an error is made in adding the amounts in the cash receipts journal or in posting one of the credit entries, the total debits will not equal the total credits.

Recording the Memorandum Entry

The cash receipts journal should be totaled and ruled at the end of the month. The credits, of course, are posted to the individual accounts at frequent intervals during the month. The debit to Cash— the total of the amounts received—is posted only at the end of the month. If the end of the month is also the end of the accounting period, the balance of the Cash account is available for the memorandum entry into the cash receipts journal for the next month. If, however, the end of the month is not the end of the accounting period, the Cash account must be pencil-footed so that the balance can be obtained to prove the balance in the checkbook and the balance in the bank statement. When this cash balance has been verified, it is recorded as a memorandum entry in the cash receipts journal at the start of the next month's accumulation of cash receipts.

Recording an Opening Entry

When a cash receipts journal is used in an accounting system, all transactions involving the receipt of cash must be recorded in it. There is, however, one exception to this principle. When a set of books is first opened for a business, the complete opening entry is recorded and explained in the general journal so that a permanent record of the total financial position of the business on that day is provided in one place. For example, when John Hall started the Central Sales Company, the accountant recorded the opening entry in the general journal as follows:

		GENERAL JOURNAL			Page *1*
DATE		ACCOUNT TITLE AND EXPLANATION	POST. REF.	DEBIT	CREDIT
19— *Nov.*	*1*	*Cash*		*9,440 00*	
		Office Equipment		*7,200 00*	
		Store Equipment		*12,100 00*	
		Loans Payable			*10,000 00*
		John Hall, Capital			*18,740 00*
		Mr. Hall starts Central Sales Company with *above assets, liabilities, and owner's equity.*			

Since there will now be a balance in the cash account once this
entry is posted from the general journal, a memorandum entry is
recorded in the cash receipts journal.

		CASH RECEIPTS JOURNAL			Page *1*
DATE		ACCOUNT CREDITED	EXPLANATION	POST. REF.	AMOUNT
19— *Nov.*	*1*	*Cash Balance*	*$9,440*	—	

If the opening entry, however, consists of a cash investment only,
the opening entry can be recorded directly in the cash receipts journal.
In this case, no memorandum entry for the Cash Balance is needed.
Henceforth, all entries to record the receipt of cash for the Central
Sales Company are entered in the cash receipts journal.

Flowcharting the Cash Receipts Procedure

When cash is received, a source document—cash register tape,
sales slip, or remittance slip—is prepared. Sales slips and remittance
slips, as well as other source documents, are identified by the form
symbol, ☐. Cash-register and adding-machine paper tapes are identified by the tape symbol, ☐.

The terminal symbol, ⬭, is used to indicate a beginning, ending, or
point of interruption in a flowchart; for example, a bank, customer,
or creditor. The terminal point is usually outside the area where the
data is being processed. For example, when cash items are deposited
into the checking account, the bank is known as a terminal point
because it is the end of the physical handling of the cash.

The two operations involved in processing cash—(1) handling cash
and (2) recording cash—can be charted to show their relationship, as
shown on page 149.

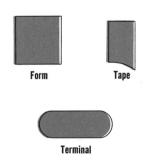

Form   **Tape**

Terminal

PROCESSING CASH RECEIPTS

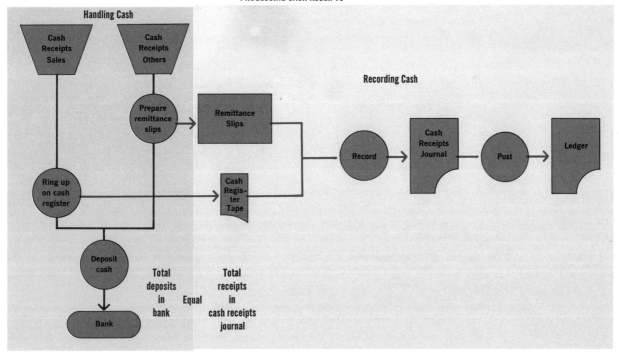

In the system illustrated, all cash received from cash sales is rung up on a cash register and all cash received from other sources is recorded on remittance slips. These source documents are sent to the accounting department to be journalized. All cash receipts are deposited in a bank. Therefore, at the end of the month, the total deposits must equal the total receipts recorded in the cash receipts journal.

In a small office, one person might handle all these operations. However, the principles of internal control of cash call for the separation of these duties where possible. Therefore, one person should deposit all the cash in the bank, while another should record the cash in the journals and maintain the financial records.

TOPIC 2 ■ PROBLEMS

5 Describe each step in the flowchart for processing cash receipts (shown above). For example: Cash is received from sales and other sources; amounts are rung up on cash register or remittance slips are prepared; etc.

6 Answer the following questions about the cash receipts journal (see page 146).

a What was the cash balance on November 1? From what other source can this information be obtained?

b Why is the amount of the November 1 cash balance shown in the Explanation column of the cash receipts journal instead of in the Amount column?

c Why is there a dash in the Posting Reference column of the cash receipts journal for the November 1 cash balance?

d If sales for the week of November 12 were recorded in a general journal instead of a cash receipts journal, what would the complete entry be?

e When the amount of total sales for the week of November 19 is posted from the cash receipts journal, is the debit to Cash posted at the same time? Why or why not?

f If the transaction of November 25 were recorded in a general journal, what would the complete entry be?

g When a $300 credit is posted from the cash receipts journal to the Smith & Adams account, is the Cash debit posted at the same time? Explain.

h On what date was $5,000 received? From what source?

i What amount was posted to the Cash account on November 30? Was the account debited or credited?

j Was $7,475 posted as a credit to any account on November 30? Why or why not?

7 Harold Watson owns and operates an accounting service in a medium-size community. Some of his customers pay in cash and some have accounts.

a Open ledger accounts and enter account balances for May 1 as follows: Cash, $845; Accts. Rec./Raymond Beale, $375; Accts. Rec./Marian Gibson, $360; Harold Watson, Capital, $1,580; and Sales. Allow three lines for each account and assign an appropriate number to each account (based on the chart of accounts on page 142).

b Using a cash receipts journal, make an appropriate memorandum entry for the May 1 cash balance and then journalize the following transactions:

May 6	Sold services for $435 in cash.	May 19	Received $360 from Marian Gibson on account.
11	Sold services for $265 in cash.		
13	Received $125 from Raymond Beale on account.	26	Received $125 from Raymond Beale on account.

c Post the credit entries from the cash receipts journal.
d Foot and rule the cash receipts journal.
e Post the debit entry from the cash receipts journal.
f Prepare a trial balance.

8 The S. Morton Company has the transactions for October listed below.
a Open ledger accounts and enter account balances for October 1 as follows: Cash, $1,780; Accts. Rec./Thomas Garrison, $560; Accts. Rec./Elizabeth Woodson, $480; Stanley Morton, Capital, $2,820; and Sales. Allow three lines for each account, and assign an appropriate number to each account.
b Using a cash receipts journal, make an appropriate memorandum entry for October 1 and then journalize the following transactions:

Oct. 5	Received $280 from Thomas Garrison on account.	Oct. 14	Stanley Morton invested an additional $1,000 in the business.
11	Sold services for $490 in cash.		

c Post these credit entries.
d Journalize the following transactions:

Oct. 20	Received $240 from Elizabeth Woodson on account.	Oct. 28	Sold services for $330 in cash.

e Foot and rule the cash receipts journal.
f Complete the posting from the cash receipts journal.
g Prepare a trial balance.

The Language of Business

The following terms are important. Do you understand the meaning of each? Can you define each term and use it in an original sentence?

accounting system	remittance slip	memorandum entry
special journal	change fund	Posting Reference column
cash register	cash receipts journal	CR
prenumbered forms	general journal	terminal point

Chapter Questions

1 List and explain the essential principles for the control of cash receipts.

2 Why should the function of receiving cash be separated from the function of paying cash?

3 Why should the function of handling cash be separated from the function of recording cash?

4 Why are prenumbered source documents used to record cash receipts?

5 In what way do good control procedures for cash receipts contribute to good employer-employee relations?

6 Explain the ways in which the use of a cash receipts journal simplifies the journalizing and posting of cash receipts.

7 When a cash receipts journal is used, what procedure is needed to prepare a trial balance during the month?

8 What is done to complete the cash receipts journal at the end of the month?

Management Cases

Control of Cash Receipts A large number of the total transactions of a business involve cash receipts and payments. Every business should set up safeguards to control cash because this asset is more susceptible to theft than any other.

Case M-1

The owner of the Royale Parking Lot charges 50 cents for the first hour and 25 cents for each additional half hour, up to a maximum of $3. The lot is in the heart of the shopping district, and two large department stores in the area have arranged for their customers to get special rates. Up to six o'clock, most customers park for about an hour; after six, they average about three hours.

There is an attendant on duty from 8 a.m. to 12 midnight, seven days a week. When a customer drives into the lot, he parks and locks his own car, and the attendant gives him a ticket on which the time of arrival is written. When the customer returns to get his car, he surrenders the ticket, and the attendant writes the time of departure and the parking fee right on the ticket. The attendant turns in the tickets with the cash receipts.

a The owner has been suspicious that his attendants have not been turning in all the money they collected. Can you suggest a system to prevent this possibility?

b A number of customers who park daily from 9 a.m. to 5 p.m. have asked for a special weekly rate. What factor should be considered?

c The owner wants to lower his payroll costs. Is there some way he can modify his fee schedule to reduce the hours an attendant is on duty?

Case M-2

At the Snack Spot, customers can be served at the counter or at tables inside the restaurant, or they can remain in their cars and be served by carhops (outside attendants). Most of the Snack Spot's business is handled by the carhops.

When a waitress inside takes an order, she fills out an order slip. When a customer pays her, she inserts the order slip into a printing device on the cash register so that the amount of the sale is imprinted on the slip at the same time it is imprinted on the tape. The cash and the order slip are then placed in the register drawer.

The carhops also record their orders on an order slip, but they do not ring up payments on the cash register. Instead they keep all the money they have collected until the end of their day's work. At that time, they turn in all the order slips and the money.

a What are some reasons for using different methods with the inside waitresses and the carhops?

b How does the manager check on the honesty of inside waitresses? of carhops?

Case M-3

In a large school, most of the faculty members belong to the local, state, and national teachers' organizations. They pay their dues to an office clerk, who then issues a separate receipt for each payment of dues to any one of the three organizations. In order to reduce her work, the clerk has requested that she be permitted to issue only one receipt to a person (even when the dues are payable to more than one organization).

a Under the separate-receipt method, how would each of the three organizations obtain full information about the payment of dues and the members in good standing?

b Under the one-receipt method, how would the same information be reported to each organization? How could each be sure that all dues collected were sent?

c Design a receipt that can be used for all three organizations at one time.

Working Hint

Errors Made in Copying Numbers

When numbers are copied, errors often occur because a number has been left out or has been mistaken for another number.

Omitting a Number When listing a series of numbers, you can guard against accidentally omitting one of them by counting the items you copied. Then count the items in the original listing. The total number of items in both lists must equal.

Misreading a Figure When recording numbers, always use well-formed figures. This will help guard against misreading the number. The figures most likely to be misread when carelessly or poorly written are these: 9 and 7; 1 and 7; 4 and 7; 2 and 0; 2 and 3; 3 and 5; 6 and 0; 8 and 0; 2 and 7.

Chapter 2
Processing
Cash Payments

A system for the control of cash involves not only cash receipts but also cash payments. The owner of a business wants to be certain that payments are made for the correct amount and then only for goods and services actually ordered and received. In addition, each employee wants to avoid suspicion if there is a shortage in cash.

TOPIC 1 ■ THE CASH PAYMENTS JOURNAL

Any accounting system must provide for adequate controls to ensure accuracy, honesty, efficiency, and speed in processing cash payments.

Principles for the Control of Cash Payments

The following principles should be a part of any system designed for the control of cash payments.

Check the Bill   No bill should be paid until it has been verified that the goods or services itemized on the bill were actually ordered and received and that the amount of the bill is computed accurately.

Pay by Check   Since all cash receipts should be deposited intact in the bank, no payments should be made from cash receipts. *All* payments (except petty cash expenditures) should be made by check. The petty cash fund is established and replenished by check.

Use Prenumbered Checks   Prenumbered checks should be used to keep track of the checks issued. Voided checks should be kept on file so that every check can be accounted for in numerical sequence.

Divide the Responsibility   The responsibility for handling the checks and recording the disbursements should be divided so that the work of one employee can be checked against that of another.

Prepare a Cash Proof   When all cash receipts are deposited in the bank and all bills are paid by check, two independent records of cash receipts and cash payments are available. The business has a record of receipts in the cash receipts journal and of disbursements in its checkbook and petty cash book. The bank has a record of all deposits and withdrawals in the checking account.

When the business receives a copy of the bank's record (in the form of the monthly bank statement), it prepares a bank reconciliation statement to verify the accuracy of the records.

Journalizing Cash Payments

The most common reasons for disbursing cash are to pay operating expenses, to pay creditors, and to pay for assets purchased. In each case, the asset Cash decreases when cash is paid out. Therefore, every cash payment involves a credit to the Cash account. When cash payments are recorded in a general journal, every debit entry must be accompanied by a credit entry involving the Cash account. If the Central Sales Company recorded all its cash payments in a general journal, the November entries would look like this:

GENERAL JOURNAL					Page 2
DATE	ACCOUNT TITLE AND EXPLANATION	POST. REF.	DEBIT	CREDIT	
19—					
Nov. 1	*Rent Expense*..........................	514	300 00		
	Cash................................	*101*		300 00	
	Rent for November, Check 201				
8	*Accts. Pay./Dixon & Hicks*..............	201	400 00		
	Cash................................	*101*		400 00	
	On account, Check 202				
26	*Salaries Expense*.......................	515	800 00		
	Cash	*101*		800 00	
	Salaries for November, Check 204				
28	*Office Equipment*......................	121	220 00		
	Cash................................	*101*		220 00	
	New adding machine, Check 205				
29	*Utilities Expense*.......................	517	80 00		
	Cash................................	*101*		80 00	
	Gas and electricity, Check 206				

```
          Cash      101
          _____|_____
                  |  → 300
                  |  → 400
                  |  → 800
                  |  → 220
                  |  → 80
```

To save time in journalizing and in posting, many businesses use a special journal known as a *cash payments journal* to record all cash payments. In this way, only the debit entries need to be recorded and posted individually. The related credit entries to Cash can be accumulated until the end of the month and then totaled. The total is then posted as a credit to the Cash account.

The advantages of using a cash payments journal may be seen in the November 1 transaction, involving a $300 payment by the Central Sales Company for the November rent. This entry, when recorded in a general journal, requires three lines. When recorded in the cash payments journal, however, this same entry takes only one line and the amount is written only once. Since all checks must be accounted for, a special column is provided in the cash payments journal for recording check numbers. Note that even if a check is voided, the number is listed; however, a line is drawn in the Account Debited column, Posting Reference column, and Amount column, and "Voided" is recorded in the Explanation column.

CASH PAYMENTS JOURNAL					Page 1
DATE	ACCOUNT DEBITED	EXPLANATION	CHECK NO.	POST. REF.	AMOUNT
19— Nov. 1	Rent Expense............	Rent for November...	201		300 00
8	Accts. Pay./Dixon & Hicks..	On account.........	202		400 00
15	———————————	Voided...........	203	—	———
26	Salaries Expense..........	Salaries for November.	204		800 00
28	Office Equipment........	New adding machine..	205		220 00
29	Utilities Expense........	Gas and electricity...	206		80 00

For every debit in the cash payments journal, it is understood that there will be a credit entry to the Cash account.

The other cash payments would be recorded in the cash payments journal in a similar manner.

Debits: posted individually during month.

Posting from the Cash Payments Journal

The accounts debited in the cash payments journal are posted individually to the proper ledger accounts. This posting usually takes place at intervals during the month. To identify those entries already posted, the account number is entered in the Posting Reference column of the cash payments journal next to each item posted. In the ledger accounts, the letters CP and the number of the cash payments journal page are written in the Posting Reference column to indicate that the entry was posted from the cash payments journal. In the following illustration of the Rent Expense account, the posting reference CP1 indicates that the $300 debit to the account was journalized on page 1 of the cash payments journal.

Credit to Cash: total posted at end of month.

CASH PAYMENTS JOURNAL Page 1			
DATE	ACCOUNT DE	POST. REF.	AMOUNT
19— Nov. 1	Rent Expense.......	514	300 00

			Rent Expense				Account No. 514	
DATE	EXPLANATION	POST. REF.	DEBIT	DATE	EXPLANATION	POST. REF.	CREDIT	
19— Nov. 1	Rent for Nov.	CP1	300 00					

CP: cash payments journal.

Totaling the Cash Payments Journal   In order to determine the amount that should be posted from the cash payments journal to the Cash account at the end of the month, the cash payments journal should be totaled and ruled as shown on page 156.

1 Draw a single rule under the last figure in the Amount column.
2 Write the last date of the month in the Date column.
3 Write "Cash Credit" in the Account Debited column.
4 Write "Total payments" in the Explanation column.
5 Add the amounts in the Amount column and pencil-foot the total. Check the addition, and write the total in ink beneath the single rule.

6 Draw a double rule under the Date, Posting Reference, and Amount columns to show that the journal is completed for the month.

7 After the total credit of $1,800 is posted to the Cash account, enter the number of the Cash account, 101, in the Posting Reference column of the cash payments journal.

	CASH PAYMENTS JOURNAL				Page *1*
DATE	ACCOUNT DEBITED	EXPLANATION	CHECK NO.	POST. REF.	AMOUNT
19—					
Nov. 1	*Rent Expense*	*Rent for November* . . .	201	514	300 00
8	*Accts. Pay./Dixon & Hicks* . .	*On account*	202	201	400 00
15		*Voided*	203	—	—
26	*Salaries Expense*	*Salaries for November* .	204	515	800 00
28	*Office Equipment*	*New adding machine* .	205	121	220 00
29	*Utilities Expense*	*Gas and electricity* . . .	206	517	80 00
					1,800 00
30	*Cash Credit* 4	*Total payments*	7	101	1,800 00

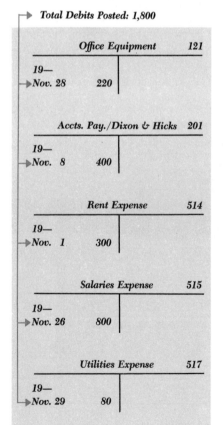

Total Debits Posted: 1,800

Office Equipment   121
19—	
Nov. 28 220	

Accts. Pay./Dixon & Hicks   201
19—	
Nov. 8 400	

Rent Expense   514
19—	
Nov. 1 300	

Salaries Expense   515
19—	
Nov. 26 800	

Utilities Expense   517
19—	
Nov. 29 80	

After the cash credit is posted, the accounts in the ledger appear as follows. Note that the total credit of $1,800 posted to the Cash account equals the total of the individual debits previously posted from the cash payments journal to the various accounts.

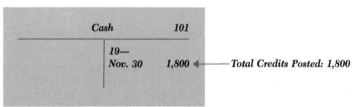

Cash   101
19—
Nov. 30   1,800 ◄——— *Total Credits Posted: 1,800*

Since the credit to the Cash account is not posted until the end of the month, a trial balance taken during the month would be out of balance. However, once the credit is posted, a trial balance can be taken because the ledger should now be in balance.

The use of the cash payments journal, like the use of the cash receipts journal, reduces the number of entries made in the general journal but does not eliminate the need for the general journal. The general journal is still used as the book of original entry for transactions that are not provided for in any of the special journals.

Flowcharting Cash Payments

The steps in the control of cash payments are shown in the flowchart on page 157. Two new symbols are used to show that the bill is approved for payment, stamped "Paid," and then filed for reference.

The *addition-to-a-form symbol*, ⊘, indicates an addition to a form or record, such as making an approval for payment, stamping a bill "Paid," or listing discounts.

The *storage (or file) symbol*, ▽, shows that the item is placed or stored in a file.

Addition
to a Form

Storage
or File

PROCESSING CASH PAYMENTS

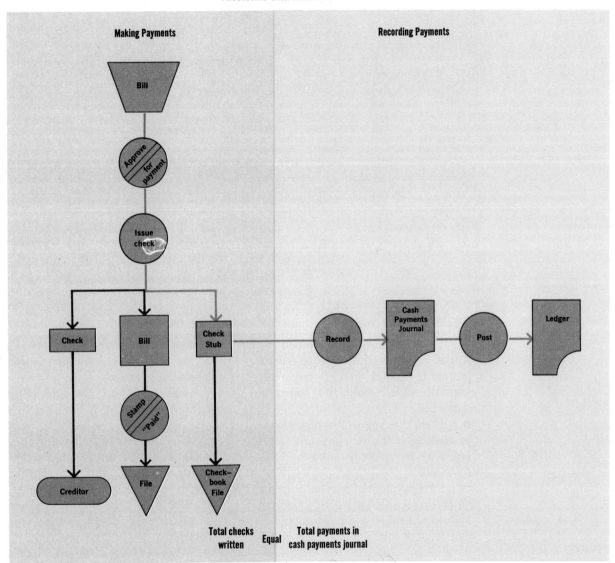

TOPIC 1 ■ PROBLEMS

9 Describe each step in the flowchart for processing cash payments (shown above). For example: bill is received from supplier; bill is approved for payment.

10   Study the following cash payments journal and Cash account. Then answer the questions that follow.

CASH PAYMENTS JOURNAL						Page *1*
DATE	ACCOUNT DEBITED	EXPLANATION	CHECK NO.	POST. REF.	AMOUNT	
19—						
Aug. 2	*Equipment*.............	*New tools*.........	21	105	120 00	
4	*Rent Expense*...........	*August rent*........	22	501	130 00	
12	*Accts. Pay./B. J. Carter*....	*On account*........	23	201	210 00	
22	*Utilities Expense*.........	*August bill*........	24	502	15 00	
23	*Adam Bartley, Capital*.....	*Personal use*........	25	302	90 00	
31	*Cash Credit*...........	*Total payments*......		101	565 00	

			Cash			Account No. *101*	
DATE	EXPLANATION	POST. REF.	DEBIT	DATE	EXPLANATION	POST. REF.	CREDIT
19—				19—			
Aug. 1	*Balance*.......	√	630 00	Aug. 31	*Payments*.....	CP1	565 00
31	*Receipts*......	CR1	940 00	31	*Balance*.......	√	1,005 00
			1,570 00				1,570 00
19—							
Sept. 1	*Balance*.......	√	1,005 00				

a   If the purchase of equipment on August 2 was recorded in a general journal instead of the cash payments journal, what would the complete entry be?

b   When the August 2 transaction is journalized in the cash payments journal, why is no credit entry to Cash recorded?

c   If the payment of rent on August 4 had been recorded in a general journal instead of in the cash payments journal, what would the complete entry have been?

d   When the rent expense transaction is posted from the cash payments journal, is the credit to Cash for $130 posted at the same time? Why or why not?

e   What amount is posted to the Cash account from the cash payments journal on August 31? Is the account debited or credited?

f   Is $565 posted to the debit of any account on August 31? Why or why not?

g   Why was Check 23 issued?

h   In what account is Mr. Bartley's withdrawal of August 23 recorded? Why?

i   Where does the August 1 balance of $630 in the Cash account come from?

j   Where does the August 31 debit of $940 in the Cash account come from?

k   Why are the August 31 and September 1 balances checked in the Posting Reference column of the Cash account?

11   David Crouse runs a small engineering consulting service. You have been asked to handle his books for the month of September.

a   Open ledger accounts and record September 1 balances as follows: Cash, $1,800; Accts. Pay./Leroy Roberts, $400; David Crouse, Capital, $1,400; Rent Expense; Telephone Expense; and Utilities Expense. Allow three lines for each account, and assign an appropriate number to each account.

b   Record in a cash payments journal the appropriate entries for the following transactions.

Sept. 1   Issued Check 172 for $110
        for September rent.
   8   Issued Check 173 for $200
        to Leroy Roberts on account.
  12   Issued Check 174 for $80 to
        David Crouse, the owner.

Sept. 18   Issued Check 175 for $24 for
        September telephone bill.
  27   Issued Check 176 for $18 for
        September utilities.

c   Foot and rule the cash payments journal.
d   Post the entries from the cash payments journal.
e   Prepare a trial balance.

12   Edward Trainor is the owner of a mailing service. You have been asked to perform the following functions.

a   Open ledger accounts and record February 1 balances as follows: Cash, $3,400; Equipment, $600; Accts. Pay./James Engle, $1,200; Edward Trainor, Capital, $2,800; Telephone Expense; Utilities Expense. Allow three lines for each account, and assign an appropriate number to each account.

b   Rule a cash payments journal, and record the appropriate entries for the following transactions.

Feb. 1   Issued Check 304 for $300 to
        James Engle on account.
  11   Issued Check 305 for $150
        for equipment.
  24   Issued Check 306 for $30 for
        February utilities bill.

Feb. 27   Issued Check 307 for $20 for
        February telephone bill.
  28   Issued Check 308 for $300 to
        James Engle on account.

c   Foot and rule the cash payments journal.
d   Post the entries from the cash payments journal.
e   Prepare a trial balance.

TOPIC 2 ■ THE CASH PROOF

Any method used to verify that the amount of cash recorded equals the amount of cash handled is known as a *cash proof*. You have already observed how a cash proof is made when the total shown on a cash register tape (the amount recorded) is compared with the amount in the cash drawer (the amount handled). Still another kind of cash proof is taken when the balance in one's checking account is compared with the balance shown in the Cash account or with the balance shown on a bank statement.

Cash proof: a method used to prove that the amount of cash recorded equals the amount of cash handled.

In this topic we shall review these various cash proofs and describe related procedures that grow out of the use of a special account in the ledger (Cash Short and Over) and the use of special cash journals.

Cash Short and Over

CASH PROOF

Date _December 2, 19—_

Register No. _III_

Cash Received		_180_ _00_
Less: Cash Paid Out		—
Net Cash Received		180 00
Cash in Drawer	_191_ _00_	
Less: Change Fund	_10_ _00_	
Net Cash Handled		_181_ 00
~~Short or~~ Over		_1_ 00

Clerk _James Amos_

Supervisor _L. Carson_

Cash	?	Sales
181	1	180

Cash overage: credit Cash Short and Over

When cash is handled in over-the-counter transactions, differences sometimes occur between the amount of cash that is in the drawer at the end of the day and the amount that is recorded on the cash register tape. The amount of cash in the drawer might be more than the amount shown on the tape, or less. When the reason for a cash discrepancy cannot be traced to an error, it is assumed the difference was caused by a mistake in making change.

Cash Over   If there is more cash in the drawer than there ought to be (according to the cash proof), then the cash is "over." For example, the cash register tape for December 2 indicates that net receipts from daily cash sales are $180. The supervisor copies this amount on the cash proof form. He then counts the actual cash in the drawer ($191) and subtracts the amount of the change fund ($10). This leaves a balance of $181. The cash proof shows that he should have received only $180, but the cash in the drawer is $181. Thus cash is "over" by $1. If no error can be located in the records, it must be assumed that an error was made in making change.

This cash proof is sent to the accounting department, where it becomes the source document for an entry in the journal. The debit entry is clear: the Cash account must be debited for $181 because this is the actual amount of cash that will be deposited in the bank. The credit entry, however, should show the Sales account credited for only $180. Since the debit and credit amounts must be equal, the overage of $1 must be credited to some account.

This overage could, of course, be lumped together with sales income and recorded in the Sales account. However, if this practice were followed over a period of time, the business would have a distorted record of its sales income. The solution used in most accounting systems is to set up a temporary owner's equity account entitled *Cash Short and Over.* An overage is treated as income because it increases owner's equity. Therefore, in this case, the overage of $1 is credited to the Cash Short and Over account. This transaction would be recorded in a cash receipts journal as follows:

CASH RECEIPTS JOURNAL					Page 2	
DATE	ACCOUNT CREDITED	EXPLANATION	POST. REF.	AMOUNT	
19—					
Dec. 2	Sales.	*Daily sales*.		180	00
2	Cash Short and Over.	*Cash overage*.		1	00

If these entries were posted individually to the proper accounts, the accounts would appear as follows:

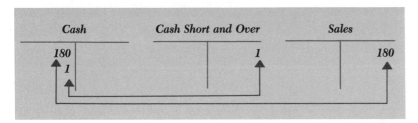

Cash	Cash Short and Over	Sales
180	1	180
1		

These T accounts demonstrate that when an overage is treated as income, the effects of the transaction can be properly assigned and the equality of debits and credits can be preserved.

Cash Short   If there is less cash in the drawer than there ought to be (according to the cash proof), then the cash is "short." Thus, if the net cash received is $318 and the net amount of cash in the drawer is $315, cash is short by $3. If the money cannot be located, it is necessary to record this shortage of $3.

Any shortage is treated like an expense because it decreases owner's equity. Therefore, the $3 shortage just described should be debited to the Cash Short and Over account. To understand the relationships in this transaction, it is again helpful to use T accounts for analysis.

Cash	Cash Short and Over	Sales
315	3	318

The debit to Cash should be only $315 because this is the actual amount that will be deposited in the bank. However, the full amount of $318 should be credited to the Sales account because this is the true income that was earned. This income, of course, is reduced by an expense of $3 (which is what the $3 shortage represents).

Cash shortage: debit Cash Short and Over

If this transaction were recorded in a general journal, it would be entered as follows:

Dec.	3	Cash............................	315	00		
		Cash Short and Over..........	3	00		
		Sales........................			318	00

However, when special cash journals are used, the transaction must be recorded in a different way. Here are the steps the accounting clerk would take.

CASH PROOF

Date _December 3, 19—_

Register No. _II_

Cash Received		318	00
Less: Cash Paid Out			
Net Cash Received		318	00
Cash in Drawer	340 00		
Less: Change Fund	25 00		
Net Cash Handled		315	00
Short ~~or Over~~		3	00

Clerk _Barbara Brown_
Supervisor _L. Carson_

1 Record a $318 credit to Sales in the cash receipts journal. (Such an entry, however, implies a $318 debit to Cash.)

CASH RECEIPTS JOURNAL					Page 2
DATE	ACCOUNT CREDITED	EXPLANATION	POST. REF.	AMOUNT	
19— Dec. 3	Sales......................	Daily sales..........		318 00	

Cash		Sales	
318			318

2 Record the $3 shortage in the cash *payments* journal. (Such an entry implies a $3 credit to Cash.)

CASH PAYMENTS JOURNAL					Page 2
DATE	ACCOUNT DEBITED	EXPLANATION	CHECK NO.	POST. REF.	AMOUNT
19— Dec. 3	Cash Short and Over......	Cash shortage.......	—		3 00

Cash		Cash Short and Over		Sales	
318	3	3			318
315					

If these entries were posted individually, the balance of the Cash account would be $315 (as in the analysis above), the Cash Short and Over account would have a $3 debit balance, and the Sales account would have a $318 credit balance.

The Cash Short and Over account summarizes the various shortages and overages in making change during an accounting period. Thus the balance of the Cash Short and Over account is considered either an expense or income, depending on whether it has a debit balance or a credit balance. When Cash Short and Over has a debit balance, it is shown as an expense item on the income statement because it decreases owner's equity. When it has a credit balance, however, it is shown as an income item because it increases owner's equity.

The Cash Short and Over account is listed in the chart of accounts for the Central Sales Company as account 511 under expenses. It is

Cash Short and Over	
Debit Balance Expense	Credit Balance Income

understood, however, that if at the end of the accounting period, the account has a credit balance, the balance will be considered as income rather than as an expense. In either case, however, the Cash Short and Over account is a temporary owner's equity account and is closed into the Income and Expense Summary account at the end of the accounting period.

The Cash Short and Over account is a useful device for reconciling accounting records when discrepancies in cash cannot be traced to actual errors. This device, however, is not a substitute for locating actual errors. It is used only when absolutely necessary.

Verifying the Cash Account Balance and the Checkbook Balance

Under an effective system of cash control, all cash receipts are deposited in a checking account and all cash payments are made by checks drawn against that account. The checkbook stubs, which carry a running record of all deposits and withdrawals to the account, serve as source documents for the journal entries. Postings are made to the Cash account from the cash receipts journal only at the end of each month. At that time, a figure representing total debits is posted from the cash receipts journal, and a figure representing total credits is posted from the cash payments journal.

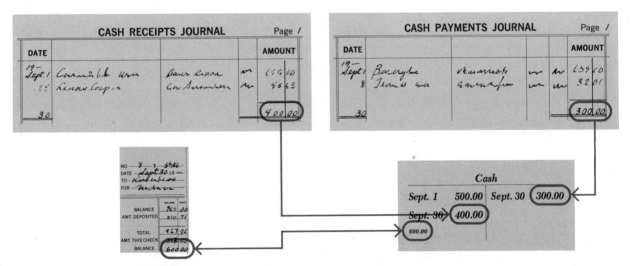

When the postings are made and the balance of the Cash account has been pencil-footed, the balance in the Cash account should be equal to the balance shown for that date in the checkbook. If there have been no errors in any of the entries or the computations, the cash proof is quite easy to make: simply compare the two totals. If they are equal, the proof is complete.

If, however, you want to take a cash proof at some time other than at the end of the month, the procedure is slightly more involved. The balance in the Cash account will not be up to date because the cash debits and credits that have been accumulating in the special journals since the end of last month have not yet been posted to the Cash account. Here, for example, are the steps you would have to take to prepare a cash proof for the Central Sales Company on November 15.

1   Obtain the balance of the Cash account as it stood at the start of the month. The memorandum entry in the cash receipts journal indicates that the balance of the Cash account as of November 1 was $9,440.00. (Here lies the advantage of entering this balance in the cash receipts journal at the start of each month; after making a cash proof, the accounting clerk can quickly locate this figure without having to look in the ledger. The fast availability of this figure is particularly helpful if one prepares a cash proof frequently.)

2   Add all the amounts recorded in the cash receipts journal between November 1 and November 15, and pencil-foot the total in the Amount column. This figure ($5,950.00) represents the total of the accumulated debits to Cash during the new month.

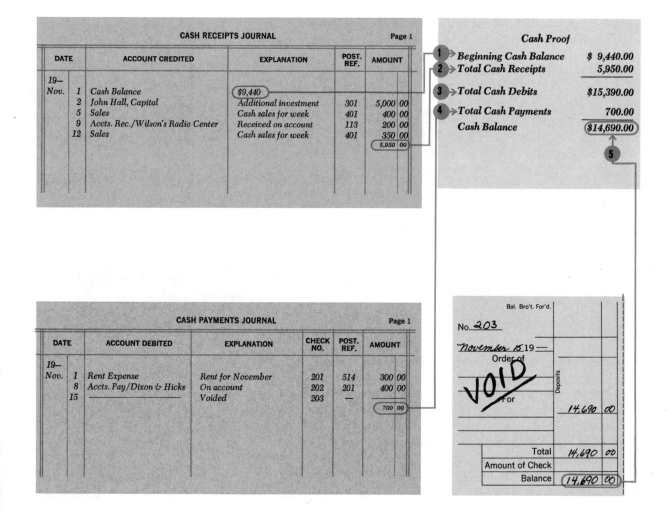

3 Add these two amounts—the debit balance at the start of the new month ($9,440.00) and the total of the accumulated debits ($5,950.00)—to obtain the total debits to Cash as of November 15.

4 Add the amounts accumulated in the cash payments journal between November 1 and November 15, and pencil-foot this total in the Amount column. This figure ($700.00) represents the total of the accumulated credits to Cash during the new month.

5 Subtract the accumulated credits ($700.00) from the total debits ($15,390.00) to determine the balance of the Cash account on November 15. This amount ($14,690.00) should equal the amount shown on the checkbook for the same date.

This kind of cash proof may be prepared any time; many businesses prepare it at regular intervals, such as daily or weekly.

It is also desirable to make this kind of cash proof at the end of the month, after the cash receipts journal and the cash payments journal have been pencil-footed but before they have been totaled and ruled. Thus discrepancies can be detected before final entries are made in ink.

Verifying the Checkbook Balance and the Bank Statement Balance

A system for cash control also requires verification that the checkbook balance equals the bank statement balance. Since there is usually a delay between the date on which a check is recorded in the checkbook and the date on which the bank pays it, the checkbook balance seldom agrees with the bank statement balance. There are, in addition, many other factors that could create an apparent discrepancy between the balance shown on the bank statement and the one shown on the latest stub of the checkbook. A bank reconciliation statement is prepared, therefore, to find out why these balances do not agree.

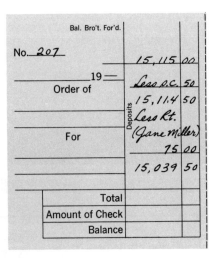

On November 30, the latest stub on the Central Sales Company's checkbook showed a balance of $15,115.00. The bank statement for the period ending November 30 showed a balance of $14,859.50. The bank reconciliation statement that was prepared for November 30 indicates that when a deposit in transit, an outstanding check, a service charge, and a dishonored check are taken into consideration, the two balances are, in fact, equal. (See page 166.)

After the bank reconciliation has been prepared, the balance on the latest checkbook stub must be brought into agreement with the final amount shown on the reconciliation statement as the "adjusted checkbook balance." In short, from the existing checkbook balance of $15,115.00, two deductions need to be made: one for a service charge of $.50, and one for a dishonored check of $75.00. When these deductions are actually recorded on the check stub, the checkbook balance will then agree with the adjusted balance shown on the reconciliation statement.

Since these deductions constitute a decrease in cash, they must be journalized and posted so that the balance in the Cash account will

Depositor *Central Sales Company*

BANK RECONCILIATION STATEMENT

November 30 19 —

BALANCE SHOWN ON BANK STATEMENT $ *14,859.50*   BALANCE SHOWN ON CHECKBOOK STUB $ *15,115.00*

Plus: Deposits in Transit

Date	Amount	
11/26	$400	00
Total Deposits in Transit	$ 400.00	

SUBTOTAL $*15,259.50*

Less: Checks Outstanding

Number	Amount	
205	$220	00
Total Checks Outstanding	$ 220.00	

Less: Charges and Fees

Description	Amount	
Service Charge	$	50
Returned check *(Jane Miller)*	75	00
Total Charges and Fees	$ 75.50	

ADJUSTED BANK BALANCE $*15,039.50*   ADJUSTED CHECKBOOK BALANCE $*15,039.50*

also agree with the adjusted balance on the reconciliation statement. Here is the procedure for journalizing such transactions.

1   To record the service charge of $.50, make an entry in the cash payments journal and debit the amount to the Miscellaneous Expense account. At the time of posting, a $.50 credit will be entered against the Cash account and thereby decrease the balance by that amount.

	CASH PAYMENTS JOURNAL				Page 2

DATE	ACCOUNT DEBITED	EXPLANATION	CHECK NO.	POST. REF.	AMOUNT
19—Dec. 2	*Miscellaneous Expense*.....	*Bank service charge*..	—	513	50

2   To record the return of a dishonored check, make an appropriate entry in the cash payments journal. This transaction is not, strictly speaking, a cash payment; however, it is treated as if it were in order to undo the original recording of this transaction as a cash receipt.

CASH RECEIPTS JOURNAL				Page 1
DATE	ACCOUNT CREDITED	EXPLANATION	POST. REF.	AMOUNT
19— Nov. 16	Accts. Rec./Jane Miller.........	On account...........	111	75 00

The dishonored check in question was originally received from Jane Miller on November 16 in partial payment of her account. At the time the check was received, the preceding entry was made in the cash receipts journal. When this entry was posted to the ledger, the Cash account was increased by $75.00 and the account receivable in Jane Miller's name was decreased by the same amount. Now that the check has been returned as uncollectible, $75.00 must be deducted from the Cash account and added back to Jane Miller's account. To do this, the following entry must be made in the *cash payments journal.*

CASH PAYMENTS JOURNAL					Page 2
DATE	ACCOUNT DEBITED	EXPLANATION	CHECK NO.	POST. REF.	AMOUNT
19— Dec. 2	Accts. Rec./Jane Miller.....	Ret'd check of Nov. 16.	—	111	75 00

TOPIC 2 ■ PROBLEMS

13 During the month of March, Warren Young, owner of Young's Delivery Service, completed the transactions below.

a Record the entries for the following transactions in a cash payments journal.

Mar. 2 Issued Check 39 for $110 for March rent.

6 Issued Check 40 for $126 to Martin Glenn on account.

12 Issued Check 41 for $24 for March telephone bill.

Mar. 13 The cash in the cash register was short $10.

14 Issued Check 42 for $140 for equipment.

b The cash receipts journal shows a pencil footing of $280 at the close of business on March 14. The beginning cash balance for the month was $760. After Check 42 has been deducted, the checkbook shows a balance of $630. Prepare a cash proof.

c Record the entries for the following transactions.

Mar. 16 Issued Check 43 for $130 to Craig Gibson on account.

19 Issued Check 44 for $80 to Warren Young, the owner, for personal use.

Mar. 23 Received the bank statement which shows a service charge of $4.50. Record the appropriate entry.

25 Issued Check 45 for $21 for utilities.

d Foot and rule the cash payments journal.

14 The Ski Shop uses a special journal to record all cash payments transactions.
a Record the following entries in a cash payments journal.

May 1 Issued Check 103 for $75 for advertising in *Our Times* magazine.

2 Issued Check 104 for $140 for May rent.

May 5 Issued Check 105 for $200 to Ann Blaine on account.

9 Issued Check 106 for $100 to Mary Browne, the owner, for her personal use.

b At the close of business on May 9, the cash receipts journal shows a pencil footing of $170. The beginning cash balance for the month was $1,120. After Check 106 is deducted, the total cash in the bank is $760. There is, however, $15 that has not been marked on the check stub because it has not been deposited yet. Prepare a cash proof.

c Record the entries for the following transactions.

May 12 Issued Check 107 for $220 for drafting tools.

15 Cash proof of the cash register shows a shortage of $5.

16 Issued Check 108 for $25 to establish a petty cash fund.

May 19 Issued Check 109 for $70 to Peter Brock on account.

20 Received the bank statement which shows a service charge of $7. Make the appropriate journal entry.

d Foot and rule the cash payments journal for the end of the month.

The Language of Business

The following terms are important. Do you understand the meaning of each? Can you define each term and use it in an original sentence?

cash payments journal	voided	Cash Short and Over
cash short	CP	storage symbol
cash over	addition-to-a-form symbol	cash proof

Chapter Questions

1 List and explain the essential procedures that are used in an accounting system for the control of cash payments.

2 Explain how the monthly bank statement provides an excellent external control of cash receipts and cash payments.

3 What are the steps involved in completing the cash payments journal at the end of the month?

4 Why are cash proofs prepared during the month?

5 When a cash receipts journal and a cash payments journal are used, how are cash proofs made during a month?

6 At the end of the accounting period, the Cash Short and Over account showed total debits of $4.80 and total credits of $3.90. Is the balance of this account considered income or an expense?

7 For the month of August, the Cash Short and Over account has total debits of $97 and total credits of $3. The accountant feels that the procedure for handling shortages and overages should be investigated. Do you agree? Why?

8 What source documents serve as the basis of the entries in the cash payments journal?

Management Cases

Control of Cash Disbursements Many businesses lose large sums of money through the petty theft of cash. Small amounts taken by dishonest employees can add up to a sizable sum over a period of time. Reports of the embezzlement of large sums are frequent news items. A business should set up safeguards to control cash in order to (1) remove temptations to theft and (2) protect the reputations of all employees.

Case M-4

The Rose Social Club plans to hold a dance to raise money for a recreation center. The treasurer has planned the following system for handling and recording cash.

1 The dance committee chairman will issue ten unnumbered dance tickets to each committee member for advance sale.

2 Whenever the committee members need more tickets, they will turn in the cash from tickets they have sold and receive enough new tickets to bring the total number of tickets in their possession up to the original number of ten.

3 The chairman will pay expenses for the dance from the ticket receipts on hand at the time.

4 Tickets will not be issued on the night of the dance; people without tickets will pay cash at the door.

Analyze the merits of this system by answering the following questions:

a What are the advantages of using prenumbered tickets?

b Why should the chairman turn in all ticket receipts to the treasurer?

c Would you bother selling tickets at the door on dance night? Why?

d What proof should the chairman submit to verify that he paid the expenses?

Case M-5

The Classic Sign Company, a manufacturer of signs and billboards, has branches in a number of cities. Assume that you have been appointed manager of a branch office. In addition to the people who work in the shop, there are five people in the office: the manager (your position), a secretary, a bookkeeper, and two clerks. The secretary and the bookkeeper have been with the branch office for a number of years. These procedures are followed in the handling of cash:

1 The manager, the secretary, and the bookkeeper are authorized to sign checks.

2 Money is received primarily through the mail, which is opened by any office employee whose time permits. The person who opens the mail fills out a remittance slip for each amount received and gives the slip to the bookkeeper and places all cash receipts in a locked box.

3 Because the bank is a thirty-minute drive from the office, deposits are usually made once a week. Any member of the office staff may be given the responsibility of taking the deposit to the bank. Weekly deposits total approximately $2,000.

4 A cash receipts journal and a cash payments journal are kept, and all cash receipts and cash expenditures are recorded in these journals by the bookkeeper only.

5 All bills are checked, approved, and paid by check either by the bookkeeper or by the secretary, whoever has the time. Since both are authorized to write checks, they and the manager have access to the checkbook and can write and sign checks.

6 All checks are numbered. When an error is made in preparing a check, the check is discarded and a note is made on the checkbook stub.

7 Small expenditures are made from a petty cash fund. Although a careful record is kept of the amounts put in the fund, no record is kept of the payments from it. The fund is kept in a small box in the secretary's desk. Either she, the bookkeeper, or the manager may take money from the box to pay for small items. (Each withdrawal usually is less than $1, but no uniform policy is observed.) When the fund in the box is exhausted, cash is taken from the cash deposit and placed in the petty cash box.

What specific recommendations would you make to provide better cash control?

Case M-6

The Sussex Building Supply Company started as a very small business. In the beginning, there were only a few transactions each week. The owner kept all the records, which consisted of a two-column journal (in which all transactions were journalized) and a ledger (in which all ledger accounts were kept). As business increased, a clerk was employed to do the office work, including keeping the records. Later, another clerk was employed to do the general office work. The first clerk was given the title of accounting clerk and was to spend full time on the books.

At present time, the business has grown significantly. The accounting clerk finds that she cannot keep up with all the work; she has asked the owner to employ another person to help with the journal and the ledger. Although the number of transactions has greatly increased, the record system being used is the same as the one originally set up by the owner. All entries are first recorded in the two-column general journal and then posted to the accounts in the ledger.

If you were the owner, what steps would you take to determine whether or not the accounting clerk needs an assistant? Support your recommendation with suggestions.

Working Hint

Common Errors in Recording Amounts

Here are some practical tips for avoiding the most common types of errors made in recording amounts.

Doubling the Wrong Digit This type of error occurs when a number is misread or miscopied: for example, copying $1.19 as $1.99 or $2.99 as $2.29. Such errors may be avoided by grouping the numbers as you read them; for example, read "one nineteen" instead of "one, one, nine" or "two ninety-nine" instead of "two, nine, nine."

Transposing Digits Digits are sometimes transposed when they are copied. For example, $.56 may be erroneously written as $.65, or $89 may be written as $98. This kind of error can be avoided by rechecking each figure after you have written it.

Changing the Magnitude This type of error results from writing the initial digit of a number in the wrong column: for example, writing $4,000 for $400 or $500 for $5,000. When the Amount column contains only one vertical rule to separate dollars and cents, errors may be avoided by using a comma to divide thousands from hundreds.

Chapter 3
Processing Purchases of Merchandise

Business firms that obtain income through buying and selling goods are known as *merchandising businesses*. These firms may be *retailers* (who sell directly to consumers) or *wholesalers* (who sell to retailers and sometimes to large consumers). The goods purchased for resale are known as *merchandise*. The merchandise that a business has in stock is known as *merchandise inventory*.

In any merchandising business, regardless of its size or the nature of its operations, some system must be established to control the way in which the merchandise is purchased and handled.

Merchandise: goods purchased for resale.

Merchandise inventory: merchandise in stock.

TOPIC 1 ■ A SYSTEM FOR THE CONTROL OF PURCHASES

In any accounting system designed to control the purchase of merchandise, forms and procedures must be established for the four primary operations involved: (1) ordering the merchandise, (2) receiving the merchandise, (3) accounting for the merchandise, and (4) storing the merchandise.

Ordering the Merchandise

In a small business, all the activities involved in ordering merchandise may be handled by the owner. In a large organization, however, the ordering operation is usually handled by a special purchasing department, headed by a purchasing agent. Regardless of the size of the firm, the ordering operation involves (1) determining what needs to be purchased, (2) selecting the supplier, and (3) placing the order.

Determining Needs In a small business, a notation on a piece of paper or in a book could be a signal that the supply of some item of merchandise is low and thus needs to be reordered. In a large business like the Central Sales Company, where there are a number of separate merchandising departments, the signal that merchandise needs to be reordered comes from *inventory cards*.

The inventory card provides a record of the stock of only one item—in this case, Curtis AM/FM Portable Radios (27-P12). The

INVENTORY CARD

No. 27-P12

Item Curtis AM/FM Portable Radio

Location: Aisle 18   Bin 7

Maximum 22   Minimum 10

Date	Quant. Rec'd	Unit Cost	Quant. Sold	Balance
19— 11/13	22	31.50		22
11/20			3	19
11/27			2	17
12/4			1	16
12/12			1	15
12/18			2	13
12/23			3	10

minimum stock for reordering this item has been set at 10. Thus, on December 23, when the inventory of these radios drops to 10, the manager of the radio department knows that it is time to order additional stock. Since the maximum stock of Curtis radios of this model has been set at 22, the manager can quickly determine that he needs to purchase 12 additional radios in order to replenish his stock. These quantities set as the minimum and the maximum are established in terms of the average volume of sales and how long it takes to get new stock.

To initiate the entire purchasing function, the department manager prepares a written request, called a *purchase requisition,* asking the purchasing agent to order the necessary merchandise. The purchase requisition provides the following information: WHO is making the request, WHAT is to be purchased, and WHEN it is needed.

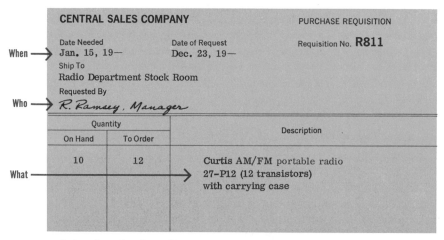

Selecting the Supplier The purchasing agent has a list of suppliers for most items that are to be purchased. From this list he selects the supplier who is best able to provide the merchandise needed. The supplier may be selected because of the price that he quotes. For example, the price list published by George Young quotes Kool-Ray electric fans at $4.60 each, whereas a competitor might quote the same fans at $5.00 each. The supplier may be selected because of the items he carries. For example, George Young carries the Kool-Ray electric fans, which are described in his catalog as 12-inch fans, whereas a competitor carries 10-inch electric fans. Finally, the selection of the supplier might be based solely upon the service and satisfactory delivery he gave on previous purchases.

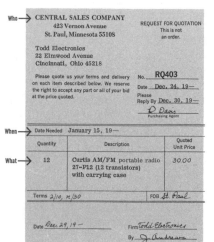

If the items requisitioned have not been previously ordered, or if the purchasing agent wants to consider other sources of supply, the purchasing agent might need to request prices from prospective suppliers. He requests these prices by sending a letter or a special form called a *request for quotation.* The form tells the prospective supplier WHO is making the request for a quotation, WHAT items and quantities are wanted, and WHEN the goods are needed.

The request for quotation illustrated on page 172 was prepared by the purchasing agent of the Central Sales Company upon receipt of a purchase requisition for 12 Curtis radios. One copy is retained on file by the purchasing agent; other copies are sent to prospective suppliers. One of these suppliers, Todd Electronics, indicates on the form that it can supply the needed items at $30 per unit at the terms shown. Todd Electronics then signs the form and returns it to the Central Sales Company.

On the request for quotation, Todd Electronics shows the credit terms of 2/10, n/30. The expression "2/10" means that the buyer can deduct 2 percent of the total bill if he pays it within 10 days from the date of the bill. In the expression "n/30," the *n* stands for *net;* the complete expression signifies that if the buyer does not want to take advantage of the discount, he has 30 days in which to pay the full (net) amount. (If the terms were n/EOM, the net amount would have to be paid at the end of the month.)

> 2/10, n/30: 2% discount if bill paid in 10 days; otherwise net amount due in 30 days.

In addition to specifying credit terms, Todd Electronics indicates that the goods will be shipped "FOB St. Paul." The expression *FOB* stands for *free on board;* thus Todd Electronics will pay the shipping charges from Cincinnati to St. Paul. (If the form showed "FOB Cincinnati," Central Sales would have to pay the shipping charges.)

> FOB: free on board.

Since the price quoted by Todd Electronics is lower than what other wholesalers have quoted, the purchasing agent of Central Sales decides to order the radios from this company. Having selected the supplier, the purchasing agent must now initiate the form that will establish a firm legal agreement between Central Sales and Todd Electronics. This form is called a *purchase order.*

Placing the Order   The purchase order that is drawn up by the purchasing agent authorizes the supplier to ship the merchandise specified and to charge the purchaser for these goods at the quoted price. For each item listed on the purchase order there should be (1) a figure indicating the quantity ordered; (2) a stock number for the item, if the number is known; (3) a brief description of the item; (4) the unit price, taken either from the supplier's catalog or from his signed copy of the request for quotation; (5) the terms for paying the bill; and (6) instructions for shipping the goods.

The number of copies of the purchase order that are prepared varies with the size of the business and the kind of control system used. Under the system used by the Central Sales Company, purchase orders are prepared on prenumbered forms, each of which contains five copies. Copy 1 is sent to the supplier, in this case Todd Electronics, who customarily returns an acknowledgment of this order. Copy 2 is sent to the department that submitted the purchase requisition to confirm that the needed merchandise is now on order. The purchasing department retains Copy 3 for its own numerical files in order to keep a record of all purchase orders issued. Copies 4 and 5 are sent to the receiving department, where they are held until the goods ordered actually arrive.

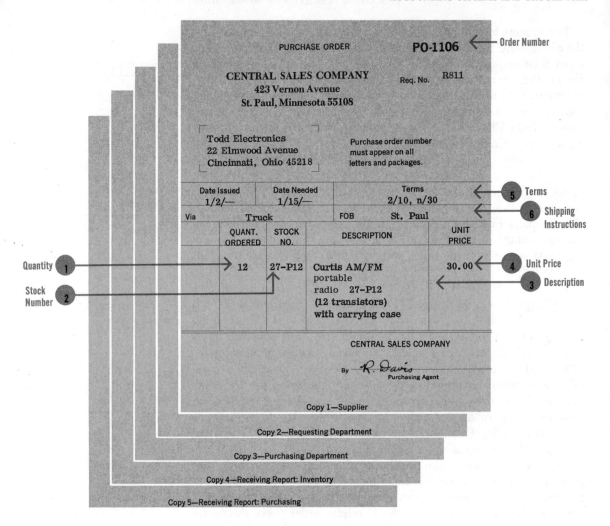

Receiving the Merchandise

When the merchandise is received from the supplier, (1) it must be unpacked, inspected, and counted; (2) it must be recorded as being received; and (3) it must be moved to the storage or sales area of the department that submitted the purchase requisition. All these activities make up the second major operation in the purchasing procedure—receiving the merchandise.

When merchandise comes into the receiving department, the receiving clerk must check the merchandise to determine any shortages, errors, or damages in the shipment. The receiving clerk enters his count of the goods actually received on Copy 4 of the purchase order. If any items are damaged or missing or do not agree with the description on the purchase order, the receiving clerk holds the shipment and notifies the purchasing agent to find out how the shipment should be handled. If, however, the merchandise is received in good

INVENTORY CARD

No. *27-P12*

Item *Curtis AM/FM Portable Radio*

Location: *18* Bin *7*

Maximum *22* Minimum *10*

Date	Quant. Rec'd	Unit Cost	Quant. Sold	Balance
19— 11/13	22	31.50		22
11/20			3	19
11/27			2	17
12/4			1	16
12/12			1	15
12/18			2	13
12/23			3	10
12/28			2	8
1/2			3	5
1/8			1	4
1/10	12	30.00		16

PURCHASE ORDER **PO-1106**

CENTRAL SALES COMPANY Req. No. R811
423 Vernon Avenue
St. Paul, Minnesota 55108

Todd Electronics
22 Elmwood Avenue
Cincinnati, Ohio 45218

Goods Received 1/10/—
Quantity Checked *On*
Quality Checked *GA*

Date Issued 1/2/—	Date Needed 1/15/—	Terms 2/10, n/30
Via Truck	FOB	St. Paul

QUANT. REC'D	QUANT. ORDERED	STOCK NO.	DESCRIPTION	UNIT PRICE
12	12	27-P12	Curtis AM/FM portable radio 27-P12 (12 transistors) with carrying case	30.00

CENTRAL SALES COMPANY

By *R. Davis*
Purchasing Agent

Copy 4—Receiving Report: Inventory

condition and agrees with the description on the purchase order, the receiving clerk indicates that the shipment is accepted by initialing the appropriate items in the approved section of Copy 4—the receiving report. The goods are then sent, along with Copy 4, to the stockroom or the department that requisitioned these items. There the shipment is again counted and checked before being put into inventory. Copy 4 serves as the source document for updating the inventory cards for the items received. Copy 5, which also carries the receiving clerk's initials of approval, is sent to the purchasing agent to inform him that the shipment has been received and accepted.

Accounting for the Merchandise

When the purchasing agent receives Copy 5 from the receiving department (confirming that all the items ordered have been received in good condition), he holds this copy of the purchase order until he receives an *invoice* (a bill) from the supplier. To the purchaser, this bill is a *purchase invoice* because it lists the items that he has purchased. To the supplier who has issued this form, it is a *sales invoice* because it lists the items he has sold. The invoice on page 176 would be considered a purchase invoice by the Central Sales Company and a sales invoice by Todd Electronics.

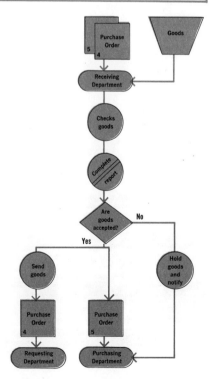

Invoice: bill.

Purchase invoice:
bill for merchandise
purchased.

Sales invoice: bill
for merchandise
sold.

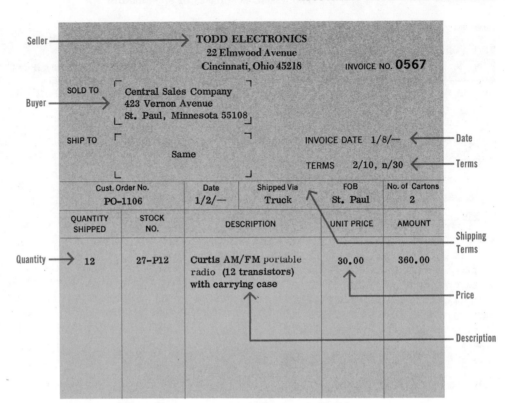

Seller →	**TODD ELECTRONICS**			
	22 Elmwood Avenue			
	Cincinnati, Ohio 45218		INVOICE NO. **0567**	

SOLD TO — Buyer →
Central Sales Company
423 Vernon Avenue
St. Paul, Minnesota 55108

SHIP TO
Same

INVOICE DATE 1/8/— ← Date

TERMS   2/10, n/30 ← Terms

Cust. Order No. PO-1106	Date 1/2/—	Shipped Via Truck	FOB St. Paul	No. of Cartons 2
QUANTITY SHIPPED	STOCK NO.	DESCRIPTION	UNIT PRICE	AMOUNT
12	27-P12	Curtis AM/FM portable radio (12 transistors) with carrying case	30.00	360.00

Quantity →

Shipping Terms

Price

Description

Extension: unit price
multiplied by
number of units
purchased.

GEORGE YOUNG		INVOICE NO. **P903**
318 Howell Street		
St. Paul, Minnesota 55119		

SOLD TO Central Sales Company
423 Vernon Avenue
St. Paul, Minnesota 55108

SHIP TO
Same

Invoice Date 1/27/—

Terms 1/10, n/30

Purchase Order No. PO-1112	Date 1/20/—	Shipped Via Truck	FOB St. Paul	No. of Cartons 6
QUANTITY	DESCRIPTION		UNIT PRICE	AMOUNT
12	76-A Minute Man Timers		2.50	30.00
10	213-J Kool-Ray Elec. Fan 12 in.		4.60	46.00
	TOTAL			76.00

The invoice form sent by the supplier contains almost the same kind of information that was supplied on the purchase order by the buyer. It shows the name and address of the seller and the buyer; the invoice number and the date; the terms; the buyer's purchase order number and date (for cross reference); the method of shipment; and, most important, the quantity, price, and description of each item shipped. Unlike the purchase order, the invoice contains a computation of the amount owed. Each amount shown in the Amount column is called an *extension*. The extension is determined by multiplying the unit price of the item by the number of units shipped. The amount shown in the invoice above ($360) was computed by multiplying the unit price ($30) by the number of units shipped (12). If the invoice showed more than one extension in the Amount column (as would occur if more than one kind of merchandise has been shipped), then the extensions would be added to show the total amount owed.

When the purchasing agent of Central Sales Company receives the invoice from Todd Electronics, he compares it with Copy 5 of the purchase order to make sure he has been billed only for the merchandise actually received. If there are any discrepancies between the purchase order and the invoice, he notifies the supplier to resolve them. However, if the invoice is correct as submitted, the purchasing agent stamps the invoice with a special "Approved" stamp and initials those items that he has checked and verified as being correct. He forwards the invoice to the accounting department for further checking and then journalizing and payment. Copy 5 is entered in numerical sequence in the purchasing department's permanent file of completed purchase orders.

When the purchase invoice comes to the accounting department, the extensions and the totals are rechecked and the invoice is journalized. Finally, when the invoice is due, a check is issued for the correct amount. As the invoice passes through each step in the accounting department, the person responsible initials the invoice to indicate which items he has checked and approved. In the next topic, we shall discuss how a purchase invoice is journalized and paid.

The flowchart on page 178 illustrates various operations involved in the purchasing procedure described in this topic. The activities (numbered 1 through 17) are described briefly under the various departments and the selected supplier headings. By reading the activities and following the flowchart, you can see how each activity is related to the operations of ordering the merchandise, receiving the merchandise, and accounting for the merchandise.

Storing the Merchandise

The merchandise that a business keeps on hand for sale is called *inventory*. Since goods are continually being purchased and sold, the inventory changes frequently. An effective system for the control of purchases must also provide for (1) controlling the quantity of items held in inventory, (2) keeping an accurate, up-to-date record of the inventory, and (3) storing the goods in such a way as to avoid deterioration or loss of value.

Quantity Control To satisfy potential customers, a merchandising business should have a large assortment of goods on hand, in a wide variety of sizes, styles, or models (as appropriate) so that the customer has a good selection to choose from and can obtain immediate delivery. If a merchandising business cannot provide a broad selection and provide fast delivery, it will lose its customers. Thus it must establish a minimum inventory on every item in stock. Whenever the quantity drops to this minimum, additional merchandise must be requisitioned.

While it is important to keep inventories from being exhausted, it is equally important for a merchandising business not to carry a greater quantity of any item than it can sell in a reasonable amount of time. There are several reasons why this is so. First, excess inventory ties up money that could be invested in other assets. For example, a hardware store that sells no more than 50 snow blowers a winter would be foolish to order 100 snow blowers at a time; the money needed to pay for the second winter's supply of snow blowers could be better spent on some other kind of merchandise. A second reason

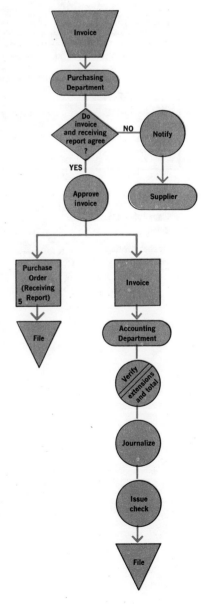

FLOWCHART OF A PURCHASING SYSTEM

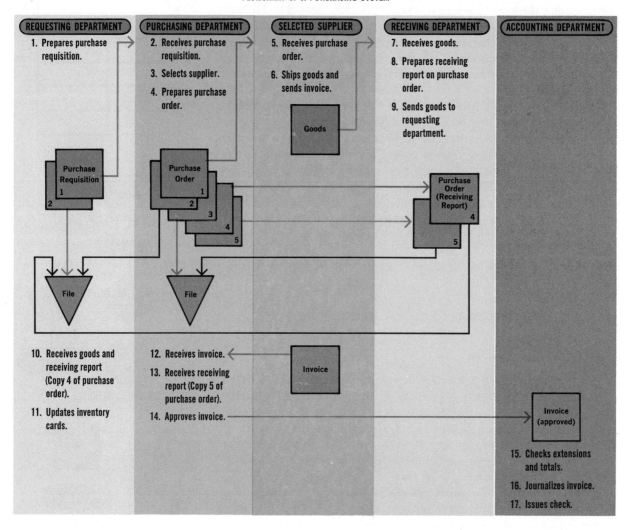

for establishing a maximum quantity for each item in inventory is to avoid the expense of building or renting additional storage space. If 100 snow blowers were ordered, the excess 50 blowers might well be taking up space the hardware store needs for lawn mowers during the spring and summer season. A third reason for setting a maximum stock quantity for each item is that most kinds of merchandise decrease in value after a certain period of time, either because of physical deterioration or because of changes in style (as in the case of dresses) or because of innovations in new products that make the current stock obsolete. Thus, if a more efficient and less expensive snow blower is developed in the coming six months, the owner might find it difficult to sell his remaining stock the following winter.

In setting minimum and maximum quantities for each item in inventory, a manager should consider (1) what quantity of this item is sold, on the average, during a week or a month or a year (whichever is the most appropriate span); (2) how long it takes to have new stock delivered after an order has been placed, and (3) how fast the stock might decrease in value because of deterioration or obsolescence.

Keeping Up-to-Date Inventory Records Some businesses keep a continuous day-to-day record of each item they have in their merchandise inventory. This type of inventory system is known as a *perpetual inventory* and requires a separate inventory card to be kept for each item. Whenever new merchandise is received or sold, the changes in quantity are subtracted or added so that each card will show the current balance of the quantity on hand for each item. If the unit cost of each item is also provided on the inventory card, the accountant can quickly compute the total cost of the current merchandise inventory.

However, many small retail stores, such as grocery stores, hardware stores, and drugstores, find it impractical to record each sale and purchase on an inventory card for each of the low-priced items that it handles. For example, it would be too expensive and time-consuming to have an inventory clerk in a drugstore record each sale of aspirin on an inventory card. These businesses use the *periodic inventory method.* In this method, the merchandise in inventory is counted at regular intervals in order to determine the total number of items in inventory at that time. This periodic inventory is taken at specified times, such as every month, every six months, or every year.

A druggist, for example, might order additional aspirin every two weeks. He uses an order sheet which lists the items he generally carries. Beside each item on the order sheet he lists the maximum and minimum numbers that he should have in stock. When he is ready to place an order, he simply counts the bottles of aspirin he has on hand and then determines the quantity he wants to order.

Whenever inventory is actually counted, it is called a *physical inventory* because every item must be counted and listed on a sheet.

Perpetual inventory: continuous record of each item in stock.

Periodic inventory: inventory counted at regular intervals.

Physical inventory: inventory actually counted.

ORDER FORM

BEELINE DRUGS, INC.

August 14, 19—

Description and Size	Stock No.	Max.	Min.	On Hand	Order
Aspirin, 100	0870	100	50	40	60
Aspirin, 50	0871	200	100	75	125
Aspirin, 25	0872	300	150	180	—

INVENTORY SHEET

CENTRAL SALES COMPANY
423 Vernon Avenue
St. Paul, Minnesota 55108

Date December 31, 19— Sheet No. 8

Counted By M. West Recorded By J. Mann Figured By G. Rice

STOCK NO.	QUANTITY	UNIT OF COUNT	DESCRIPTION	UNIT PRICE	EXTENSION
30-P10	5	ea.	AM Portable Radio (10 transistors, 6x4 speaker)	21 00	105 00
937-R48	3	ea.	4-Band Receiver (with ...)	125 00	375 00
				TOTAL	1,751 50

In order to have accurate financial statements, every merchandising business needs to take physical inventory at the end of the accounting period. All businesses should therefore take a physical inventory at least once a year. An actual count of the items for the inventory is the only way the accountant can have an accurate record of the goods actually on hand. Even if perpetual inventory cards are kept for each item, a business will not know how many units have been lost as a result of theft or breakage, unless a physical inventory is taken.

TOPIC 1 ■ PROBLEMS

15 Answer the following questions about the purchase requisition on page 172, the request for quotation on page 172, the purchase order on page 174, the receiving report on page 175, and the purchase invoice on page 176.

a What is the date of the requisition?
b What is the requisition number?
c Who requested the goods?
d To what location were the goods to be shipped?
e What quantity was requisitioned and what amount was on hand?
f What unit price was quoted by Todd Electronics?
g Who signed and approved the purchase order?

h What is the purchase order number?
i What is the order date?
j How are the goods to be shipped?
k What are the terms of the purchase?
l When were the goods received?
m What quantity was received?
n What is the invoice number?
o What is the invoice date?
p What is the total invoice price?

16 On a form similar to the one below, answer the following questions based on the flowchart of a purchasing system on page 178.

Form	Disposition	Purpose
EXAMPLE: Purchase Requisition Copy 1	Purchasing Department	Tells the purchasing agent what is needed, when it is needed, and by whom.
Purchase Requisition Copy 2		

a What is the disposition of the two copies of the purchase requisition? What is the purpose for making each copy?
b What is the disposition of the five copies of the purchase order? What is the purpose for making each copy?
c What is the disposition of the two copies of the receiving report? What is the purpose for making each copy?
d What is the disposition of the approved invoice? What is the purpose?

17 On two inventory cards like the one on page 175, record these items.

Item 35: steam iron, aisle 12, bin 4, maximum 72, minimum 18, balance of 28 on June 1, unit cost $8.

Item 63: portable mixer, aisle 13, bin 8, maximum 60, minimum 12, balance of 17 on June 1, unit cost $9.50.

The following quantities received and sold were taken from receiving reports and shipping reports.

June 3 Sold 8 Item 35.
4 Sold 6 Item 63.
9 Sold 8 Item 35.
12 Received 49 Item 63; unit cost, $9.50.
13 Sold 12 Item 63.
16 Received 60 Item 35; unit cost, $8.
17 Sold 12 Item 35.
Sold 8 Item 63.
18 Sold 12 Item 35.

June 19 Sold 12 Item 35.
Sold 12 Item 63.
23 Sold 15 Item 35.
24 Sold 18 Item 63.
26 Sold 6 Item 35.
July 1 Received 50 Item 63; unit cost, $9.25.
3 Received 57 Item 35; unit cost, $8.50.
6 Sold 8 Item 63.
7 Sold 2 Item 63.

a Record the quantities received and sold; update the inventory cards.

b Report on what dates purchase requisitions should be issued.

TOPIC 2 ■ THE PURCHASES JOURNAL

Before a business can sell merchandise, it must spend money to purchase the goods to be resold. The amounts paid for the merchandise are called *costs*. The amounts received from the sale of the merchandise are considered *income*. The relationship between costs and income determines whether a business will have a gross profit from which to pay its expenses. If the gross profit is larger than the expenses, the company will have a net income. If the expenses are greater than the gross profit, the company will suffer a net loss.

Income	(from sale of goods)
− Cost	(of goods sold)
Gross Profit	(on sales)
− Expenses	(to operate business)
Net Income or Net Loss	

Accounting for Purchases of Merchandise

To have a gross profit, a merchandising business must sell its goods at a price higher than it pays for them. For example, the Central Sales Company buys the portable radios for $30 and sells them for $40. Expressing this relationship in accounting terms, we would say that the *income* from the goods sold is $40, the *cost* of the goods is $30, and the gross profit on the sale is $10. This gross profit of $10 is used to cover the expenses incurred in operating the business.

Purchasing goods for resale is much like incurring an expense in operating a business. Until the merchandise has been sold, the cost of the merchandise decreases owner's equity. In order to record the costs of all merchandise purchased during an accounting period, a temporary owner's equity account called *Purchases* is established. The amounts in this account can be viewed as costs that decrease owner's equity *until the merchandise is sold*. Cost accounts are similar

Income from Goods Sold	$40
Less: Cost of Goods Sold	30
Gross Profit	$10

Purchases account: temporary owner's equity account to record cost of merchandise purchased.

**CENTRAL SALES COMPANY
CHART OF ACCOUNTS**

COSTS AND EXPENSES

501 *Purchases*
511 *Cash Short and Over*
512 *Insurance Expense*
513 *Miscellaneous Expense*
514 *Rent Expense*
515 *Salaries Expense*
516 *Supplies Expense*
517 *Utilities Expense*

to expense accounts because both decrease owner's equity and both are temporary accounts. Accountants generally group these accounts and call them "Cost and Expense Accounts." (Remember, that expenses are amounts spent to operate the business, whereas costs are amounts spent to acquire merchandise to be resold.) In the Central Sales Company, Purchases is number 501.

Purchases for Cash   When a business pays cash for merchandise, the asset Cash is credited because cash decreases. The owner's equity account Purchases is debited because there is a decrease in owner's equity until the merchandise is sold.

January 2:   The Central Sales Company purchases merchandise for $100 and immediately issues Check 130 in payment.

WHAT HAPPENS	ACCOUNTING RULE	ENTRY
Cost of merchandise decreases owner's equity by $100.	*To decrease owner's equity, debit the account.*	*Debit: Purchases, $100.*
The asset Cash *decreases by $100.*	*To decrease an asset, credit the account.*	*Credit: Cash, $100.*

Purchases on Credit   When merchandise is purchased on credit, a liability is incurred. Thus the liability Accounts Payable is credited because liabilities increase.

January 10:   The Central Sales Company purchases merchandise from Todd Electronics for $360 on credit.

WHAT HAPPENS	ACCOUNTING RULE	ENTRY
Cost of merchandise decreases owner's equity by $360.	*To decrease owner's equity, debit the account.*	*Debit: Purchases, $360.*
The liability Accounts Payable *increases by $360.*	*To increase a liability, credit the account.*	*Credit: Accts. Pay./Todd Electronics, $360.*

The Purchases account is used *only* for merchandise acquired for resale; assets acquired for business use (such as trucks) are debited to the appropriate asset account, *not* the Purchases account.

Journalizing Purchases for Cash

When merchandise is purchased for cash, the entry is recorded in the cash payments journal because the transaction involves a credit to

Cash. The entry to record the January 2 transaction for the cash purchase of merchandise for $100 would be recorded as follows:

CASH PAYMENTS JOURNAL					Page 3
DATE	ACCOUNT DEBITED	EXPLANATION	CHECK NO.	POST. REF.	CASH CREDIT
19— Jan. 2	Purchases.............	Fisher Co............	130		100 00

Journalizing Purchases on Credit

The purchase invoice is the source document that supplies the information for the journal entry. Thus the journal entry to record the purchase of merchandise on credit cannot be made until the purchase invoice has been approved by the purchasing department. Once approved, an invoice for the purchase of merchandise on credit is the basis for a debit to Purchases and a credit to the creditor's account. This transaction cannot be recorded in the cash payments journal, however, because the account credited is Accounts Payable, not Cash.

This transaction is journalized as illustrated below:

GENERAL JOURNAL					Page 5
DATE	ACCOUNT TITLE AND EXPLANATION	POST. REF.	DEBIT	CREDIT	
19— Jan. 10	Purchases..............................	501	360 00		
	Accts. Pay./Todd Electronics.............	202		360 00	
	Inv. 0567; (1/8); 2/10, n/30.				
11	Purchases..............................	501	1,204 00		
	Accts. Pay./Dixon and Hicks.............	201		1,204 00	
	Inv. 82A; (1/10); n/EOM.				

Purchases	501		Accts. Pay./Dixon and Hicks	201		Accts. Pay./Todd Electronics	202
19— Jan. 10 J5 360			19— Jan. 11 J5 1,204			19— Jan. 10 J5 360	
11 J5 1,204							

When a business has many transactions involving purchases on credit, a purchases journal may be used to save time and space. A one-column purchases journal can be used because each entry has a debit to Purchases; only the credit entries to the individual accounts change. As in the previous special journals, the credit part of the entry can be recorded on one line, and the debits to Purchases can be accumulated for one entry (the total) at the end of the month.

Purchases journal: book of original entry to record purchases of merchandise on credit.

PURCHASES JOURNAL						Page *1*
DATE	ACCOUNT CREDITED	INVOICE		TERMS	POST. REF.	AMOUNT
		NO.	DATE			
19—						
Jan. 10	*Todd Electronics*	0567	1/8	2/10, n/30	202	360 00
11	*Dixon & Hicks*	82A	1/10	n/EOM	201	1,204 00
14	*George Young*	P876	1/14	1/10, n/30		200 00
22	*Vista Corporation*	106A	1/20	2/10, n/30		240 00
25	*Todd Electronics*	0664	1/22	2/10, n/30		850 00
27	*George Young*	P903	1/27	1/10, n/30		76 00

Posting entries from a purchases journal is similar to posting entries from other one-column journals. The invoice number is shown in the explanation section of the account. Thus, anyone can quickly trace the entry to the original invoice should a question arise.

Accts. Pay./Todd Electronics								Account No. *202*
DATE	EXPLANATION	POST. REF.	DEBIT	DATE	EXPLANATION	POST. REF.	CREDIT	
				19—				
				Jan. 10	*Inv. 0567*	P1	360 00	

Accts. Pay./Dixon & Hicks								Account No. *201*
DATE	EXPLANATION	POST. REF.	DEBIT	DATE	EXPLANATION	POST. REF.	CREDIT	
				19—				
				Jan. 11	*Inv. 82A*	P1	1,204 00	

Each credit entry in the purchases journal is posted individually to the appropriate creditor's account. The credit postings are usually made daily so that the accountant will know at all times how much is owed to each creditor. The account numbers placed in the Posting Reference column indicate those accounts that have been posted. In the creditors' accounts, the letter P and the page number indicate

P: purchases journal.

that the amount has been posted from the purchases journal.

At the end of each month, the purchases journal should be totaled in order to determine the debit amount that should be posted to the Purchases account. The same procedure is used for totaling and ruling the purchases journal as was used for the cash receipts journal and the cash payments journal. The only difference is that the words "Purchases Debit" are written in the Account Credited column.

DATE	ACCOUNT CREDITED	INVOICE		TERMS	POST. REF.	AMOUNT
		NO.	DATE			
19—						
Jan. 10	Todd Electronics.........	0567	1/8	2/10, n/30	202	360 00
11	Dixon & Hicks...........	82A	1/10	n/EOM	201	1,204 00
14	George Young...........	P876	1/14	1/10, n/30	204	200 00
22	Vista Corporation.........	106A	1/20	2/10, n/30	203	240 00
25	Todd Electronics.........	0664	1/22	2/10, n/30	202	850 00
27	George Young...........	P903	1/27	1/10, n/30	204	76 00
31	Purchases Debit........				501	2,930 00

PURCHASES JOURNAL Page 1

After the journal is totaled and ruled, the total amount of the purchases is posted to the debit side of the Purchases account. When the amount is posted, the number of the Purchases account is written in the Posting Reference column of the purchases journal.

After all entries for January have been posted for the Central Sales Company, the Purchases account will show only one debit of $2,930 for all purchases on credit during the entire month. The total of the credits posted from the purchases journal to the various creditors' accounts in the ledger also equals $2,930. Thus the debit posted equals the total credits posted.

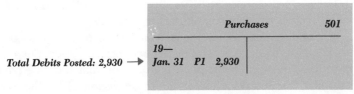

Total Debits Posted: 2,930 → Purchases 501
Jan. 31 P1 2,930

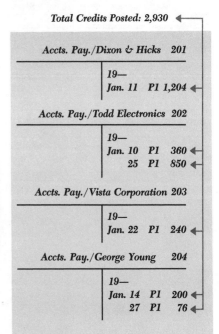

Total Credits Posted: 2,930 ←

Accts. Pay./Dixon & Hicks 201
19—
Jan. 11 P1 1,204 ←

Accts. Pay./Todd Electronics 202
19—
Jan. 10 P1 360 ←
25 P1 850 ←

Accts. Pay./Vista Corporation 203
19—
Jan. 22 P1 240 ←

Accts. Pay./George Young 204
19—
Jan. 14 P1 200 ←
27 P1 76 ←

The purchases journal, like the other special journals, saves time and space in journalizing and in posting and permits more than one person to work on the books at one time. One person might be assigned to record all invoices in the purchases journal; another might be responsible for the cash receipts journal; another, for the cash payments journal; and still another, for the general journal.

When a purchases journal is used, however, only purchases *on credit* can be recorded in the purchases journal. If the merchandise is purchased for cash, the transaction should be recorded in the cash payments journal. If an asset other than merchandise for resale is bought—furniture, for example—then the appropriate asset account (not the Purchases account) is debited for the amount of the invoice.

Purchases journal: merchandise purchased on credit.

Cash payments journal: merchandise purchased for cash.

Trade Discounts

Many wholesalers and manufacturers publish catalogs in which they describe their products and list the retail prices. They frequently

Trade discount:
deduction from list
price.

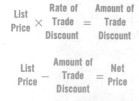

$$\begin{array}{ccc} \text{List} \\ \text{Price} \end{array} \times \begin{array}{c} \text{Rate of} \\ \text{Trade} \\ \text{Discount} \end{array} = \begin{array}{c} \text{Amount of} \\ \text{Trade} \\ \text{Discount} \end{array}$$

$$\begin{array}{ccc} \text{List} \\ \text{Price} \end{array} - \begin{array}{c} \text{Amount of} \\ \text{Trade} \\ \text{Discount} \end{array} = \begin{array}{c} \text{Net} \\ \text{Price} \end{array}$$

VISTA CORPORATION
16 Remington Street
Detroit, Michigan 48217

Sold To: Central Sales Company
423 Vernon Avenue
St. Paul, Minnesota 55108

Invoice No. **106A**
Date January 20, 19—
Terms 2/10, n/30

| Salesman | Your Order No. | Shipped By | | FOB |
| Hunt | PO1135 | Truck | | St. Paul |

QUANTITY	STOCK NO.	DESCRIPTION	UNIT PRICE	EXTENSION
2	84–576	Vista television sets	200.00	400.00
		Less 40% discount		160.00
			Invoice Total	240.00

CASE STEEL PRICE LIST

107-7

STOCK NO.	LIST PRICE	DISCOUNT
16940	$101.00	25%
16945	116.00	25
24839	47.00	23
24950	37.00	23
32725	86.00	35
32740	137.00	35
32755	177.00	35

offer deductions from these *list prices* to dealers or to individual customers who buy large quantities. These deductions in price are called *trade discounts.*

Suppose the Central Sales Company wants to purchase a certain kind of television set from the Vista Corporation. In its catalog, Vista advertises this television set at a list price of $200 (the price to retail customers). However, Vista offers this television set to dealers at a trade discount of 40%, which amounts to $80 (40% of $200). Thus a dealer has to pay $120 a set ($200 less $80). Central Sales Company has ordered two of these television sets from Vista Corporation and has received the invoice shown in the margin. Trade discounts are usually shown in this manner.

By offering trade discounts, a business can adjust the prices at which it is willing to bill its merchandise without changing the list price it quotes in the catalog. For example, suppose that Vista Corporation wants to continue advertising its Vista television set at a list price of $200, but because of rising prices it must increase its cost to the dealers from $120 to $130. It simply issues a new price list on which the trade discount is reduced from 40% to 35%. Central Sales, as a dealer, would now receive a trade discount of only $70 (35% of $200). Central Sales would have to pay $130 ($200 less $70) for each set. By issuing a revised price list, Vista does not have to reissue a complete catalog just to change the price on a few items.

The trade discount can also be increased so as to offer merchandise to the dealers at a lower cost. For example, when new models of television sets come out, Vista might increase the trade discount on older models to encourage dealers to purchase them.

Trade discounts are not recorded in the accounting records because they are used only to determine the *net* purchase price. For accounting purposes, the significant price is the price that must be paid to the supplier (the list price minus the trade discount). In the case of the January 20 invoice from Vista, the purchase price of $240 for the two sets is the amount to be recorded in the purchases journal and it is the amount to be posted to the creditor's account.

TOPIC 2 ■ PROBLEMS

18 Answer the following questions about the purchases journal and the ledger accounts shown on pages 184 and 185.

a The purchase recorded on January 14 was made from whom?

b What would the entry have been if the purchase recorded on January 10 had been entered in a general journal?

c When the January 10 purchase is posted as a credit to the Todd Elec-

tronics account, is the Purchases account debited at the same time for $360? Why or why not?

d What would the entry have been if the purchase recorded on January 11 was made in a general journal?

e When the January 11 purchase is posted as a credit to the Dixon & Hicks account, is the Purchases account debited at the same time? Why or why not?

f On what date was merchandise purchased for $200, and from whom?

g What amount was posted to the Purchases account on January 31? Was this account debited or credited? Why?

h Was $2,930 posted to the credit of any account on January 31? Why or why not?

i How much is owed to Todd Electronics as of January 31? Where do you find this information?

j What does the P1 mean in the Posting Reference column of the Todd Electronics account?

k How many purchases were made from George Young during the month? Where is this information?

l What is the last date on which Invoice 0567 from Todd Electronics should be paid?

19 On January 20, the invoice below was received by Denton's Paint Shop. It has been checked and verified by the purchasing department, and has been submitted to the accounting department. Verify the extensions, the totals, and the amount of the trade discount. If there are any errors, what are the correct amounts?

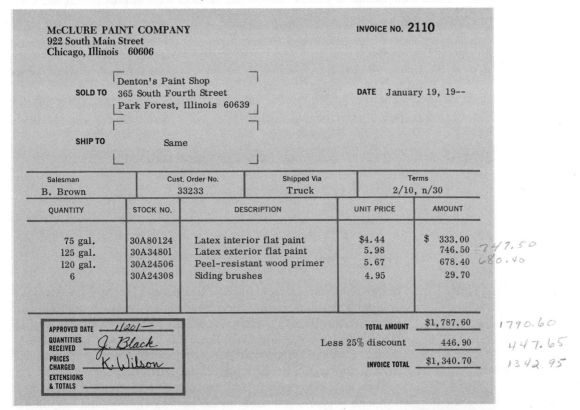

QUANTITY	STOCK NO.	DESCRIPTION	UNIT PRICE	AMOUNT	
75 gal.	30A80124	Latex interior flat paint	$4.44	$ 333.00	
125 gal.	30A34801	Latex exterior flat paint	5.98	746.50	747.50
120 gal.	30A24506	Peel-resistant wood primer	5.67	678.40	680.40
6	30A24308	Siding brushes	4.95	29.70	

McCLURE PAINT COMPANY
922 South Main Street
Chicago, Illinois 60606

INVOICE NO. 2110

SOLD TO
Denton's Paint Shop
365 South Fourth Street
Park Forest, Illinois 60639

DATE January 19, 19--

SHIP TO   Same

Salesman	Cust. Order No.	Shipped Via	Terms
B. Brown	33233	Truck	2/10, n/30

APPROVED DATE 1/20/—
QUANTITIES RECEIVED J. Black
PRICES CHARGED K. Wilson
EXTENSIONS & TOTALS

TOTAL AMOUNT $1,787.60   1790.60
Less 25% discount 446.90   447.65
INVOICE TOTAL $1,340.70   1342.95

20 During the month of May, the purchasing agent for the Elite Dress Shop approved the following invoices.

May 1 Invoice B73, dated April 29; from Agnes Russell; terms n/30; $360.

May 10 Invoice 3637, dated May 5; from David Hayes; terms n/60; $500.

May 15 Invoice 237-846, dated May 12; from the F and R Company; terms 2/10, n/20; $190.

23 Invoice B114, dated May 20; from Agnes Russell; terms n/30; $85.

May 27 Invoice 237-910, dated May 24; from the F and R Company; terms 2/10, n/30; $230.

a Open ledger accounts as follows: Accts. Pay./F and R Company, Accts. Pay./David Hayes, Accts. Pay./Agnes Russell, Purchases. Allow four lines for each account, and assign an appropriate number to each account.

b Journalize the invoices into a purchases journal on the date on which they were approved.

c Foot and rule the purchases journal.

d Post the entries from the purchases journal.

NOTE: Save the purchases journal for use in Problem 21.

21 During the month of June, the following invoices were approved.

June 5 Invoice 3702, dated June 1; from David Hayes; terms n/60; $421.

11 Invoice B173, dated June 8; from Agnes Russell; terms n/30; $225.

16 Invoice 238-004, dated June 13; from the F and R Com-

pany; terms 2/10, n/30; $184.

June 24 Invoice B202, dated June 21; from Agnes Russell; terms n/30; $77.

28 Invoice 3786, dated June 24; from David Hayes; terms n/60; $108.

a Journalize these invoices in the purchases journal used in Problem 20.

b Foot and rule the purchases journal.

c Post the entries from the purchases journal.

d Prepare a trial balance.

TOPIC 3 ■ THE ACCOUNTS PAYABLE LEDGER

SUBSIDIARY LEDGERS

In previous illustrations, the Central Sales Company has had four creditors: Dixon & Hicks, Todd Electronics, Vista Corporation, and George Young. Most businesses have many more creditors; some businesses have several hundred. Thus the ledger of a large business would become very crowded if it contained accounts for all assets, all liabilities, all owner's equity, all income, and all expenses.

Such an arrangement would be difficult for several reasons. First, only one person could work on the posting at one time. Second, the trial balance prepared from the ledger would be extremely long. Moreover, if the trial balance were out of balance, it would be extremely difficult to find an error because all the accounts would have to be checked. In order to avoid these difficulties, the ledger is commonly divided into separate subsidiary ledgers.

Subsidiary Ledgers

A business that has many creditors commonly pulls all the creditors' accounts out of the general ledger and puts them into a separate ledger called the *accounts payable ledger* (or the *creditors ledger*). Similarly, if the business has many charge customers, the customers' accounts are pulled out of the ledger and placed in an *accounts receivable ledger* (or *customers ledger*). To illustrate why subsidiary ledgers are desirable, consider how the balance sheet for the Central Sales Company might look if it had all accounts in one ledger.

As you can see, the total of the accounts payable, rather than the individual creditors' amounts, is the significant figure used in computing the total liabilities. Therefore, instead of listing four accounts payable accounts, only one account—Accounts Payable—could be shown and the balance sheet would still be in balance.

Likewise, the individual customers' accounts can be replaced with one main account called Accounts Receivable, with a balance equal to the total of the customers' accounts. The accounts receivable ledger will be explained in the next chapter.

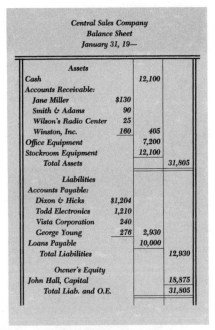

Central Sales Company
Balance Sheet
January 31, 19—

Assets			
Cash		12,100	
Accounts Receivable:			
Jane Miller	$130		
Smith & Adams	90		
Wilson's Radio Center	25		
Winston, Inc.	160	405	
Office Equipment		7,200	
Stockroom Equipment		12,100	
Total Assets			31,805
Liabilities			
Accounts Payable:			
Dixon & Hicks	$1,204		
Todd Electronics	1,210		
Vista Corporation	240		
George Young	276	2,930	
Loans Payable		10,000	
Total Liabilities			12,930
Owner's Equity			
John Hall, Capital			18,875
Total Liab. and O.E.			31,805

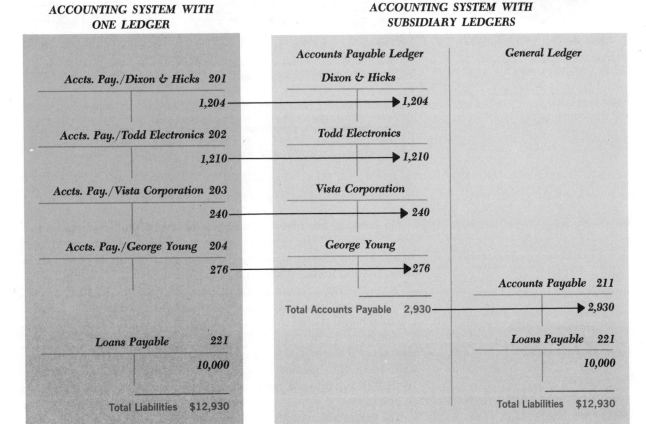

ACCOUNTING SYSTEM WITH ONE LEDGER

Accts. Pay./Dixon & Hicks 201
1,204

Accts. Pay./Todd Electronics 202
1,210

Accts. Pay./Vista Corporation 203
240

Accts. Pay./George Young 204
276

Loans Payable 221
10,000

Total Liabilities $12,930

ACCOUNTING SYSTEM WITH SUBSIDIARY LEDGERS

Accounts Payable Ledger

Dixon & Hicks
1,204

Todd Electronics
1,210

Vista Corporation
240

George Young
276

Total Accounts Payable 2,930

General Ledger

Accounts Payable 211
2,930

Loans Payable 221
10,000

Total Liabilities $12,930

Remington Rand

Wilson Jones Co.

The Accounts Payable Ledger

When the individual creditors' accounts are removed from the general ledger and placed in a subsidiary ledger, an account entitled Accounts Payable is kept in the general ledger to keep the ledger in balance. This account is called a *controlling account* because it shows the total of the individual creditors' accounts.

The individual creditors' accounts are usually kept in a loose-leaf binder or file so that accounts can be added or deleted. These loose cards are filed in alphabetic sequence so that they can be located rapidly. Because of the alphabetic sequence, no numbers are assigned to the accounts in the subsidiary ledger.

Posting to the Subsidiary Ledger   During the month, the individual credit entries are posted from the purchases journal to the individual creditors' accounts in the subsidiary ledger. Since the individual accounts in the subsidiary ledger are not numbered, a check mark ($\sqrt{}$) is used in the Posting Reference column of the purchases journal to show that the amount has been posted.

				PURCHASES JOURNAL			Page *1*
DATE	ACCOUNT CREDITED	INVOICE		TERMS	POST. REF.	AMOUNT	
		NO.	DATE				
19— Jan. 10	Todd Electronics..........	0567	1/8	2/10, n/30	$\sqrt{}$	360 00	

			Todd Electronics, 22 Elmwood Avenue, Cincinnati, Ohio 45218				
DATE	EXPLANATION	POST. REF.	DEBIT	DATE	EXPLANATION	POST. REF.	CREDIT
				19— Jan. 10	Inv. 0567......	P1	360 00

No postings are made to the general ledger until the end of the month, when all the amounts are accumulated in one total. At that time, the total amount of purchases for the month is posted as a debit to the Purchases account and as a credit to the Accounts Payable controlling account in the general ledger. The total of all the credit amounts posted to the accounts payable ledger should equal the total credit posted to the controlling account in the general ledger.

Note that the accounts in the accounts payable ledger contain the address of the creditor. It is a common practice to show the creditor's address in the heading of each account in the subsidiary ledger so that all the information needed to mail a check to him is located in one place.

The use of an accounts payable ledger does not change the method for journalizing the approved purchase invoices in the purchases

---

CENTRAL SALES COMPANY CHART OF ACCOUNTS

ASSETS

101   Cash
111   *Accounts Receivable*
121   *Office Equipment*
122   *Store Equipment*

LIABILITIES

211   *Accounts Payable*
221   *Loans Payable*

journal. There is, however, a difference in the method of posting from the journal. In the process of totaling the purchases journal, "Purchases Debit/Accts. Pay. Credit" is written in the Account Credited column, and a diagonal line is drawn across the Posting Reference column to indicate that the total is to be posted to two accounts. The total is posted as a debit to the Purchases account and also is posted as a credit to the Accounts Payable controlling account in the general ledger. The number of the Purchases account is written above the diagonal line, and the number of the Accounts Payable account is written below the line. Thus an account number in the Posting Reference column indicates that the amount was posted to the general ledger, whereas a check mark indicates that it was posted to the subsidiary ledger.

When the posting from the purchases journal is completed for the month, the ledgers will be in balance if no errors were made. The total of the credit postings to the accounts payable ledger should agree with the amount posted to the Accounts Payable controlling account. In addition, the credit to the Accounts Payable account in the general ledger should equal the debit posted to the Purchases account.

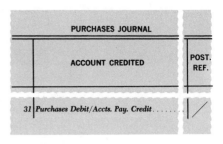

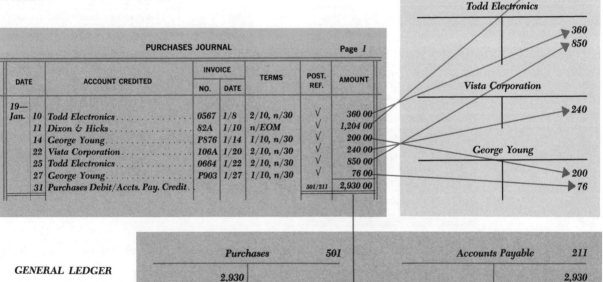

The procedure for posting from the purchases journal to the general ledger and the subsidiary ledger involves the following sequence:

1 During the month, the individual credits are posted to the creditors' accounts in the subsidiary ledger.

2 At the end of the month, the total purchases is posted as a debit to the Purchases account and a credit to the Accounts Payable controlling account in the general ledger.

Schedule of Accounts Payable

Schedule of accounts payable: list of balances in all creditors' accounts.

It is necessary to prove periodically that the subsidiary ledger is in agreement with the controlling account in the general ledger. The total of all the balances can be obtained by simply adding the balances and verifying the total with the balance of the controlling account. However, the owner frequently wants to know the individual creditors' names and the amounts owed them. Thus a listing called a *schedule of accounts payable* is usually prepared.

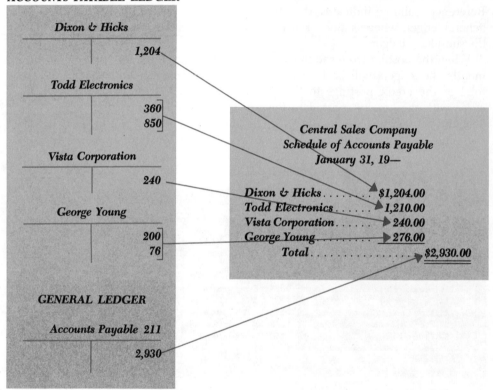

This proof must be prepared at the end of the accounting period before the trial balance is prepared as a proof of the general ledger. If the total of the subsidiary ledger accounts does not agree with the balance of the controlling account in the general journal, the error should be located and corrected before a trial balance of the general ledger is prepared. To locate the error, the accountant should use the same process he would use to locate an error on the trial balance.

As in the case of the trial balance, the fact that the two totals agree is no assurance that the books are completely accurate. It merely indicates that the total of the balances of the accounts in the subsidiary ledger is equal to the balance of the controlling account in the general ledger. The types of errors that are not revealed on the trial balance are not revealed on the schedule of accounts payable.

TOPIC 3 ■ PROBLEMS

22 Answer the following questions about the purchases journal, the general ledger accounts, and the subsidiary ledger accounts shown on page 191.

a What was the date of Invoice 82A from Dixon & Hicks? When was it recorded?

b What would the complete entry have been if the purchase recorded on January 14 had been entered in a general journal instead of in a purchases journal?

c When the January 14 purchase is posted, is the Purchases account debited for $200 at the same time?

d When the January 14 purchase is posted, what account is credited? In which ledger?

e What would the complete entry have been if the purchase recorded on January 22 had been entered in a general journal?

f When the January 22 purchase is posted, is the credit posted to both the Accounts Payable account in the general ledger and to Vista Corporation's account in the subsidiary ledger? Why or why not?

g What amount was posted to the Purchases account on January 31? Was this amount debited or credited? Why?

h Is any account credited for $2,930 on January 31?

i What do the 501 and 211 in the Posting Reference column on January 31 indicate?

j Where is the information for the schedule of accounts payable obtained?

k When a trial balance is prepared, will both the Accounts Payable controlling account and the individual subsidiary ledger accounts be listed? Why or why not?

l How is the accuracy of the subsidiary ledger proved?

23 Richard Delman has received the invoices listed below for merchandise he purchased for resale in his hardware store.

a Open general ledger accounts for Accounts Payable and Purchases. Assign an appropriate number to each account. Also open subsidiary ledger accounts for the following creditors: Delta Supply Company, James Dye, and Ronald Wilson. Allow four lines for each account.

b Journalize the following approved purchase invoices in a purchases journal.

Oct. 3 Invoice 3822, dated September 28; from the Delta Supply Company; terms 2/10, n/30; $205.

11 Invoice D155, dated October 6; from James Dye; terms n/30; $310.

16 Invoice 743, dated October 13; from Ronald Wilson; terms n/60; $286.

Oct. 22 Invoice D237, dated October 17; from James Dye; terms n/30; $422.

28 Invoice 3909, dated October 23; from the Delta Supply Company; terms 2/10, n/30; $400.

c Foot and rule the purchases journal.

d Post the entries from the purchases journal to the ledger accounts.

e Prepare a schedule of accounts payable.

NOTE: Save the journal and ledgers for use in Problem 24.

24 Use the purchases journal and ledger accounts used in Problem 23 to perform the following activities.

a Journalize the following approved purchase invoices.

Nov. 5 Invoice 776, dated November 2; from Ronald Wilson; terms n/60; $338.

   11 Invoice D278, dated November 6; from James Dye; terms n/30; $330.

   16 Invoice 3992, dated November 12; from the Delta Sup-

ply Company; terms 2/10, n/30; $215.

Nov. 22 Invoice 808, dated November 19; from Ronald Wilson; terms n/60; $502.

   28 Invoice D296, dated November 23; from James Dye; terms n/30; $94.

b Foot and rule the purchases journal.
c Post the purchases journal entries to the ledger accounts.
d Prepare a schedule of accounts payable.

TOPIC 4 ■ PURCHASES RETURNS AND ALLOWANCES

Merchandise sometimes arrives in an unacceptable condition. The goods may be damaged, the quantity may be greater or less than was ordered, or the wrong merchandise may have been sent. In such cases, the receiving clerk must ask the purchasing agent for a decision on what to do with the merchandise.

In other cases, the business might find that the goods received are not needed or are not what the purchaser thought they would be. Thus the purchasing department may want to return the merchandise to the supplier. The procedures involved in resolving these problems relate to the concept of purchases returns and allowances.

Purchase Returns and Purchase Allowances

Purchase return: merchandise sent back to the supplier.

Purchase allowance: reduction from purchase price for damages or other causes.

When merchandise arrives in an unacceptable condition, the purchasing agent normally has two alternatives: (1) he may return the merchandise, or (2) he may agree to keep it if he is allowed a reduction on the purchase price. As an example, recall the order for two television sets that Central Sales Company placed with Vista Corporation. Assume that one of the two sets was scratched while in shipment and that the receiving clerk has notified the purchasing agent of this damage. If the purchasing agent returns the television set to Vista, this transaction will be, in accounting terminology, a *purchase return*. However, Vista may offer to reduce the purchase price on the scratched television set and Central Sales may decide to keep the set on these terms. In this case, the difference between the original price and the reduced price will be a *purchase allowance*.

Receiving Cash for Purchases Returns and Allowances

When a buyer has paid cash for the merchandise, he expects to have his cash returned to him when he returns the goods. If he is allowed a reduction in the price that he has already paid, he may expect to have the allowance returned to him in cash.

Suppose the supplier agrees to take back merchandise that the Central Sales Company purchased for $100 in cash on January 2. To understand how this transaction is recorded, let's review the original entry. Since the merchandise was purchased for cash, the transaction was recorded in the cash payments journal. In effect, this entry resulted in a credit to Cash for $100 and a debit to Purchases for $100.

CASH PAYMENTS JOURNAL					Page 3
DATE	ACCOUNT DEBITED	EXPLANATION	CHECK NO.	POST. REF.	AMOUNT
19— Jan. 2	Purchases.............	Fisher Co..........	130	501	100 00

When some merchandise recorded in the Purchases account is returned, the total amount of Purchases shown on the records must be reduced. This could be done by crediting the Purchases account. (Since purchases decrease owner's equity, the return of purchases increases owner's equity.) However, it is a better practice to keep a separate record of purchases returns and allowances. By recording purchases in one account and the returns and allowances for purchases in another, information about each activity is readily available. Thus, when Central Sales Company receives $100 in cash for returning merchandise, Purchases Returns and Allowances is credited. Since cash was received, the entry is made in the cash receipts journal.

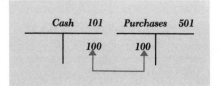

Purchases returns and allowances: decrease cost of merchandise purchased.

CASH RECEIPTS JOURNAL				Page 3
DATE	ACCOUNT CREDITED	EXPLANATION	POST. REF.	AMOUNT
19— Jan. 10	Purchases Returns and Allowances	Returns to Fisher Co...	502	100 00

Cash 101		Purchases 501		Purchases Returns and Allowances 502	
100	100	100			100

Purchases	
(Debit) *For amount* *of all merchandise* *purchased for resale*	

Purchases Returns and Allowances	
	(Credit) *For amount of* *all returns and* *allowances on* *merchandise pur-* *chased for resale*

Purchases $4,000	
Less: Purchases Returns	
and Allowances	600
Net Purchases $3,400	

CENTRAL SALES COMPANY
CHART OF ACCOUNTS

COSTS AND EXPENSES

501   Purchases
502   Purchases Returns and Allowances

The Purchases Returns and Allowances account, like the Purchases account, is a temporary owner's equity account. The information supplied by the Purchases Returns and Allowances account is used to help analyze the operations of the business. For example, if the amount of the returns and allowances becomes large, the owner or manager might want to investigate the reason. Are errors being made on purchase orders? Is poor merchandise being bought? Is too much merchandise arriving in damaged condition? Is there a breakdown in the purchasing procedure? Such information helps to guide management in taking the proper action to correct a poor purchasing situation.

To find the net amount of purchases, all one has to do is to subtract the balance of the Purchases Returns and Allowances account from the balance of the Purchases account. Because of the relationship between these two accounts, the accountant for the Central Sales Company assigned Purchases Returns and Allowances account number 502 following Purchases in the chart of accounts.

Receiving Credit for Purchases Returns or Allowances

When a buyer has not yet paid for the merchandise that he is returning, the supplier grants him credit to apply against the amount he owes. To understand how the entry is made to record a purchase return or allowance for credit, think again of the situation where Central Sales Company received two television sets from Vista Corporation. Suppose the purchasing agent tells Vista that he wants to return one set because of damage to the cabinet, and Vista agrees to take the set back. When the set is returned, Vista issues a credit memorandum to the Central Sales Company for $120, the cost of the set. The credit memorandum acknowledges that the amount owed by Central Sales to Vista on Invoice 106A ($240) will be reduced by the amount of the set returned ($120).

VISTA CORPORATION
16 Remington Street
Detroit, Michigan 48217

Sold To: Central Sales Company
423 Vernon Avenue
St. Paul, Minnesota 55108

Invoice No. **106A**
Date January 20, 19—
Terms 2/10, n/30

Salesman Hunt	Your Order No. PO1135	Shipped By Truck		FOB St. Paul
QUANTITY	STOCK NO.	DESCRIPTION	UNIT PRICE	EXTENSION
2	84-576	Vista television sets Less 40% discount	200.00	400.00 160.00
			Invoice Total	240.00

VISTA CORPORATION
16 Remington Street
Detroit, Michigan 48217

CREDIT MEMORANDUM

No. **1254**

Date Jan. 27, 19—

TO: Central Sales Company
423 Vernon Avenue
St. Paul, Minnesota 55108

Sold on
Invoice No. PO1135

Your Order No. 106A

We have credited your account as follows:

Quantity	Description	Price	Amount
1	84-576 Vista television set returned	120.00	120.00

A credit memorandum issued by a supplier indicates the amount for which the purchaser's account is to be credited and the reason for the credit. Thus a credit memorandum is the source document for recording a purchase return or purchase allowance in the journal.

To understand how the data on the credit memorandum should be journalized, it will help to review the earlier transaction.

1 When the purchase invoice was recorded, an entry was made in the purchases journal for the amount of the invoice, $240. Thus Vista Corporation's account in the accounts payable ledger was credited for $240 to show the increase in the amount owed to this creditor. Assume that this was the only entry made in the purchases journal during the month. Then, at the end of the month, a debit of $240 would be posted to the Purchases account in the general ledger and a credit for $240 would be posted to the Accounts Payable account.

Credit memorandum: source document that grants credit to buyer for purchase return or allowance.

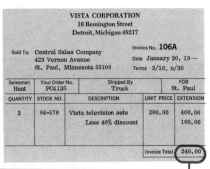

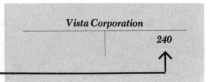

2 When the set is returned, Vista Corporation sends its credit memorandum to Central Sales Company. The credit memorandum verifies that Central Sales now owes less money to Vista Corporation —$120 less, the cost of one television set. When the credit memorandum is recorded, an entry is made in the general journal for the amount of the allowance, $120. Thus a debit of $120 must be posted to Vista's account in the accounts payable ledger to show the decrease in the amount owed to it. Moreover, the entries to the accounts in the general ledger must involve a debit to the Accounts Payable controlling account and a credit to the Purchases Returns and Allowances account. The debit entry decreases the accounts payable liability and the credit entry reduces the total amount of purchases. (The entry required to record the credit memorandum is analyzed on page 198.)

The diagonal line drawn in the posting reference column of the general journal indicates that the debit of $120 to decrease the liabilities is posted to two accounts—the controlling account in the general ledger and the creditor's account in the subsidiary ledger. The 211 in the Posting Reference column indicates that the debit has been posted to the Accounts Payable controlling account (211) in the general ledger. The check mark (√) indicates that the debit has been posted to Vista Corporation's account in the subsidiary ledger (accounts payable ledger). After these entries are posted, the total of the subsidiary ledger will be in agreement with the balance of the controlling account.

The credit of $120 to show the reduction in the total amount of purchases is posted to the Purchases Returns and Allowances account.

January 28:   Central Sales Company receives credit memorandum for $120 from Vista Corporation for the return of merchandise purchased on credit.

WHAT HAPPENS	ACCOUNTING RULE	ENTRY
The liability Accounts Payable decreases by $120.	*To decrease a liability, debit the account.*	*Debit: Accounts Payable, $120 (also the creditor's account).*
The reduction in costs caused by a return of purchases increases owner's equity by $120.	*To increase owner's equity, credit the account.*	*Credit: Purchases Returns and Allowances, $120.*

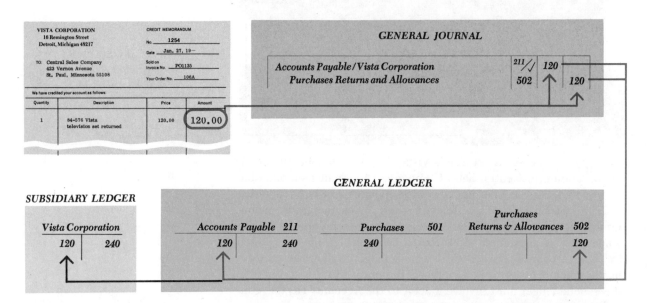

If a business has numerous purchases returns and allowances, it might use a special journal to record them. If no special journal is used, the purchases returns and allowances are journalized in a general journal.

When a two-column general journal is used to record entries that affect accounts in the general ledger and the subsidiary ledger, every entry must be double-posted. For example, the debit of $120 must be posted to the controlling account in the general ledger (indicated by the 211 in the Posting Reference column) and also to the individual creditor's account in the subsidiary ledger (indicated by the check

		GENERAL JOURNAL			Page 3
DATE	ACCOUNT TITLE AND EXPLANATION	POST. REF.	DEBIT	CREDIT	

19—
Jan. 28
	Accounts Payable/Vista Corporation........
	    Purchases Returns and Allowances........
	        Credit Memorandum 1254 of 1/27.......
		211/√
		502
			120 00	120 00	

Double-posting: posting to the controlling account in the general ledger and also to the individual account in the subsidiary ledger.

mark in the same column). When subsidiary ledgers are used, posting can be speeded up by using a four-column general journal.

The Four-Column General Journal

The general journal is used to record all entries that cannot be recorded in the special journals used by the business. A four-column general journal differs from a two-column general journal in that two special columns have been added for recording entries—an Accounts Payable Debit column and an Accounts Receivable Credit column. All entries that are debits to the Accounts Payable account (and to the individual creditor's account in the subsidiary ledger) are entered in the *Accounts Payable Debit column.* All other debit entries are entered in the General Ledger Debit column. All entries that are credits to the Accounts Receivable account (and to the individual customer's account) are entered in the *Accounts Receivable Credit column.* All other credit entries are entered in the General Ledger Credit column. For example in the entry for the credit memorandum received from Vista Corporation, the debit of $120 to the Accounts Payable controlling account and the creditor's account in the subsidiary ledger is recorded in the Accounts Payable Debit column. Since there is no special column for credits to Purchases Returns and Allowances, the credit of $120 is placed in the General Ledger Credit column.

			GENERAL JOURNAL			Page 3
ACCOUNTS PAYABLE DEBIT	GENERAL LEDGER DEBIT	DATE	ACCOUNT TITLE AND EXPLANATION	POST. REF.	GENERAL LEDGER CREDIT	ACCOUNTS RECEIVABLE CREDIT

120 00		19—
		Jan. 28
			Vista Corporation.......................
			    Purchases Returns and Allowances..........
			        Credit memorandum 1254 of 1/27.
				√
				502
					120 00	

During the month, all amounts in the Accounts Payable Debit column and Accounts Receivable Credit column are posted to the individual accounts in the subsidiary ledgers. The entries recorded in the General Ledger Debit and Credit columns are also posted. However, the debits to the Accounts Payable controlling account and the credits to the Accounts Receivable controlling account are not posted until the end of the month. For example, during January the $120 debit is posted to Vista Corporation's account in the subsidiary ledger. A check mark is placed in the Posting Reference column to show that the amount was posted to the subsidiary ledger. The credit to Purchases Returns and Allowances is posted to the general ledger as indicated by (502) in the Posting Reference column.

ACCOUNTS PAYABLE LEDGER

Vista Corporation, 16 Remington Street, Detroit, Michigan 48217

DATE	EXPLANATION	POST. REF.	DEBIT	DATE	EXPLANATION	POST. REF.	CREDIT
19— Jan. 28	Return........	J3	120 00	19— Jan. 22	Inv. 106A......	P1	240 00

GENERAL LEDGER

Purchases Returns and Allowances   **Account No. 502**

DATE	EXPLANATION	POST. REF.	DEBIT	DATE	EXPLANATION	POST. REF.	CREDIT
				19— Jan. 28	Vista Corporation	J3	120 00

Accounts Payable Debit...............	$150
General Ledger Debit..................	750
Total debits......................	$900
Total credits.....................	$900

At the end of the month, the journal is footed. The equality of the debits and credits may be checked by adding the two debit amounts together and comparing this sum with the sum of the two credit columns. If both amounts are equal, the columns are totaled and ruled.

GENERAL JOURNAL							Page 3
ACCOUNTS PAYABLE DEBIT	GENERAL LEDGER DEBIT	DATE	ACCOUNT TITLE AND EXPLANATION	POST. REF.	GENERAL LEDGER CREDIT	ACCOUNTS RECEIVABLE CREDIT	
120 00		19— Jan. 28	Vista Corporation........................ Purchases Returns and Allowances......... Credit memorandum 1254 of 1/27.	√ 502	 120 00		
150 00 150 00	750 00 750 00	31	Totals		900 00 900 00		
(211)	(√)				(√)		

1 The total of the Accounts Payable Debit column ($150) is posted to the debit side of the Accounts Payable controlling account in the general ledger. The account number of Accounts Payable (211) is written beneath the double ruling to indicate that it has been posted. Since the debits to the individual creditors' accounts have been posted during the month, no additional posting to the subsidiary ledger is required at this time.

		Accounts Payable						Account No. *211*		
DATE		EXPLANATION	POST. REF.	DEBIT	DATE		EXPLANATION	POST. REF.	CREDIT	
19—					*19—*					
Jan.	*31*	*Returns*	*J3*	*150 00*	*Jan.*	*31*	*Total purchases*	*P1*	*2,930 00*	

2 The totals of the General Ledger Debit ($750) and General Ledger Credit ($900) columns are not posted because the amounts were posted individually to the various accounts in the general ledger. A check mark ($\sqrt{}$) is placed beneath the double ruling in each column to indicate that these totals are not posted to the general ledger.

3 The Accounts Receivable Credit column is commonly used with the sale of goods. The procedure for using this column will be fully discussed in the next chapter.

Double Postings

Some entries recorded in the four-column general journal still require double postings. For example, when store equipment is purchased on credit from Yuma Steel, Inc., the entry must be made in the general journal. The account to be debited is Store Equipment—*not* Purchases. Since no special column is provided for debits to Store Equipment, the amount must be recorded in the General Ledger Debit column. The account to be credited is the Accounts Payable controlling account and, in the subsidiary ledger, the Yuma Steel account. Since there is no special column for accounts payable credits, the amount must be entered in the General Ledger Credit column.

ACCOUNTS PAYABLE DEBIT	GENERAL LEDGER DEBIT	DATE	ACCOUNT TITLE AND EXPLANATION	POST. REF.	GENERAL LEDGER CREDIT	ACCOUNTS RECEIVABLE CREDIT
			GENERAL JOURNAL			Page 2
		19—				
	525 00	*Jan. 25*	*Store Equipment*	*122*		
			Accounts Payable/Yuma Steel, Inc.	*211/$\sqrt{}$*	*525 00*	

GENERAL JOURNAL			
EXPLANATION	POST. REF.	GENERAL LEDGER CREDIT	AC RE
. . . .	122		
Steel, Inc. .	211/√	525 00	

The debit is posted to the Store Equipment account (122) in the general ledger, and the account number is entered in the Posting Reference column. The credit for $525, however, must be double-posted, that is, posted to the Accounts Payable controlling account in the general ledger and also to the creditor's account in the accounts payable ledger. To indicate that this entry must be double-posted, a diagonal line is placed in the Posting Reference column when the entry is journalized.

When the credit entry to the Accounts Payable controlling account in the general ledger is posted, the account number (211) is written above the diagonal line. When the entry to the Yuma Steel account is posted in the subsidiary ledger, a check mark (√) is written beneath the line. Both amounts do not have to be posted at the same time. For example, all amounts may be posted to the accounts payable ledger one day and all amounts to the general ledger the next day.

At the end of the month, an examination should be made to confirm that (1) for every amount in the General Ledger Debit column and the General Ledger Credit column there is an indication in the Posting Reference column that the amount has been posted; (2) for every amount in the Accounts Payable Debit column and the Accounts Receivable Credit column there is a check mark in the Posting Reference column to indicate that the amount has been posted to the subsidiary ledger; and (3) the totals of the Accounts Payable Debit column and the Accounts Receivable Credit column have the account numbers written beneath the double rule to indicate that they have been posted to the controlling accounts in the general ledger.

Special columns may be added to any journal as a time-saving device for recording and posting transactions of a similar nature. The transactions should be numerous enough, of course, to justify the addition of a special column. For example, some companies might add an Accounts Payable Credit column to avoid the double posting that is required when a four-column journal is used.

TOPIC 4 ■ PROBLEMS

25 Answer the following questions about the general journal, general ledger accounts, and subsidiary ledger account shown on pages 200 and 201.

a What journal entry was made on January 28 to record the credit memorandum received for the return of purchases?

b Why was the Vista Corporation account debited on January 28 instead of credited when merchandise was returned to Vista? Why was Purchases Returns and Allowances credited?

c When the $120 item of January 28 was posted as a debit to the Vista Corporation account, was the Accounts Payable controlling account debited for $120 at the same time?

d In the January 28 journal entry, why was the debit amount entered in the Accounts Payable Debit column and the credit amount entered in the General Ledger Credit column?

e What is the purpose of the check mark in the Posting Reference column for the January 28 journal entry?

f What is the purpose of the notation (211) beneath the $150 in the Accounts Payable Debit column?

g What is the purpose of the check marks under the General Ledger Debit and General Ledger Credit columns?

h Tell the source of the debit and the credit in the Accounts Payable controlling account, and explain why each was made.

i How much was owed to Vista Corporation on January 31?

26 During March the Maple Grocery Store received the invoices and credit memorandums listed below.

a Open general ledger accounts and assign appropriate numbers for Accounts Payable, Purchases, and Purchases Returns and Allowances. In the subsidiary ledger, open accounts for R. D. Ellis and Sunrise Company. Allow three lines for the first two accounts and four lines for the remaining ones.

b Record in a purchases journal and in a four-column general journal the following transactions.

Mar. 2 Purchased merchandise for $500 from Sunrise Company on Invoice 663, dated March 1; terms 1/10, n/30.

5 Received Credit Memorandum 47 for $50 to cover merchandise returned to Sunrise Company.

13 Purchased merchandise for $280 from R. D. Ellis on In-voice 22-84, dated March 10; terms 2/10, n/60.

Mar. 22 Purchased merchandise for $405 from Sunrise Company on Invoice 711, dated March 21; terms 1/10, n/30.

25 Received $25 allowance from Sunrise Company for damaged merchandise on Credit Memorandum 51.

c Foot and rule both journals for the end of the month.

d Post the entries from the journals to the ledgers.

e Prepare a schedule of accounts payable.

NOTE: Save the journals and ledgers for use in Problem 27.

27 Using the journals and ledgers prepared in Problem 26, perform the activities listed below and on page 204.

a Record the entries for the following transactions.

Apr. 5 Purchased merchandise for $336 from R. D. Ellis on In-voice 22-113, dated April 2; terms 2/10, n/60.

9 Received Credit Memorandum 15-2 for $50 to cover merchandise returned to R. D. Ellis.

17 Purchased merchandise for $266 from Sunrise Company on Invoice 802, dated April 16; terms 1/10, n/30.

Apr. 21 Received $40 allowance from Sunrise Company on Credit Memorandum 57 for scratched merchandise.

28 Purchased merchandise for $80 from R. D. Ellis on In-voice 22-137, dated April 25; terms 2/10, n/60.

b Foot and rule the journals for the end of the month.
c Post the entries from the journal to the ledgers.
d Prepare a schedule of accounts payable.

TOPIC 5 ■ MAKING PAYMENTS TO CREDITORS

The terms shown on the purchase order and purchase invoice indicate the agreement between the seller and the buyer as to when the invoice is to be paid. The terms granted by a seller will vary from customer to customer. A business with a reputation for paying its bills promptly will be given more liberal credit terms than a business with a poor record. Thus a seller may demand payment from some customers immediately but may offer other customers 30, 60, 90, or some other specified number of days in which to pay the invoice.

If the agreement between the buyer and the seller calls for payment immediately upon delivery of the merchandise, the terms on the invoice will be "Cash" or "Net Cash." However, if the buyer has been granted a *credit period* (that is, a period of time in which to pay the invoice), the terms on the invoice will state exactly what period of time is meant.

> Credit period: period of time within which invoice is to be paid.

Credit Periods

For most businesses, the credit period begins with the date of the invoice. If payment is due 30 days from the invoice date, the symbol "n/30" is used. The "n" (for *net*) means that the full amount of the invoice (less any *trade* discount) is due within 30 days after the invoice date. If the authorized credit period is 60 days, the terms would be shown as n/60. If payment is required at the end of the month in which the purchase is made, the terms would be n/EOM (for end of month).

Cash Discounts

As a means of encouraging customers to pay their invoices during the first part of the credit period, many businesses offer a cash discount to their customers. A cash discount entitles the purchaser to deduct a certain amount from the amount of the invoice if he pays the bill within the specified period. For example, when a purchase invoice provides credit terms of 1/20, n/30, the buyer is authorized a total credit period of 30 days and a discount period of 20 days. He may deduct 1 percent of the amount of the invoice if he pays within the 20-day discount period—this is the meaning of 1/20. However, if he pays the bill within the last 10 days of the period, he must pay the full amount—n/30. This deduction for prompt payment is known generally

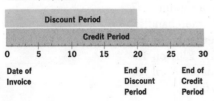

Terms: 1/20, n/30

Discount Period
Credit Period
0   5   10   15   20   25   30
Date of Invoice   End of Discount Period   End of Credit Period

as a *cash discount*. A cash discount applied to a purchase invoice is called a *purchase discount*.

Purchase Discounts   A purchase discount is not recorded at the time an invoice is journalized because the buyer gets the cash discount *only* if he pays the invoice within the discount period. To understand how purchase discounts are used, refer to the January 8 purchase invoice from Todd Electronics for $360. The terms of this purchase are 2/10, n/30. Thus, if the Central Sales Company mails its check on or before January 18 (10 days after the date of the invoice), it may deduct 2 percent of $360 ($7.20) from the invoice and may pay $352.80 ($360 − $7.20). If the Central Sales Company does not pay within this discount period, it may postpone payment for an additional 20 days until February 7 (the end of the credit period); however, it must then pay the full amount of $360. Because the business has a choice of paying early, or not, the discount is not recorded until after the check is drawn to pay the invoice. Thus, when the purchase invoice is journalized, the creditor's account is credited for the full amount of the invoice, $360. The entry in the purchases journal has the following effects.

Purchase discount: cash discount deducted from purchase invoice.

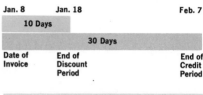

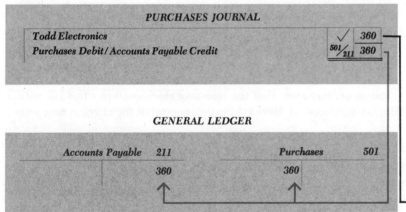

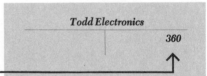

To take advantage of the discount period and to keep a good credit rating, a business must have an efficient method for keeping track of when each invoice should be paid. One method is to file the invoices in a tickler file according to the dates on which they must be considered for payment. A file folder is established for each day of the month (from 1 to 31). The accounting clerk then files each purchase invoice under the day that it must be paid in order to obtain the cash discount. On that day, the invoice is considered for payment. If the person in charge of making cash payments decides to pay the invoice, the discount is deducted from the amount due and a check is drawn for the net amount. However, if he decides not to pay the invoice, the invoice is then filed under the day that marks the end of the credit period.

Making Payments

In the Central Sales Company, the treasurer of the business decides when the invoices are to be paid. Assume that he decides not to take advantage of the cash discount offered by Todd Electronics, but decides instead to delay payment of the invoice until the last day of the credit period, which is February 7. He then has a check drawn for $360, the full (net) amount of the invoice. The check issued to pay this invoice is recorded in the cash payments journal and affects the following accounts.

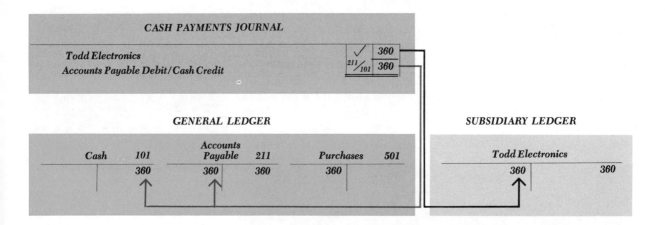

Suppose, however, that the treasurer decides to pay this bill within the discount period. Here is how the amount of the check is computed.

Rate of cash discount = 2%
2% × $360 = $7.20 (amount of discount)
$360 − $7.20 = $352.80 (amount of payment)

Although the Central Sales Company is charged $360 on the purchase invoice, Todd Electronics agrees to accept a check for $352.80 in full settlement of the account if the check is sent within the discount period. On January 18, therefore, the treasurer has a check drawn for $352.80 and sends it to Todd Electronics. This transaction is analyzed as follows:

1　Since the creditor's account shows a credit balance of $360, the account must be debited for $360 to show that this amount has been satisfied in full. Regardless of the actual amount of the check, Todd Electronics' account must be debited for $360 to reduce the credit balance to zero.

2　The check drawn to fulfill the obligation amounts to $352.80. Thus the Cash account must be credited for $352.80 because this is the actual amount of cash that was paid.

3　Since the debit and credit amounts must be equal, the cash discount of $7.20 must be credited to some account. This discount,

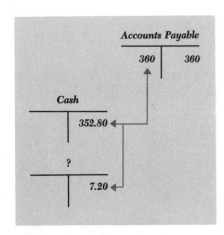

in reality, reduces the cost of the merchandise. For example, the 12 radios are recorded as costing $360. However, Central Sales paid only $352.80 for them; thus the purchase discount reduces the cost of the merchandise by $7.20. This reduction in cost actually increases owner's equity. Thus an owner's equity account must be credited.

This credit entry could be to the Purchases account. Instead, however, it is a common accounting practice to record a purchase discount in a special temporary owner's equity account called Purchases Discount. This practice provides the owner or the manager with a record of all discounts taken. It enables him to see quickly whether bills are being paid in time to take advantage of discounts. If not, he must answer such questions as these: Does the business have insufficient cash available to pay its bills within the discount period? Does the system have to be changed so that bills are approved more quickly? To find the net cost of merchandise purchased, all one needs do is subtract the balance of the Purchases Discount account from the balance of the Purchases account. However, since the Purchases Returns and Allowances account may also have a balance, the amount of net purchases are computed as shown in the margin.

Since these accounts are related, they are assigned account numbers 501, 502, and 503 in the Central Sales Company.

The entry to record a purchase discount of $7.20 taken on a payment of $360 is analyzed below.

	Purchases Discount	503
		7.20

Purchases		$4,000
Less: Purchases Returns		
and Allowances . $600		
Purchases Discount 20		620
Net Purchases		$3,380

CENTRAL SALES COMPANY
CHART OF ACCOUNTS

COSTS AND EXPENSES

501   *Purchases*
502   *Purchases Returns and Allowances*
503   *Purchases Discount*

WHAT HAPPENS	ACCOUNTING RULE	ENTRY
The liability Accounts Payable *decreases by $360.*	*To decrease a liability, debit the account.*	*Debit:* *Accounts Payable, $360 (also the creditor's account).*
The asset Cash *decreases by $352.80.*	*To decrease an asset, credit the account.*	*Credit:* *Cash, $352.80.*
The cash discount on purchases increases owner's equity by $7.20.	*To increase owner's equity, credit the account.*	*Credit:* *Purchases Discounts, $7.20.*

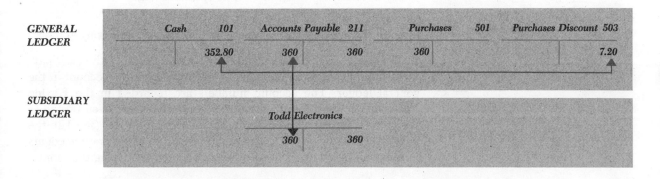

Recording Purchase Discounts in the Cash Payments Journal

All cash payments are recorded in the cash payments journal. As you have seen from the previous analysis, the entry to record the payment of cash with a purchase discount involves a debit to the Accounts Payable controlling account (and the individual creditor's account), a credit to the Purchases Discount account, and a credit to the Cash account. Since this entry involves a credit to the Purchases Discount account as well as a credit to the Cash account, it is impossible to record this type of entry in a one-column cash payments journal. Thus most businesses adapt the cash payments journal to their needs by providing a special column for credits to the Purchases Discount account in addition to the column for a credit to Cash.

The special columns shown in the following cash payments journal are frequently added to facilitate the recording of cash payments.

CASH PAYMENTS JOURNAL								Page *1*
DATE	ACCOUNT DEBITED	EXPLANATION	CHECK NO.	POST. REF.	GENERAL LEDGER DEBIT	ACCOUNTS PAYABLE DEBIT	PURCHASES DISCOUNT CREDIT	NET CASH CREDIT
19—								
Jan. 18	Todd Electronics...	Inv. 0567.........	308			360 00	7 20	352 80

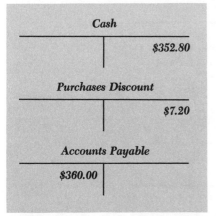

Cash

| | $352.80 |

Purchases Discount

| | $7.20 |

Accounts Payable

| $360.00 | |

$360 = $352.80 + $7.20

The Net Cash Credit column is used to record the total amount of cash paid. An entry here represents a credit to the Cash account. The Purchases Discount Credit column is used to record the amount of the purchases discount taken, if any. An entry recorded in this column represents a credit to the Purchases Discount account.

The Accounts Payable Debit column is used to record all debits to creditors' accounts for payments of invoices. The amount entered in this column ($360) must be equal to the total amount of the credits ($352.80 + $7.20). This column is added to the cash payments journal to facilitate the double posting that must be done to the Accounts Payable controlling account and to the creditor's account.

The General Ledger Debit column is used for recording debits to any account for which there is no special column.

Posting from the Cash Payments Journal During the Month

Each amount in the General Ledger Debit column of the cash payments journal is posted individually to the appropriate account in the general ledger. The account numbers are recorded in the Posting Reference column to indicate that the amounts have been posted to the general ledger. For example, the first three entries (see 1 in the illustration) involve debit amounts to be posted to separate accounts in the general ledger. These entries can be posted during the month.

CASH PAYMENTS JOURNAL								Page 3
DATE	ACCOUNT DEBITED	EXPLANATION	CHECK NO.	POST. REF.	GENERAL LEDGER DEBIT	ACCOUNTS PAYABLE DEBIT	PURCHASES DISCOUNT CREDIT	NET CASH CREDIT
19— Jan. 2	Rent Expense.....	January rent.......	305	514	310 00			310 00
3	Utilities Expense...	Gas & electricity.	306	517	42 00			42 00
4	Office Equipment..	Typewriter........	307	121	450 00			450 00
18	Todd Electronics...	Inv. 0567.........	308	√		360 00	7 20	352 80
24	George Young.....	Inv. P876.........	309	√		200 00	2 00	198 00
28	Dixon & Hicks....	Inv. 82A.........	310	√		1,204 00		1,204 00

① Debits posted during the month to accounts in general ledger.

② Debits posted during the month to creditors' accounts in subsidiary ledger.

③ Amounts in these two columns are not posted separately during the month.

Each of the three entries in the Accounts Payable Debit column is posted individually to the creditor's account in the subsidiary ledger. A check mark (√) is placed in the Posting Reference column to show that the amount has been posted. Note that the fourth and fifth entries (for January 18 and 24) entail purchases discounts whereas the sixth entry (for January 28) does not. None of the items in the Cash Credit column or Purchases Discount Credit column are posted during the month.

Postings at the End of the Month

At the end of the month, all the money columns are pencil-footed and a check is made of the equality of the debit and credit totals. To check the equality, add the two debit totals together and then add the two credit totals together; these two sums must be equal. After the equality of the debits and credits has been proved, the journal is totaled and ruled.

The total of the General Ledger Debit column is not posted because the amounts in the column have been posted individually to accounts in the general ledger. So to indicate that the total is not to be posted, a check mark (√) is placed in the amount column on the line beneath the double rules.

The total of the Accounts Payable Debit column is posted to the debit side of the controlling account in the general ledger. The individual amounts in this column were posted to the subsidiary ledger during the month. The account number (211) is recorded beneath the double rule.

General Ledger Debit.........	$ 802.00
Accounts Payable Debit......	1,764.00
Total debits...........	$2,566.00
Purchases Discount Credit....	$ 9.20
Net Cash Credit...........	2,556.80
Total credits...........	$2,566.00

	CASH PAYMENTS JOURNAL							Page 3
DATE	ACCOUNT DEBITED	EXPLANATION	CHECK NO.	POST. REF.	GENERAL LEDGER DEBIT	ACCOUNTS PAYABLE DEBIT	PURCHASES DISCOUNT CREDIT	NET CASH CREDIT
19—Jan. 2	Rent Expense.....	January rent.......	305	514	310 00			310 00
3	Utilities Expense...	Gas & electricity....	306	517	42 00			42 00
4	Office Equipment..	Typewriter........	307	121	450 00			450 00
18	Todd Electronics...	Inv. 0567..........	308	√		360 00	7 20	352 80
24	George Young.....	Inv. P876.........	309	√		200 00	2 00	198 00
28	Dixon & Hicks....	Inv. 82A..........	310	√		1,204 00		1,204 00
31	Totals...........	....			802 00 802 00	1,764 00 1,764 00	9 20 9 20	2,556 80 2,556 80
					(√)	(211)	(503)	(101)

The total of the Purchases Discount Credit column is posted to the Credit side of the Purchases Discount account in the general ledger. The account number (503) is then recorded beneath the double rule. The total of the Net Cash Credit column is posted to the credit side of the Cash account. The Cash account number (101) is then recorded beneath the double rule.

Summary of Transactions Involving Purchases

This chapter began with a discussion of the various operations involved in the function of purchasing. As a result of these operations, an approved purchase invoice was submitted to the accounting department for journalizing. In some cases, the full amount of the invoice was paid when due. In other cases, a deduction for purchases returns or allowances was made from the total amount of the invoice. In others, a deduction for purchase discounts was also made.

The chart at the top of page 211 summarizes the types of transactions and shows in each case how the transactions should be recorded.

TOPIC 5 ■ PROBLEMS

28 Answer the questions below and on pages 211 and 212 about the cash payments journal illustrated above.

a What accounts were debited and credited in the cash payments journal entry of January 24? What were the amounts debited and credited?

b Why are two credit entries needed in the cash payments journal for the January 24 transaction?

c Why is a check mark placed in the Posting Reference column for the January 24 entry?

d When the January 24 entry was posted, was $2 posted as a credit to Purchases Discount? Was $198 posted as a credit to Cash?

RECORDING THE TRANSACTIONS INVOLVING PURCHASES

Transaction	Source Document	Recorded in	Posted in General Ledger					Posted in Accounts Payable Ledger
			Cash	Accounts Payable	Purchases	Purchases Returns & Allowances	Purchases Discounts	Individual Creditor Account
Purchases for Cash	Check Stub	CASH PAYMENTS JOURNAL	XXXX		XXXX			
Return or Allowance for Cash	Remittance Slip	CASH RECEIPTS JOURNAL	XXXX			XXXX		
Purchases on Credit	Purchase Invoice	PURCHASES JOURNAL		XXXX	XXXX			XXXX
Return or Allowance for Credit	Credit Memorandum	GENERAL JOURNAL		XX		XX		XX
Payment with Purchase Discount	Check Stub	CASH PAYMENTS JOURNAL	XXX	XXXX			X	XXXX
Payment without Purchases Discount	Check Stub	CASH PAYMENTS JOURNAL	XXXX	XXXX				XXXX

e How will the $2 discount be posted to the Purchases Discount account? How will the $198 cash payment be posted to the Cash account?

f What account was debited in the entry of January 3?

g When the January 3 entry was posted, was $42 posted as a credit to Cash at the same time?

h When the January 18 entry was posted as a debit to the Todd Electronics account, was the Accounts Payable controlling account in the general ledger debited for $360 at the same time?

i How will the payment of January 18 be posted to the Accounts Payable controlling account?

j Why is a check mark placed under the General Ledger Debit column?
k Why is (211) placed under the Accounts Payable Debit column?
l Why is (503) placed under the Purchases Discount Credit column?

m Is there any way to prove the amounts in the cash payments journal?
n Can you tell by looking at subsidiary ledger accounts whether or not a discount was deducted on the payments made?

29 Process the following transactions for Albert Baker's Garden Center.
a Open general ledger accounts and record July 1 balances for Cash (debit balance, $9,600); Equipment; Accounts Payable; Albert Baker, Capital (credit balance, $9,600); Purchases; Purchases Discount; Rent Expense. Open accounts payable ledger accounts for Walter Brady and the Troy Supply Company. Allow two lines for each account except in the subsidiary ledger, where five lines should be allowed. Assign an appropriate number to each account.
b Using a purchases journal and a cash payments journal, record the entries for the following transactions.

July 1 Issued Check 103 for $140 for July rent.
  5 Purchased merchandise for $250 from Walter Brady on Invoice 482, dated July 2; terms 2/10, n/30.
  8 Issued Check 104 for $260 for equipment.
  8 Purchased merchandise for $400 from the Troy Supply Company on Invoice S252, dated July 5; terms 1/10, n/60.
  11 Issued Check 105 for $245 to Walter Brady to pay Invoice 482, less discount.
  13 Purchased merchandise for $320 from Walter Brady on

Invoice 524, dated July 10; terms 2/10, n/30.
July 14 Issued Check 106 for $396 to Troy Supply Company to pay Invoice S252, less discount.
  18 Purchased merchandise for $230 from Troy Supply Company on Invoice S371, dated July 15; terms 1/10, n/60.
  24 Issued Check 107 for $100 to Albert Baker, the owner, for personal use.
  26 Purchased merchandise for $80 from Walter Brady on Invoice 566, dated July 23; terms 2/10, n/30.
  30 Issued Check 108 for $320 to Walter Brady to pay Invoice 524.

c Foot and rule the journals.
d Post the journal entries to the ledgers.
e Prepare a schedule of accounts payable.
f Prepare a trial balance.

NOTE: Save the journals for use in Problem 30.

30 Using the journals prepared in Problem 29, complete the following assignments:
a Record the entries for the following transactions.

Aug. 1 Issued Check 109 for $140 for August rent.
  5 Purchased merchandise for

$380 from Walter Brady on Invoice 624, dated August 2; terms 2/10, n/30.

Aug. 9 Issued Check 110 for $372.40 to Walter Brady to pay Invoice 624, less discount.

12 Purchased merchandise for $550 from the Troy Supply Company on Invoice S480, dated August 9; terms 1/10, n/60.

15 Issued Check 111 for $125 to Albert Baker, the owner, for personal use.

18 Issued Check 112 for $544.50 to Troy Supply Company to pay Invoice S480, less discount.

Aug. 21 Issued Check 113 to Walter Brady to pay Invoice 566, dated July 26.

24 Purchased merchandise for $270 from Walter Brady on Invoice 711, dated August 23; terms 2/10, n/30.

28 Purchased merchandise for $185 from the Troy Supply Company on Invoice S523, dated August 25; terms 1/10, n/60.

b Foot and rule the journals.
c Post the journal entries to the ledgers.
d Prepare a schedule of accounts payable.
e Prepare a trial balance.

The Language of Business

The following terms are important. Do you understand the meaning of each? Can you define each term and use it in an original sentence?

merchandising business	extension	trade discount
merchandise	periodic inventory	subsidiary ledger
inventory cards	perpetual inventory	controlling account
purchase requisition	physical inventory	purchase return
request for quotation	costs	purchase allowance
purchase order	gross profit	credit period
purchase invoice	Purchases (account)	cash discount

Chapter Questions

1 Explain in detail the four operations involved in a purchasing procedure.

2 What is the purpose of preparing a schedule of accounts payable? In what ways is it like a trial balance?

3 Why are purchases returns and allowances not recorded directly in the Purchases account?

4 How does the use of a four-column general journal simplify journalizing and posting entries to the ledger?

5 What is the difference between a trade discount and a purchase discount? How are they entered in the accounting records?

6 Why are purchase discounts not recorded directly in the Purchases account?

7 Name and describe the source document for journalizing each of the following: purchases on credit, purchases returns and allowances, purchase discounts, and payments to creditors.

8 What procedure should be followed in posting the entries from a one-column purchases journal?

9 Explain how the use of a four-column cash payments journal simplifies journalizing and posting entries to the subsidiary ledger.

10 What sequence is followed in posting from a four-column general journal? from a four-column cash payments journal?

Management Cases

Quantity Purchases To encourage dealers to purchase a large quantity of an item at one time, manufacturers frequently offer reduced prices on quantity purchases. The dealer or his purchasing agent must analyze the purchase records carefully to determine what quantity of merchandise he should purchase to make the best investment. He may find that the price advantage of a quantity purchase is offset by the following disadvantages: (1) A large amount of money is tied up in merchandise inventory, (2) costs of storage increase, (3) items lose value because of deterioration and style changes from one season to the next.

Case M-7

The Fulton Appliance Store can purchase a Frosty home freezer for $210 with credit terms of n/30. The manufacturer will pay the shipping charges to the store. If, however, the store purchases a carload of 50 freezers, the cost is reduced to $198 each. The lower price results from the quantity price offered by the manufacturer and the reduced transportation costs of a carload shipment.

Last year the store sold 40 freezers. The sales were distributed throughout the entire year. Sales have been increasing gradually, and the store is expecting a 20 percent increase in sales in the coming year.

Would you recommend that the store purchase a carload of freezers? Explain the reasons for your answer.

Case M-8

Yeager Brothers purchased a shipment of water coolers from the Ajax Manufacturing Company. The invoice for the coolers is for $3,600, is dated June 1, and has terms of 2/10, n/30. On June 11, the company does not have sufficient cash to pay the invoice; but it will have the money by July 1. In order to take advantage of the 2 percent cash discount, Mr. Yeager is considering borrowing from a bank the money to pay the invoice. The company has a good credit rating and can borrow the necessary amount at 6 percent interest. Mr. Yeager wants to know the answer to this question: Would it pay to borrow the money and take advantage of the discount, or is it wiser to pay the net invoice on June 30?

The following facts must be considered: (1) The amount Mr. Yeager needs to borrow is the amount that he would need to pay the invoice on June 11. (2) The interest on the loan will be calculated for only 20 days because there are 20 days between June 11 and July 1, the date on which the full amount of the invoice is due. The invoice is, therefore, being prepaid by 20 days.

What is your recommendation?

Case M-9

Because of the limited amount of cash it has available, the Harrison Supply Company found it impossible to pay its invoices before the expiration of the discount period. As a result, management followed a policy of paying all invoices on the final due date.

Last year, the business had a net income of $4,580. During the year the company purchased merchandise totaling $67,480. All the merchandise was purchased from wholesalers on terms of 2/10, n/30.

The manager of Harrison's estimates that if the firm had had $5,000 additional cash with which to work, it would have been able to take advantage of all cash discounts. This $5,000 could have been borrowed at 6 percent interest.

If the manager had borrowed $5,000 at the beginning of last year and paid all the invoices within the discount period, what effect would this have had on the net income for the year? What would the amount of the net income have been?

Working Hint

Ruling Creditor Accounts

A disadvantage of the standard ledger form is that it is difficult to tell the current balance in the account when several entries have been posted. To ease this problem, the accounting clerk can rule off the amount of each invoice in the creditor's account when it has been paid.

In the account shown below, goods were purchased on May 2 from Acme Distributors in the amount of $75.25. On May 15 a payment of $50 was made on account, and on May 28 a payment of $25.25 was made in settlement of the invoice. A single rule is drawn under the $75.25 credit and under the $25.25 debit to show that the May 2 invoice has now been paid in full. Thus the balance owed on a creditor's account may be easily determined. In the account illustrated below, $65 is still owed to the Acme Distributors because another purchase was made from them on May 14.

Acme Distributors, 5360 Ninth Street, Evansville, Indiana 47703

DATE		EXPLANATION	POST. REF.	DEBIT	DATE		EXPLANATION	POST. REF.	CREDIT
19—					19—				
May	15		CP1	50 00	May	2	Inv. 2061	P1	75 25
	28		CP2	25 25		14	Inv. 2974	P1	65 00

Payments   Invoice

Chapter 4
Processing Sales on Credit

The income of a merchandising business is derived chiefly from the sale of merchandise. Some businesses have a policy of selling merchandise only *for cash;* others sell both for cash and on credit.

The procedure for processing cash sales was described in Chapter 1. The sales were recorded on cash register tapes or sales slips. These source documents then served as the basis for journalizing the transactions in the cash receipts journal. In this chapter, the procedure for processing sales made on credit will be described.

TOPIC 1 ■ A SYSTEM FOR THE CONTROL OF SALES ON CREDIT

The accounting systems used by merchandising businesses vary according to the nature and size of the business. Every business, however, must have a system that provides for processing efficiently and accurately both the merchandise for delivery to the customer and the data for recording the sales transaction. Every system must ensure that (1) the customer's order is properly received and promptly approved or disapproved; (2) the goods ordered are taken from stock, packaged, and shipped; and (3) the customer is accurately billed for the merchandise. In most retail businesses, where sales are made over the counter, these three operations are performed at one time. The order is placed when the customer tells the salesclerk what he wants. Delivery is made when the clerk takes the merchandise from the shelf, wraps it, and hands it to the customer. Billing takes place when the clerk fills out a sales slip, charging the customer for the goods. Most wholesale businesses, by contrast, do not have over-the-counter sales. In these cases an order is received from a customer through the mail or from a salesman who visits the customer. Although the procedures and forms vary from business to business, they generally follow the procedures described in this topic.

Receiving and Approving the Order

Taking the Order Orders for merchandise reach a business in a number of ways. They may come in on *sales order forms* that are filled out by salesmen, who call on customers and solicit orders. They may come in on *purchase order* forms or in *letters* from customers. Or they may be jotted down on *sales slips* by clerks who take orders from behind a counter or over a telephone.

Since orders are submitted in a wide variety of ways, data is received on a multitude of odd-sized forms, letters, and slips. Any business that processes a substantial number of orders finds it desirable to transfer all the order data to standard forms. These forms are made up in multiple copies to simplify and expedite the filling of the order.

The following is a description of the way the Central Sales Company processes the orders it receives.

Preparing the Shipping Order   When an order is received by the sales department, the salesclerk verifies all the information submitted by the customer and provides any additional information (such as catalog numbers or unit prices) that will expedite the filling of the order. The salesclerk enters all the necessary data on a prenumbered, multiple-copy form known as a *shipping order*. Here is a *shipping order* prepared on the basis of a purchase order submitted to the Central Sales Company by Wilson's Radio Center.

PURCHASE ORDER

WILSON'S RADIO CENTER
37 Penton Street
Duluth, Minnesota 55808

No. **69458**

- Purchase order numbers must appear on all papers and packages. Packing slip must accompany shipments.

TO Central Sales Company
423 Vernon Avenue
St. Paul, Minnesota 55108

- Terms of discount must be shown on invoice.
- Delivery schedule as indicated must be held.

Date 1/2/—	Items Needed By 1/15/—	Terms 1/20, n/30	Via Rlwy. Exp.	FOB St. Paul
QUANTITY		DESCRIPTION		UNIT PRICE
12		Radio tube No. IR5		1.47
6		Radio tube No. 3GK5		1.23
1		Antenna mast, 3-section No. 84-3		5.86

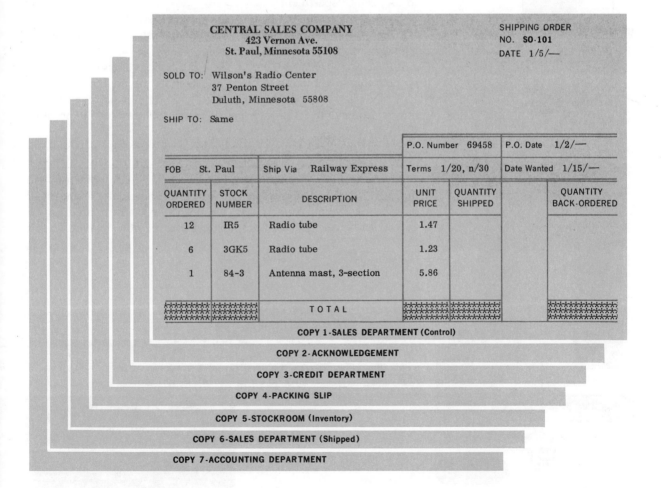

CENTRAL SALES COMPANY
423 Vernon Ave.
St. Paul, Minnesota 55108

SHIPPING ORDER
NO. **SO-101**
DATE 1/5/—

SOLD TO: Wilson's Radio Center
37 Penton Street
Duluth, Minnesota 55808

SHIP TO: Same

P.O. Number 69458	P.O. Date 1/2/—

FOB St. Paul	Ship Via Railway Express	Terms 1/20, n/30	Date Wanted 1/15/—

QUANTITY ORDERED	STOCK NUMBER	DESCRIPTION	UNIT PRICE	QUANTITY SHIPPED		QUANTITY BACK-ORDERED
12	IR5	Radio tube	1.47			
6	3GK5	Radio tube	1.23			
1	84-3	Antenna mast, 3-section	5.86			
		TOTAL				

COPY 1-SALES DEPARTMENT (Control)

COPY 2-ACKNOWLEDGEMENT

COPY 3-CREDIT DEPARTMENT

COPY 4-PACKING SLIP

COPY 5-STOCKROOM (Inventory)

COPY 6-SALES DEPARTMENT (Shipped)

COPY 7-ACCOUNTING DEPARTMENT

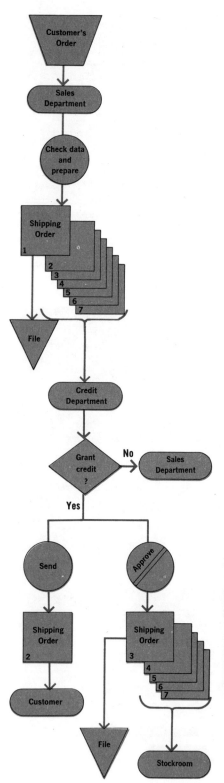

The salesclerk transfers some of the information from the purchase order without change; for example, the customer's name and address, the number and date of the customer's purchase order, the shipping terms, and the date on which the customer needs the merchandise. Some of the information on the purchase order must be verified before the shipping order can be completed. For example, the salesclerk must verify that the credit terms requested by the customer (1/20, n/30) conform to company policy before he enters these terms on the shipping order. Moreover, the clerk must verify the correctness of the stock numbers and unit prices of the items described on the purchase order.

When the salesclerk completes the shipping order, he detaches Copy 1 of the shipping order, attaches it to the purchase order, and retains it in the *unshipped order file.* Until the order is shipped and billed, this "control" copy is kept in the sales department as the only fixed record the company has of the order that has been received. The remaining copies of the shipping order are then passed on intact to the credit department.

Securing Credit Approval   The credit department determines whether or not the customer is a good credit risk, that is, whether he is likely to pay the bill when it falls due.

If the customer is a poor credit risk or if the status of his credit cannot be determined without additional information, the credit department typically will return the shipping order to the sales department with a note of explanation. The sales manager will then resolve the problem with the customer. If, however, the customer's credit is good, the credit clerk will detach Copy 2 and send it to the customer to acknowledge that the order has been received and is being processed. The clerk will then sign his name in the panel at the top of Copy 3 to indicate that the order has been approved for shipment. (By means of interleaved carbon paper or by the use of specially treated paper, the signature is transferred automatically to the other copies. In this way, anyone who uses one of these copies can be sure that the customer's credit has been checked and approved.)

The credit clerk will then detach Copy 3 of the shipping order for his own files and send the remaining copies to the stockroom, where the merchandise is stored.

Packing and Shipping the Merchandise

When the shipping order arrives in the stockroom, a clerk assembles the items specified and packs them in cartons. As he does so, he indicates on Copy 4 (the packing slip copy) and on all remaining copies (by carbon or other impression paper) whether or not he is sending the full quantity of each item ordered. As the illustration of the packing slip indicates, all the items on the order are being shipped except the IR5 radio tubes. Only 8 of the 12 tubes ordered can be supplied; therefore, the remaining 4 tubes are listed in the Quantity Back-Ordered column. This is done to inform the customer that these remaining items are not included in the current shipment but will be sent as soon as they are available. The shipping clerk then completes the shipping information at the top of the packing slip. The packing slip is then detached from the pack and separated into an address label and a packing slip. The label is attached to the outside of the package. The packing slip is enclosed in the package so that the customer can check the contents of the package against the listing on the packing slip. (Notice that on Copy 4—the packing slip—the credit approval section has been blocked out so that the customer cannot read what was written there.) The quantity shipped plus the quantity back-ordered should agree with the customer's purchase order. The stock clerk then detaches the inventory copy (Copy 5) for his own files (so that the number of items shipped can be subtracted from the appropriate inventory cards) and sends the remaining copies back to the sales department.

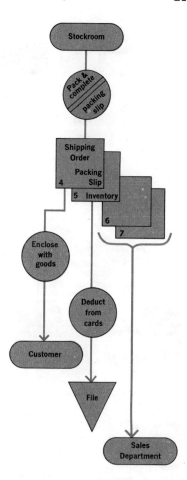

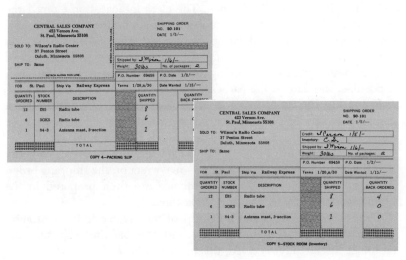

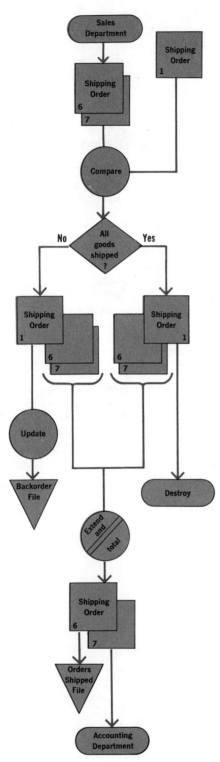

Billing for the Merchandise

When the remaining copies (6 and 7) are returned to the sales department, a salesclerk takes Copy 1 (the control copy) out of the unshipped order file. He checks Copy 1 against the shipped copy (Copy 6) to verify that no changes were made from the original specifications. If all merchandise has been shipped, then Copy 1 is destroyed. On Copies 6 and 7, the salesclerk multiplies the quantity shipped by the unit price and records the resulting extensions in the Amount column. When all the extensions are computed, he totals them, initials the pack, and separates Copies 6 and 7. Copy 6 is placed in an orders shipped file, and Copy 7 is sent to the accounting department. Copy 7 provides the data for the preparation of a *sales invoice* (the customer's bill).

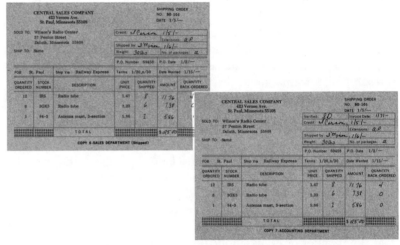

If there are any back orders, the procedure described above is changed slightly. The salesclerk computes the extensions and total for only those items actually shipped. The clerk indicates on Copy 1 the items not shipped and files this form in a back-order file. When new stock is received, he will fill out a new shipping order so that the balance of the order can be shipped to the customer. (A letter should be sent to the customer explaining the delay in shipment and indicating, if possible, the date of the earliest delivery.)

Preparing the Sales Invoice   The sales invoice looks much like a completed copy of the shipping order except that it lists only those items actually shipped and shows how much the customer owes.

An accounting clerk checks Copy 7 of the shipping order to verify that the extensions and total amount are correct on the shipping order. At least two copies of the *sales invoice* are then prepared in the billing section of the accounting department.

The accounting clerk sends Copy 1 of the invoice to the customer. Unlike the acknowledgment copy and the packing slip that the customer has already received, this invoice is his *bill*.

CENTRAL SALES COMPANY   INVOICE NO. **101**
423 Vernon Avenue
St. Paul, Minnesota 55108

SOLD TO: Wilson's Radio Center
            37 Penton Street
            Duluth, Minnesota 55808

SHIP TO: Invoice Date 1/7/ —

            Same

                                        Terms 1/20, n/30

Purchase Order No. 69458		Date 1/2/—	Shipped Via Railway Express	FOB St. Paul	No. of Packages 2
QUANTITY	STOCK NUMBER	DESCRIPTION		UNIT PRICE	AMOUNT
8	IR5	Radio tube		1.47	11.76
6	3GK5	Radio tube		1.23	7.38
1	84–3	Antenna mast, 3–section		5.86	5.86
		TOTAL			25.00

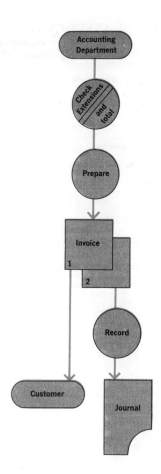

Copy 2 is kept in the accounting department as the source document for journalizing the sales transaction. Frequently, the sales invoice is prepared in three copies—Copy 3 goes to the sales department where it can be used in analyzing sales revenue. After the invoice is prepared, the invoice date is recorded at the top of the shipping order to indicate that it was billed.

In the system described for the Central Sales Company, a multiple-copy form was used to save retyping and recopying at each stage of the procedure. If this system had not been used, the shipping label and the packing slip, for example, would have had to be prepared separately. The number of copies prepared at one time will vary depending on the specific needs of the particular company.

Periodic Billing Even though a business sends an invoice to the customer at the time that the merchandise is shipped, most businesses find it useful to send the customer a statement of his account periodically. The statement that the seller sends to the customer looks something like the customer's ledger account. For example, if the statement is sent at the end of the month, the statement will show (1) the balance due at the beginning of the month, (2) all charges for sales during the month, (3) all deductions for payments received or goods returned during the month, and (4) the balance currently unpaid.

A statement may be either of two types: a *nondescriptive statement,* which shows only the dates, numbers, and total of the invoices; or a *descriptive statement,* which gives an explanation for each item that appears on the statement. The possible statements that the Central Sales Company might send to Wilson's Radio Center are illustrated on page 222.

CENTRAL SALES COMPANY
423 Vernon Avenue
St. Paul, Minnesota 55108

STATEMENT OF ACCOUNT

Wilson's Radio Center
37 Penton Street
Duluth, Minnesota 55808

Date   January 31, 19—

Please return this stub with your check

Amount Enclosed $_____

Date	Reference	Charges	Credits	Balance
Balance Forwarded				.00
Jan. 7	101	25.00		25.00
15	104	400.00		425.00
26	Cash		25.00	400.00
27	107	76.50		476.50

Nondescriptive statement: shows only dates, numbers, and total of invoices.

CENTRAL SALES COMPANY
423 Vernon Avenue
St. Paul, Minnesota 55108

STATEMENT OF ACCOUNT

Wilson's Radio Center
37 Penton Street
Duluth, Minnesota 55808

Date   January 31, 19—

Please return this stub with your check

Amount Enclosed $_____

Date	Reference	Charges	Credits	Balance
Balance Forwarded				.00
Jan. 7	IR5 radio tube	11.76		
	3GK5 radio tube	7.38		
	84-3 antenna mast	5.86		25.00
15	8C Vista television	400.00		425.00
26	Cash		25.00	400.00
27	400-M radio	76.50		476.50

Descriptive statement: shows dates, numbers, and total of invoices, as well as description of items.

When a business has only a small number of charge customers, statements are usually sent at the end of each month to show the balance due. When a business has many credit customers, it is usually not possible to send all the statements on the last day of the month because of the load that would be created at that one time. In order to distribute the job of preparing statements over the working days of the month, a process known as *cycle billing* is used. Under this plan all the customer accounts are divided into groups—usually according to alphabetical sequence of last names, as in the plan below.

Cycle billing: billing according to alphabetical sequence of last names at designated dates.

Last Names Beginning with	Billing Covers Charges and Payments for These Dates		Closing Date
A—F	8th of the month to	7th of the next month	7
G—K	15th	14th	14
L—R	22nd	21st	21
S—Z	29th	28th	28

A business that uses this plan would prepare a statement for John Adams on the 7th of the month. Therefore, his statement for March would show all the charges and payments to John Adams' account between February 8 to March 7. John Rambeck's statement for March would be prepared on March 21 and would show all charges and payments to his account between February 22 and March 21.

Flowcharting the Sales Operations

The procedures for handling the three operations of receiving and approving the order, packing and shipping the merchandise, and billing for the merchandise, can be shown in the following flowchart.

FLOWCHART OF A SALES SYSTEM

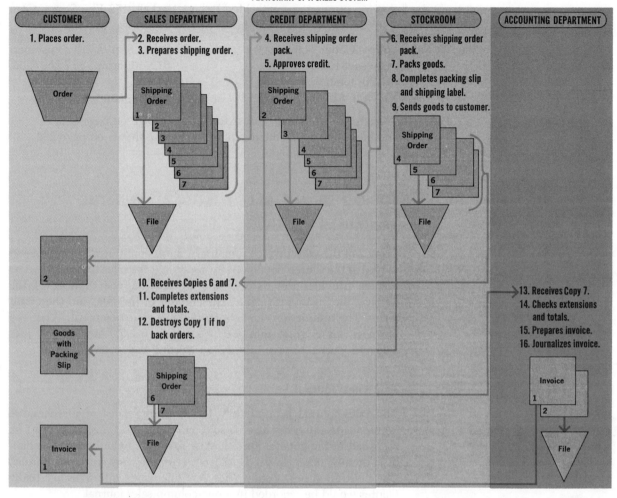

TOPIC 1 ■ PROBLEMS

31 Answer these questions about the shipping orders on pages 217 to 220.

a Who is the customer?

b Where will the goods be shipped?

c What is the shipping order number?

d How are the goods being shipped?

e How many IR5 radio tubes were ordered?

f Is the number shipped always the same as the number ordered? Why?

g What is the unit price of the IR5 radio tubes?

h What were the terms of the sale?

i Can a cash discount be received on this sale?

j When was the shipping order pack prepared? the credit approved? the goods shipped? the invoice prepared?

k Who receives Copy 2 of the shipping order? Why?

l Why does the stockroom keep Copy 5 of the shipping order?

m What happens to Copy 1 after Copy 6 is received by the sales department?

32 During March, Scott & Wilson, 36 Alden Street, Montclair, New Jersey 07015, completed the following transactions with Mrs. Robert Haskell, 172 Elm Street, Glen Ridge, New Jersey 07021. On February 28, her account balance was $12.60.

Mar. 8 Sales Slip C564: blouse, $6.90; gloves, $10.50; men's socks, $1.70; total, $19.10.

10 Received cash, $12.60.

Mar. 23 Sales Slip E715: cushions, $18.40; lamp, $27.25; total, $45.65.

25 Return, lamp, $27.25.

a Prepare a descriptive statement similar to the one shown on page 222.
b Prepare a nondescriptive statement similar to the one shown on page 222.

TOPIC 2 ■ THE SALES JOURNAL AND THE ACCOUNTS RECEIVABLE LEDGER

Copy 2 of the sales invoice remains in the accounting department and is used as the source document for recording the sales transaction. The invoice provides the date of the transaction, the number of the invoice, the customer's name, the amount of the sale, and the credit terms. The transaction can be recorded in a general journal. When the business has a great number of sales on credit, however, it uses a special journal to save time in journalizing and posting.

Sales journal: used to record merchandise sold on credit.

CENTRAL SALES COMPANY
423 Vernon Avenue
St. Paul, Minnesota 55108

INVOICE NO. **101**

SOLD TO: Wilson's Radio Center
37 Penton Street
Duluth, Minnesota 55808

SHIP TO: Same

Invoice Date 1/7/—

Terms 1/20, n/30

Purchase Order No. 69458	Date 1/2/—	Shipped Via Railway Express	FOB St. Paul	No. of Packages 2
QUANTITY	STOCK NUMBER	DESCRIPTION	UNIT PRICE	AMOUNT
8	IR5	Radio tube	1.47	11.76
6	3GK5	Radio tube	1.23	7.38
1	84-3	Antenna mast, 3-section	5.86	5.86
		TOTAL		25.00

The Sales Journal

The sales journal is used only for recording sales of merchandise on credit. If any other asset is sold on credit, the transaction must be recorded in the general journal. Any cash sale (whether of merchandise or any other asset) is recorded in the cash receipts journal. The illustration below shows how the sales invoice to Wilson's Radio Center would be recorded in a one-column sales journal.

When a one-column sales journal is used, only the debit entries are recorded. For each such debit entry, a credit to the Sales account for a like amount is understood. As in the case of other special journals, the individual debits are posted to the proper accounts during the month; the credits to the Sales account are accumulated so that only the total amount is posted to Sales at the end of the month.

		SALES JOURNAL				Page *1*
DATE	INVOICE NO.	ACCOUNT DEBITED	TERMS	POST. REF.	AMOUNT	
19— *Jan.* 7	*101*	*Wilson's Radio Center*...............	*1/20, n/30*		25 00	

The invoices are entered in the sales journal in numerical order so that every invoice is accounted for. The credit terms are entered in the journal so that they can easily be transferred to the customer's ledger account at the time of posting. For example, the sale of January 7 to Wilson's Radio Center carries terms of 1/20, n/30. By having this information in the customer's account, a person can quickly ascertain what cash discount was offered to the customer and when the credit period ends. If the company gives the same credit terms to all its customers, the Terms column could be eliminated from the sales journal. The Central Sales Company uses a Terms column, however, because it offers different credit terms to its customers.

The Accounts Receivable Ledger

In the previous chapter, the creditors' accounts were removed from the general ledger and placed in a subsidiary ledger known as the *accounts payable ledger.* For the same reasons, it is more efficient to also take the customers' accounts out of the general ledger and place them in alphabetical order in a subsidiary ledger, called the *accounts receivable ledger.* This procedure reduces the number of accounts in the general ledger and makes it easier to locate errors on the trial balance. The general ledger is kept in balance by establishing an Accounts Receivable controlling account. The balance of the Accounts Receivable controlling account must equal the total of the balances of all the customer accounts in the accounts receivable ledger.

Ledger Account Forms   The ledger form that has been used up to this point is a *standard ledger form* and is customarily used for general ledger accounts. For customers' and creditors' accounts, however, many firms use a *balance ledger form,* which is an account form with three money columns. This form is designed to show the current balance of the account at all times.

**CENTRAL SALES COMPANY
CHART OF ACCOUNTS**

ASSETS

101	Cash
111	Accounts Receivable
121	Office Equipment
122	Store Equipment

LIABILITIES

| 211 | Accounts Payable |
| 221 | Loans Payable |

OWNER'S EQUITY

| 301 | John Hall, Capital |

INCOME

| 401 | Sales |

COSTS & EXPENSES

501	Purchases
502	Purchases Returns and Allowances
503	Purchases Discount
511	Cash Short and Over
512	Insurance Expense
513	Miscellaneous Expense
514	Rent Expense
515	Salaries Expense
516	Supplies Expense
517	Utilities Expense

| Name |
| Address |

DATE	EXPLANATION	POST. REF.	DEBIT	CREDIT	BALANCE

Balance Ledger Form

A balance ledger form can be used for customers' accounts and creditors' accounts. Therefore, the heading of the balance column is not indicated as being a debit or credit. Since customer accounts normally have debit balances, it is not necessary to identify these balances (unless they are credit balances). Likewise, in creditors' accounts (which normally have credit balances), only debit balances are identified.

The account for Wilson's Radio Center may be used to illustrate how the balance ledger form is used for a customer account.

| Name | Wilson's Radio Center | | | | Credit Limit | $2,000 |
| Address | 37 Penton Street, Duluth, Minnesota 55808 | | | | Telephone | 293-5510 |

DATE		EXPLANATION	POST. REF.	DEBIT	CREDIT	BALANCE	
19—							1
Jan.	7	Inv. 101.....................	S1	25 00		25 00	2
	15	Inv. 104.....................	S1	400 00		425 00	3
	26	Cash........................	CR3		25 00	400 00	4
	27	Inv. 107.....................	S1	76 00		476 00	5
Feb.	4	Cash........................	CR4		476 00	— 00	6

S: sales journal.

1 The debit of $25 from the sale on credit of January 7 is posted from the sales journal to the Debit column of the account. The S in the Posting Reference column indicates that the debit was posted from the sales journal.

2 The account now has a debit balance of $25. This balance does not need to be identified as a debit because customer accounts normally have debit balances.

3 The second entry is also a debit from a sale on credit. This debit of $400 increases the account balance to $425.

4 On January 26, Wilson's pays $25 in cash. Since this payment reduces the amount the customer owes, his account is credited, and the balance is reduced to $400.

5 On January 27, another sale on credit is made for $76. The debit amount increases the debit balance to $476.

6 The last entry is a payment of $476.00. This credit entry reduces the balance to zero. Hereafter, additional debits will be added to the account and additional credits will be subtracted. In this way the current balance is always shown.

Order of Posting:
1. Sales journal.
2. Cash receipts journal.
3. Purchases journal.
4. Cash payments journal.
5. General journal.

When this kind of form is used for customers' accounts, the accounting clerk should post from the sales journal before he posts from the cash receipts journal. In this way he will record the debits to the accounts before he records the credits. That is, he will record the charges against the customer's account before he records any payment of those charges. If the credit amount from the cash receipts journal were posted to the account first, then the customer's account might have a credit balance until the debit is posted from the sales journal.

When using this balance ledger form for the accounts payable ledger, it is a good practice to post the entries from the purchases journal before the accounts payable entries are posted from the cash payments journal in order to avoid having debit balances in the creditors' accounts.

This balance account form is sometimes preferred for general ledger accounts as well as subsidiary ledger accounts, because it shows the current balance. If these accounts are on loose sheets, they can be inserted in a typewriter or accounting machine for rapid posting.

There are many arrangements for these ledgers. The oldest type is the bound-book ledger, but most accounts are now maintained on loose-leaf pages filed in a binder or tray. Thus the account of a customer who stops buying can easily be removed once his balance is zero, and new accounts can quickly be inserted.

Posting from the Sales Journal

Charges to the customers' accounts should be posted daily to keep the account balances up to date. The credit manager refers to the customer's account to determine whether additional orders from the customer should be approved or disapproved for credit. He also checks the customer's account balance to make sure that the customer is making payments on time. If a customer becomes delinquent in his payments, the credit manager must take steps to determine why the payment has not been made and to see that the amount is collected.

Posting entries from the sales journal is similar to posting entries from other one-column journals. Every debit entry in the sales journal is posted individually to the appropriate customer's account in the accounts receivable ledger. When the amount is posted to this subsidiary ledger, a check mark is placed in the Posting Reference column of the sales journal. (In the customer's account, the letter S is written in the Posting Reference column to indicate that the amount has been posted from the sales journal.) The illustrations on pages 228 and 229 show how the general and subsidiary ledger accounts appear when only the entries from the sales journal for January are posted.

At the end of the month, the sales journal is totaled to determine the amount that is to be posted as a debit to the Accounts Receivable controlling account and as a credit to the Sales account in the general ledger. The same procedure is used for totaling and ruling the sales journal as is used for totaling and ruling the purchases journal. The only difference is that the words "Accounts Receivable Debit/Sales Credit" are written in the Account Debited column. At the same time, a diagonal line is drawn across the Posting Reference column to indicate that the total is to be posted to two accounts. When the total amount of the sales is posted, the account number of the Accounts Receivable controlling account is entered above the diagonal line and the number of the Sales account is entered beneath.

When the posting is completed from the sales journal for the month, the total debits posted to the accounts receivable ledger should agree with the amount posted to the Accounts Receivable controlling account in the general ledger. In addition, the debit posted to the Accounts Receivable account in the general ledger should equal the credit posted to the Sales account.

		SALES JOURNAL		Page 1
DATE	INVOICE NO.	ACCOUNT	POST. REF.	AMOUNT
19—Jan.	7	101	Wilson's Radio Cen	√	25 00

Name Wilson's Radio Center
Address 37 Penton Street, Duluth Min. 808

DATE	EXPLANATION	POST. REF.	DEBIT
19—Jan.	7	Inv. 101	S1	25 00

SALES JOURNAL

Page *1*

DATE	INVOICE NO.	ACCOUNT DEBITED	TERMS	POST. REF.	AMOUNT
19—					
Jan. 7	*101*	*Wilson's Radio Center*..............	*1/20, n/30*	√	25 00
11	*102*	*Jane Miller*.....................	*2/10, n/30*	√	80 00
14	*103*	*Smith & Adams*.................	*2/10, n/30*	√	1,600 00
15	*104*	*Wilson's Radio Center*..............	*1/20, n/30*	√	400 00
20	*105*	*Winston, Inc.*...................	*1/20, n/30*	√	350 00
26	*106*	*Jane Miller*.....................	*2/10, n/30*	√	160 00
27	*107*	*Wilson's Radio Center*..............	*1/20, n/30*	√	76 00
30	*108*	*Smith & Adams*.................	*2/10, n/30*	√	200 00
31		*Accounts Receivable Debit/Sales Credit*.		111/401	2,891 00 / 2,891 00

ACCOUNTS RECEIVABLE LEDGER

Name *Jane Miller*   **Credit Limit** $1,000
Address *89 Liberty Avenue, Ashley, Ohio 43015*   **Telephone** 369-3031

DATE	EXPLANATION	POST. REF.	DEBIT	CREDIT	BALANCE
19—					
Jan. 11	*Inv. 102*......................	*S1*	80 00		80 00
26	*Inv. 106*......................	*S1*	160 00		240 00

Name *Smith & Adams*   **Credit Limit** $4,000
Address *210 Dalmeny Street, St. Paul, Minnesota 55142*   **Telephone** 453-0701

DATE	EXPLANATION	POST. REF.	DEBIT	CREDIT	BALANCE
19—					
Jan. 14	*Inv. 103*......................	*S1*	1,600 00		1,600 00
30	*Inv. 108*......................	*S1*	200 00		1,800 00

Name *Wilson's Radio Center*   **Credit Limit** $2,000
Address *37 Penton Street, Duluth, Minnesota 55808*   **Telephone** 293-5510

DATE	EXPLANATION	POST. REF.	DEBIT	CREDIT	BALANCE
19—					
Jan. 7	*Inv. 101*......................	*S1*	25 00		25 00
15	*Inv. 104*......................	*S1*	400 00		425 00
27	*Inv. 107*......................	*S1*	76 00		501 00

| Name | Winston, Inc. | | | Credit Limit | $500 |
| Address | 417 North Ninth Street, Minneapolis, Minnesota 55423 | | | Telephone | 774-7548 |

DATE	EXPLANATION	POST. REF.	DEBIT	CREDIT	BALANCE
19— Jan. 20	Inv. 105	S1	350 00		350 00

Total Accounts Receivable $2,891.00

GENERAL LEDGER

Accounts Receivable — Account No. 111

DATE	EXPLANATION	POST. REF.	DEBIT	DATE	EXPLANATION	POST. REF.	CREDIT
19— Jan. 31		S1	2,891 00				

Sales — Account No. 401

DATE	EXPLANATION	POST. REF.	DEBIT	DATE	EXPLANATION	POST. REF.	CREDIT
				19— Jan. 31		S1	2,891 00

Schedule of Accounts Receivable

At the end of the month, a proof is made to ensure that the subsidiary ledger agrees with the Accounts Receivable controlling account in the general ledger. This proof, called a *schedule of accounts receivable,* is a listing of the individual customers' names and the amounts they owe. The owner or the credit manager frequently wants to have this information available so that the business can control the amount of credit it allows to an individual customer.

Schedule of accounts receivable: list of balances of all customers' accounts.

If the individual customers' names are not needed, the arithmetic proof of the subsidiary ledger can be made by simply adding the balances of the customers' accounts and verifying that the total agrees with the balance of the controlling account. Regardless of the form, the proof is prepared at the end of the accounting period before the trial balance is prepared to prove the general ledger. If the totals do not agree, the error should be located and corrected before the trial balance is prepared for the general ledger. The same procedure is used to find the error as is used to locate an error on the trial balance.

```
        .00T
      240.00
    1,800.00
      501.00
      350.00
    2,891.00T
```

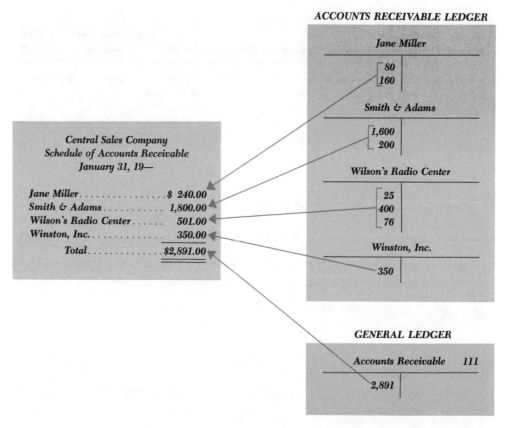

The types of errors that are not revealed on the trial balance are not revealed on the schedule of accounts receivable. Therefore, even though the two totals agree, there is no assurance that the books are completely accurate. It merely indicates that the total of the balances in the accounts of the subsidiary ledger is equal to the balance of the controlling account in the general ledger.

Sales Taxes

Most states, and many cities, collect some form of general sales tax. Sales taxes are usually charged on sales of merchandise to consumers only, but in some states they are also charged on the sale of services. Typically, a sales tax is imposed on the purchaser but collected by the seller, who remits the taxes at specified times to the state or city government.

When a sales tax is collected on a cash sale, it is ordinarily recorded as a separate item on the cash register. At the end of the day, the cash register tape shows the total amount of sales and a separate total of the sales taxes collected. If it is not possible to accumulate two separate totals on the cash register tape, some retailers record only the sale on a cash register. The money for the sales tax is then placed in a separate drawer or box. Thus at the end of the day the total on the cash register tape and the money in the main cash drawer will be the total of the sales only. By multiplying the total amount of the sales by the tax rate, the clerk can determine the amount of sales taxes that should have been collected. Then a proof of the amount of the sales tax collected is made by physically counting the money in the drawer.

When a sales tax is charged on a credit sale, the sales tax is shown separately on the invoice. When the invoice is recorded, the total amount of the invoice (the sale and the sales tax) will be charged to the customer's account. Thus at the time of the sale, the sales tax is either collected (cash sale) or is billed to the customer (credit sale).

The seller is required to report periodically to the tax collector of the state or city the total amount of sales taxes he has collected. At that time, the business forwards the total amount of the tax money to the tax collector. Suppose all businesses are required to file reports at the end of each quarter. Then on March 31, the business would file its sales tax report and remit all the sales taxes it collected from January 1 to March 31.

Recording Sales Taxes

Until the business remits the sales taxes to the tax collector, the amount of the tax collected represents a liability to the business because it is an amount owed. In order to keep a record of the amount owed the government, the sales taxes collected are credited to a separate liability account at the time they are collected or billed. For example, if the Central Sales Company had to charge a 3 percent sales tax to Jane Miller, the sales invoice would be as shown in the margin. The entry to record this sales transaction would involve this analysis.

CENTRAL SALES COMPANY CHART OF ACCOUNTS

LIABILITIES

211	Accounts Payable
221	Loans Payable
222	Sales Tax Payable

CENTRAL SALES COMPANY
423 Vernon Avenue
St. Paul, Minnesota 55108

INVOICE NO. 102

SOLD TO: Jane Miller
89 Liberty Avenue
Ashley, Ohio 43015

SHIP TO: Same

Invoice Date 1/11/—

Terms 2/10, n/30

Purchase Order No. A-738		Date 1/6/—	Shipped Via Truck	FOB St. Paul	No. of Packages 1
QUANTITY	STOCK NUMBER	DESCRIPTION		UNIT PRICE	AMOUNT
2	R-452	AM/FM deluxe clock radio		40.00	80.00
		TOTAL 3% Sales Tax			80.00 2.40
		TOTAL			82.40

WHAT HAPPENS	ACCOUNTING RULE	ENTRY
The asset Accounts Receivable *increases by $82.40.*	*To increase an asset, debit the account.*	Debit: Accounts Receivable, $82.40 (also the customer's account).
The liability Sales Tax Payable *increases by $2.40.*	*To increase a liability, credit the account.*	Credit: Sales Tax Payable, $2.40.
Income increases owner's equity by $80.00.	*To increase owner's equity, credit the account.*	Credit: Sales, $80.00.

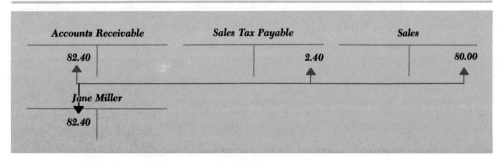

A one-column sales journal cannot be used to record this entry because it involves a credit to Sales Tax Payable as well as a credit to Sales. Therefore, a special column is added to the sales journal to accommodate the sales tax payable on credit sales. Here is how the entries would be made in the modified sales journal.

SALES JOURNAL							Page 1
DATE	INVOICE NO.	ACCOUNT DEBITED	TERMS	POST REF.	ACCOUNTS RECEIVABLE DEBIT	SALES TAX PAYABLE CREDIT	SALES CREDIT
19— Jan. 11	102	Jane Miller.........................	2/10, n/30	√	82 40	2 40	80 00
31		Totals...........................			2,977 73	86 73	2,891 00
					(111)	(222)	(401)

During the month, the amounts in the Accounts Receivable Debit column are posted individually to the customers' accounts in the subsidiary ledger. At the end of the month, the journal is totaled to obtain the amounts to be posted to the general ledger. A single rule is drawn across all money columns, and the money columns are pencil-footed. The equality of the debits and credits is proved by adding the Sales Tax Payable Credit column to the Sales Credit column. This total should agree with the total of the Accounts Receivable Debit column. After the equality is proved, the amounts are written in ink, the last line is completed, and the double rules are drawn.

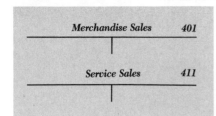

Sales Tax Payable Credit	$ 86.73
Sales Credit	2,891.00
Accounts Receivable Debit	$2,977.73

Sales Tax Payable	222
	19— Jan. 31 SI 86.73

Merchandise Sales	401

Service Sales	411

The totals of the sales journal are then posted to the appropriate accounts in the general ledger. The account numbers are written beneath the double rules to indicate that the totals have been posted. After all items have been posted, the total amount of the sales tax charged during January ($86.73) will appear on the credit side of the Sales Tax Payable account in the general ledger.

If a business sells merchandise on which sales taxes must be collected and also sells services on which no sales taxes are charged, it is good accounting practice to set up two separate sales accounts. If this is done, the accountant will know at the end of the accounting period on what income the sales taxes were collected. This information is usually requested on sales tax returns.

Remitting the Sales Tax   The data required to file the sales tax return is contained in the general ledger. For example, if the Central Sales Company were required to file a report to the state tax commission at the end of each month, the accountant would complete the return for January 31 as shown on page 233.

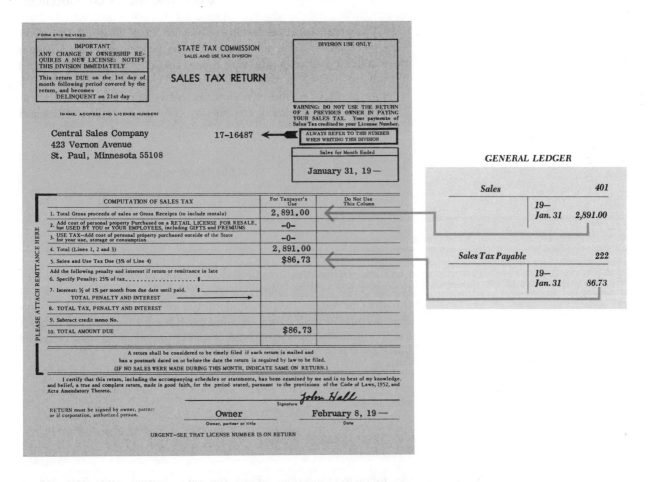

The amount of sales tax due is $86.73, the balance of the Sales Tax Payable account. A check is drawn for this amount and is entered in the cash payments journal. The debit for $86.73 will be to Sales Tax Payable because the liability account is decreased. After the cash payments journal entries are posted, the Sales Tax Payable account will have a zero balance. Of course, after the sales journal is posted for February, the account will again have a credit balance for the amount of sales tax charged or collected during February.

Sales Tax Payable 222

19—			19—		
Feb. 8 CP4	86.73		Jan. 31 SI	86.73	

CASH PAYMENTS JOURNAL								Page 4
DATE	ACCOUNT DEBITED	EXPLANATION	CHECK NO.	POST. REF.	GENERAL LEDGER DEBIT	ACCOUNTS PAYABLE DEBIT	PURCHASES DISCOUNT CREDIT	NET CASH CREDIT
19— Feb. 8	Sales Tax Payable	January return	313	222	86 73			86 73

In the preceding illustration, only sales taxes charged on credit sales were shown. The only change in the procedure to record sales taxes collected on cash sales is to record the entry in the cash receipts journal instead of in the sales journal. When a one-column cash receipts journal is used, two entries are required to record these amounts because the entry contains two credits: a credit to Sales and a credit to Sales Tax Payable.

CASH RECEIPTS JOURNAL		
Sales.	401	300
Sales Tax Payable	222	9

When the entries are posted from the journal, the amount of the sales tax will be posted to the Sales Tax Payable account in the general ledger. At the end of the month, the Sales Tax Payable account will show one posting for the sales journal (the column total) and one entry for each cash sale recorded in the cash receipts journal.

There is no change in submitting the Sales Tax Return because the accounts in the general ledger again contain all the information about sales taxes.

TOPIC 2 ■ PROBLEMS

33 Answer the following questions about the sales journal, subsidiary ledger accounts, and general ledger accounts shown on pages 228 and 229.

a Invoice 104 was sold on what date and to whom?

b If the sale recorded for January 7 had been entered in a general journal instead of the sales journal, what would the complete entry have been?

c When the January 7 sale is posted, is the Sales account credited for $25 at the same time? Why or why not?

d When the January 7 sale is posted, what account is debited? In which ledger is the account located?

e When the January 14 sale is posted, are both the Accounts Receivable controlling account in the general ledger and the Smith & Adams account in the subsidiary ledger debited? Why or why not?

f What amount was posted to the Sales account on January 31? Was this amount debited or credited? Why?

g How is the accuracy of the subsidiary accounts receivable ledger proved?

h Where is the data for the schedule of accounts receivable obtained?

i Are both the Accounts Receivable controlling account and the individual subsidiary ledger accounts listed on a trial balance? Why or why not?

j If Jane Miller paid her account on January 15, how much should she pay? Why?

k If Jane Miller paid her account on February 3, how much should she pay? Why?

34 Answer these questions about the sales tax entries in the journal on page 232.

a When the January 11 sale is posted, is the Sales Tax Payable account credited for $2.40? Why or why not?

b If the sale and sales tax recorded on January 11 had been entered in a general journal, what would the complete entry have been?

c What amount was posted to the Sales Tax Payable account on January 31? Was this amount debited or credited? Why?

d Is any account debited for $2,977.73 on January 31? Why or why not?

35 The Sun Florists issued the following invoices for sales on credit during April.

April 2   To Donald Paper Company; Invoice 348; terms 1/15, n/30; sale amount, $120.

     11   To Howard Quigley; Invoice 349; terms n/30; sale amount, $80.

     15   To Pompton Gift Shop; Invoice 350; terms 1/10, n/30; sale amount, $60.

April 23   To Howard Quigley; Invoice 351; terms n/30; sale amount, $45.

     28   To Pompton Gift Shop; Invoice 352; terms 1/10, n/30; sale amount, $110.

a Open general ledger accounts for Accounts Receivable and Sales. (Allow two lines each.) Using the balance ledger form, open subsidiary ledger accounts for the customers. (Allow four lines for each account.)

b Record the above sales transactions in a one-column sales journal.

c Foot and rule the sales journal.

d Post the entries from the journal.

e Prepare a schedule of accounts receivable.

36 The Quality Stationery Store is located in a state that has a 2% sales tax on merchandise. During March the store issued the following invoices.

March 7   Invoice 331; to Daniel Mason; terms n/30; sale amount, $90; tax, $1.80.

     12   Invoice 332; to Brown's Catering Service, Inc.; terms 1/10, n/30; sale amount, $75; tax, $1.50.

     16   Invoice 333; to Daniel Mason; terms n/30; sale amount, $45; tax, $.90.

March 22   Invoice 334; to Brown's Catering Service, Inc.; terms 1/10, n/30; sale amount, $30; tax, $.60.

     29   Invoice 335; to Bendewald Studio; terms 1/15, n/30; sale amount, $180; tax, $3.60.

a Open general ledger accounts for Accounts Receivable, Sales Tax Payable, and Sales. (Allow two lines each.) Using the balance ledger form, open subsidiary ledger accounts for the customers. (Allow four lines for each account.)

b Record the above transactions in a three-column sales journal.

c Post the debit entries from the sales journal.

d Foot and rule the sales journal.

e Post the entries at the end of the month.

f Prepare a schedule of accounts receivable.

TOPIC 3 ■ SALES RETURNS AND ALLOWANCES

At the time the merchandise is shipped, the seller sends an invoice to bill the customer for the items sent. The customer, however, sometimes receives the merchandise in an unacceptable condition. The items may be damaged, the quantity may be greater or less than was ordered, the wrong merchandise may have been sent, or the customer may find that the items do not meet his needs. In such cases, the seller generally grants the customer the privilege of returning the merchandise. The seller refers to the items returned to him as *sales returns*.

Sales return: merchandise returned to the seller.

Sometimes, instead of returning the unsatisfactory merchandise, a customer agrees to keep it if he is allowed a reduction from the original price shown on the invoice. Such a reduction in price is called a *sales allowance*.

Sales allowance: reduction from sales price for damages or other causes.

In the previous chapter, returns and allowances were discussed from the customer's point of view as purchase returns and allowances. In this topic, the accounting procedure for handling returns and allowances will be presented from the viewpoint of the seller as sales returns and allowances.

Refunding Cash for Sales Returns and Allowances

When the customer has paid cash for the items sold to him, he generally wants to have cash refunded to him when he returns the items. If he is allowed a reduction in the price he paid, he wants to have the allowance refunded to him in cash. Cash refunds are made either by (1) taking the money out of the cash register or (2) drawing a check.

Refunds in Cash. When the refund is made from the cash register, the amount paid out will be shown on the cash proof. For example, the cash proof, which the Central Sales Company prepares on a weekly basis, reports (1) cash of $380 received from sales and (2) cash of $7 paid out of the drawer for returns and allowances. When this cash proof is submitted to the accounting department, the amount of the cash sales ($380) must be recorded. In the entry, the Cash account is debited for $380 to reflect the increase in assets and the Sales account is credited for $380 to reflect the increase in owner's equity caused by the income earned.

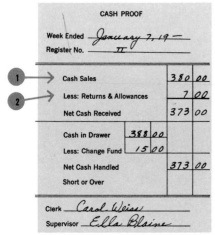

CASH RECEIPTS JOURNAL				Page 3
DATE	ACCOUNT CREDITED	EXPLANATION	POST. REF.	AMOUNT
19— Jan. 7	Sales	Cash sales for week.	401	380 00

In effect, this entry results in a debit to Cash for $380 and a credit to Sales for $380.

The amount of the cash paid out for items returned and allowances granted ($7) must also be recorded. Since cash is paid out, the Cash account must be credited to show the decrease in assets. Some of the merchandise recorded in the Sales account has been returned; therefore, the total amount of Sales shown on the records must be reduced. This could be done by debiting the Sales account. (Since sales increase owner's equity, the return of sales decreases owner's equity.) However, it is a better practice to keep a record of the amount of sales returns and allowances in a separate account. In this way, information is readily available about the amount of sales and also about the amount and frequency of sales returns and allowances. (Because of the relationship between the Sales account and the Sales Returns and Allowances account, the accountant for the Central Sales Company has assigned them consecutive account numbers 401 and 402.)

Thus Sales Returns and Allowances is debited to record the $7 in cash paid out for merchandise returned by customers. Since cash was paid out, the entry was made in the cash payments journal.

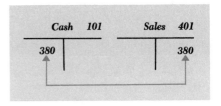

CENTRAL SALES COMPANY
CHART OF ACCOUNTS

INCOME

401   *Sales*
402   *Sales Returns and Allowances*

CASH PAYMENTS JOURNAL								**Page 4**
DATE	ACCOUNT DEBITED	EXPLANATION	CHECK NO.	POST. REF.	GENERAL LEDGER DEBIT	ACCOUNTS PAYABLE DEBIT	PURCHASES DISCOUNT CREDIT	NET CASH CREDIT
19— Jan. 7	Sales Returns and Allowances	Returns for week.	—	402	7 00			7 00

When all entries have been posted at the end of the month, the effect of these entries will be a net increase to Cash of $373 (a debit of $380 less a credit of $7), a debit to Sales Returns and Allowances of $7, and a credit to Sales of $380.

Cash	101	Sales Returns and Allowances	402	Sales	401
380		7	7		380

Cash Payments Journal

Cash Receipts Journal

The Sales Returns and Allowances account, like the Sales account, is a temporary owner's equity account. Both accounts are reported on the income statement; the amount of sales returns and allowances is subtracted from the amount of sales to determine the amount

Income from Sales:
Sales............................ $380
Less: Sales Returns and Allowances....   7
Net sales $373

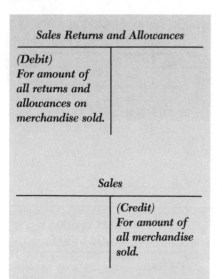

of net sales. Like the Sales account, the Sales Returns and Allowances account is closed into the Income and Expense Summary account at the end of the accounting period.

The information supplied by the Sales Returns and Allowances account helps to guide management in analyzing the operations of the business. For example, if the amount of the returns and allowances becomes large, management should investigate the reason. Are errors being made on shipping orders? Is the quality of the merchandise being sold unsatisfactory? Is the merchandise being packed in such a way that damages result in shipping? By having this information about the returns and allowances, management can take steps to correct a poor situation in its sales procedure.

Refunds by Check   When a check is drawn to make the refund, the check stub provides the data for making the journal entry. For example, on February 8 the Central Sales Company issued Check 314 to refund $20 to Charles Goodrich. The entry would be recorded in the cash payments journal.

		CASH PAYMENTS JOURNAL								Page 4
DATE	ACCOUNT DEBITED	EXPLANATION	CHECK NO.	POST. REF.	GENERAL LEDGER DEBIT	ACCOUNTS PAYABLE DEBIT	PURCHASES DISCOUNT CREDIT	NET CASH CREDIT		
19— Feb. 8	Sales Returns and Allowances	C. Goodrich	314	402	20 00			20 00		

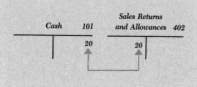

After all the entries have been posted at the end of the month, the effect of this entry will be a debit to Sales Returns and Allowances and a credit to Cash.

Granting Credit for Sales Returns and Allowances

When the customer has not yet paid for the merchandise sold to him, he is not given a cash refund for returns or allowances. Instead, the seller's sales department issues a credit memorandum to grant the customer credit to apply against the amount he owes.

Credit Memorandum   A credit memorandum is issued by the seller as evidence to the customer that the balance of his account is being reduced. The credit memorandum states the customer's name, the amount for which his account is to be credited, and the reason for the credit. For example, on January 14 Invoice 103 was issued for $1,600 to Smith & Adams, billing them for 5 television sets. The sets arrived at the customer's place of business in a damaged condition. Suppose that Smith & Adams gets permission from Central Sales Company to repair the television sets themselves instead of returning them. In exchange, Central Sales will reduce the sales price of each set by $20. The sales department of Central Sales then issues a credit memorandum CM-12 for $100 (5 sets at $20 each).

Credit memorandum: a statement granting a reduction in sales price for damaged or returned goods.

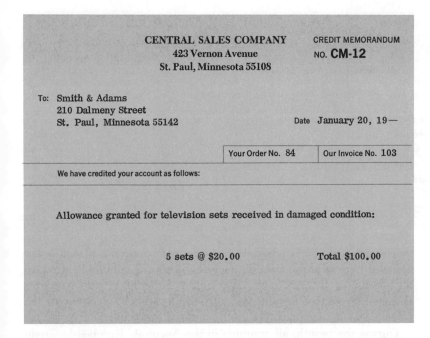

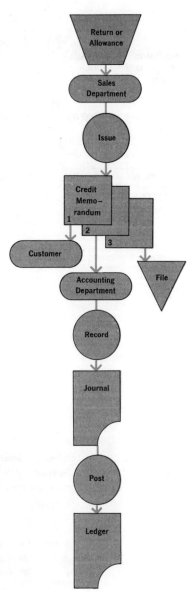

The credit memorandum is issued in three copies. One copy goes to the customer as the source document for an entry to decrease his account with Central Sales Company. The second copy goes to the seller's accounting department as the source document for crediting the customer's account. The third copy is kept by the sales department for its file. After the credit memorandum has been recorded in the seller's books and also in the customer's books, their records of how much is owed should agree as to the amount still owed.

Recording Sales Returns and Allowances When the data on the credit memorandum is recorded, the income from sales must be reduced and the amount to be received from the account receivable is reduced by a like amount. When the credit memorandum issued to Smith & Adams is recorded, an entry is made in the general journal for the amount of the allowance, $100. The debit entry must reduce the amount of the sale, and the credit entry must decrease the accounts receivable asset.

January 20: Central Sales Company issues Credit Memorandum CM-12 for $100 to Smith & Adams for allowance on merchandise sold on credit.

WHAT HAPPENS	ACCOUNTING RULE	ENTRY
The reduction in income caused by a return of sales decreases owner's equity by $100.	*To decrease owner's equity, debit the account.*	Debit: Sales Returns and Allowances, $100.
The asset Accounts Receivable *decreases by $100.*	*To decrease an asset, credit the account.*	Credit: Accounts Receivable, $100 (also the customer's account).

ACCOUNTS PAYABLE DEBIT	GENERAL LEDGER DEBIT	DATE	ACCOUNT TITLE AND EXPLANATION	POST. REF.	GENERAL LEDGER CREDIT	ACCOUNTS RECEIVABLE CREDIT
			GENERAL JOURNAL			**Page 3**
		19—				
	100 00	Jan. 20	*Sales Returns and Allowances*	402		
			Smith & Adams	√		100 00
			Credit Memorandum CM-12.			
150 00	750 00	31	*Totals*		780 00	120 00
(211)	(√)				(√)	(111)

The debit of $100 to Sales Returns and Allowances is placed in the General Ledger Debit column because no special column is provided for debits to this account. The credit of $100 to the Accounts Receivable controlling account and the customer's account in the subsidiary ledger is placed in the Accounts Receivable Credit column.

During the month, all amounts in the Accounts Receivable Credit column are posted to the customers' accounts in the accounts receivable ledger. Thus the $100 credit to the Smith & Adams account in the subsidiary ledger is posted during January. At that time, a check mark (√) is placed in the Posting Reference column.

ACCOUNTS RECEIVABLE LEDGER

Name	Smith & Adams			Credit Limit	$4,000
Address	210 Dalmeny Street, St. Paul, Minnesota 55142			Telephone	453-0701

DATE	EXPLANATION	POST. REF.	DEBIT	CREDIT	BALANCE
19—					
Jan. 14	*Inv. 103*	S1	1600 00		1600 00
20	*Allowance, CM-12*	J3		100 00	1500 00
30	*Inv. 108*	S1	200 00		1700 00

GENERAL LEDGER

DATE	EXPLANATION	POST. REF.	DEBIT	DATE	EXPLANATION	POST. REF.	CREDIT
			Sales Returns and Allowances			**Account No. 402**	
19—							
Jan. 20	Smith & Adams	J3	100 00				
29	Jane Miller	J3	20 00				

The debit to the Sales Returns and Allowances account is also posted during the month from the General Ledger Debit column. The account number (402) in the Posting Reference column indicates that this amount was posted to the general ledger.

The credits to the Accounts Receivable controlling account are not posted until the journal is footed and totaled at the end of the month. At that time, the total of the Accounts Receivable Credit column ($120) is posted to the credit side of the Accounts Receivable controlling account in the general ledger. The account number (111) is placed beneath the double rule to indicate that it has been posted.

GENERAL LEDGER

| | | | | Accounts Receivable | | | | Account No. *111* | |
DATE	EXPLANATION	POST. REF.	DEBIT	DATE	EXPLANATION	POST. REF.	CREDIT
19— Jan. 31	Total Sales.....	*S1*	2891 00	*19—* Jan. 31	Returns.......	*J3*	120 00

If a company has many sales returns and allowances, it could establish a special sales returns and allowances journal. In this case, the procedure used in recording and posting the sales returns and allowances journal is similar to that used for the sales journal.

Sales Taxes on Sales Returns and Allowances

In states and cities where sales taxes have to be collected on sales, an additional entry must be made when sales returns and allowances are recorded. Recall the transaction of January 11, where Jane Miller bought merchandise on credit for $80 and was charged an additional $2.40 as sales tax. The amount of the sale ($80) was credited to the Sales account, and the amount of the sales tax ($2.40) was credited to the Sales Tax Payable account. The customer's account and the Accounts Receivable controlling account were debited for an amount equal to the selling price of the merchandise plus the sales tax.

| | | SALES JOURNAL | | | | | | Page *1* |
DATE	INVOICE NO.	ACCOUNT DEBITED	TERMS	POST. REF.	ACCOUNTS RECEIVABLE DEBIT	SALES TAX PAYABLE CREDIT	SALES CREDIT
19— Jan. 11	102	Jane Miller........................	2/10, n/30	√	82 40	2 40	80 00

Assume that this was the only entry recorded in the sales journal during the month. Then at the end of the month the accounts would show the following entries.

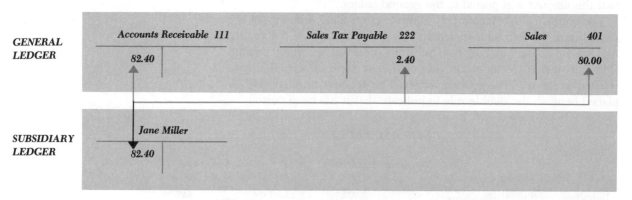

If the entire sale is returned, an entry must be made in the general journal to reverse the previous entry. Thus the accounts would all show zero balances.

ACCOUNTS PAYABLE DEBIT	GENERAL LEDGER DEBIT	DATE	ACCOUNT TITLE AND EXPLANATION	POST. REF.	GENERAL LEDGER CREDIT	ACCOUNTS RECEIVABLE CREDIT
		GENERAL JOURNAL				**Page 2**
		19—				
	80 00	Jan. 11	Sales Returns and Allowances...............	402		
	2 40		Sales Tax Payable........................	222		
			Jane Miller............................	√		82 40
			Credit Memorandum CM-10.			

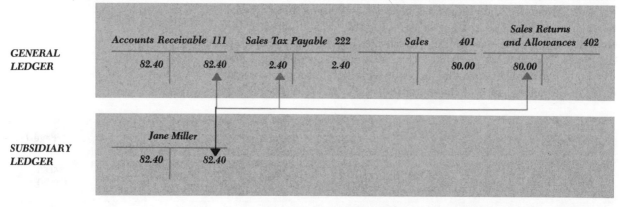

A sales tax on the original sale is no longer payable to the governmental agency. Therefore, the Sales Tax Payable account must be reduced by the amount of the tax that was charged because neither the customer nor the business is obligated to pay the tax. Therefore, the entry to record the sales return also reduced the balance of the Sales Tax Payable account. If, however, only half of the merchandise sold were returned, then the following entry would be made.

ACCOUNTS PAYABLE DEBIT	GENERAL LEDGER DEBIT	DATE	ACCOUNT TITLE AND EXPLANATION	POST. REF.	GENERAL LEDGER CREDIT	ACCOUNTS RECEIVABLE CREDIT
			GENERAL JOURNAL			**Page 2**
		19—				
	40 00	Jan. 11	*Sales Returns and Allowances*	402		
	1 20		*Sales Tax Payable*	222		
			Jane Miller	✓		41 20
			Credit Memorandum CM-10.			

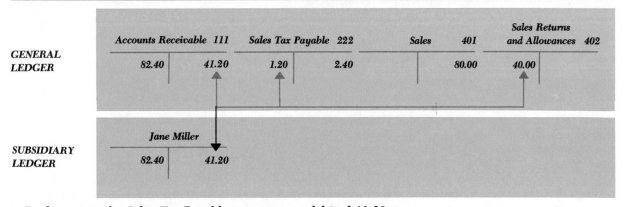

GENERAL LEDGER

Accounts Receivable 111		Sales Tax Payable 222		Sales 401		Sales Returns and Allowances 402
82.40	41.20	1.20	2.40		80.00	40.00

SUBSIDIARY LEDGER

Jane Miller	
82.40	41.20

In this entry, the Sales Tax Payable account was debited $1.20 to cancel the appropriate amount of the tax collected when the merchandise was sold. The balance of the Sales Tax Payable account is now $1.20—3 percent of the actual sale ($40).

TOPIC 3 ■ PROBLEMS

37 Answer the following questions about the credit memorandum on page 239, the journals on pages 237 and 240, and the ledger accounts on pages 240 and 241.

a What journal entry was made to record the cash paid out for the return of sales on January 7? In what journal was this entry recorded?

b What company received the credit memorandum? Who was the seller?

c In what journal was the credit memorandum recorded? Why?

d Why was the Smith & Adams account credited instead of debited in the entry to record the sales allowance issued on January 20? Why was Sales Returns and Allowances debited?

e When the $100 item of January 20 was posted to the Smith & Adams account in the subsidiary ledger, was the Accounts Receivable controlling account in the general ledger credited for $100 at the same time?

f How will the credit entry of January 20 be posted into the Accounts Receivable controlling account?

g In the January 20 general journal entry, why was the debit amount entered in the General Ledger Debit column and the credit amount in the Accounts Receivable Credit column?

h Why is the check mark placed in the Posting Reference column of the general journal entry of January 20?

i Why is (111) placed under the double rules in the Accounts Receivable Credit column?

j Why are check marks placed under the double rules in the General Ledger Debit column and the General Ledger Credit column?

k How much did Smith & Adams owe the Central Sales Company on January 21?

l From what sources were the debit entry and the credit entry posted to the Accounts Receivable controlling account? Why was each made?

38 Answer the following questions about the sales tax entries recorded in the general journal shown on page 243.

a Why was the Sales Tax Payable account debited?

b When was the $1.20 debit amount posted to the Sales Tax Payable account?

c Why were the debit amounts entered in the General Ledger Debit column?

d Why was the Jane Miller account credited for $41.20 and not $40?

39 Perform the following operations to process the sales on credit made by the Garden and Lawn Shop for the month of October.

a Open accounts in the general ledger for Accounts Receivable, Sales, and Sales Returns and Allowances. (Allow four lines for the first account and two lines for each of the others.) Open customer accounts for Robert Daniels and Karen Sterling in the subsidiary ledger. (Allow six lines for each.)

b Record each of the following transactions in the sales journal or in the general journal.

Oct. 3 Sold merchandise for $240 on credit to Robert Daniels; Invoice 2486; terms 2/10, n/30.

4 Robert Daniels returned $40 worth of merchandise; Credit Memorandum 263.

13 Sold merchandise for $460 on credit to Karen Sterling; Invoice 2487; terms 1/10, n/30.

Oct. 21 Sold merchandise for $350 on credit to Robert Daniels; Invoice 2488; terms 2/10, n/30.

26 Issued allowance of $20 to Robert Daniels for scratched merchandise; Credit Memorandum 264.

c Foot and rule both journals.

d Post the entries from the journals to the appropriate ledgers.

e Prepare a schedule of accounts receivable.

40 Perform the following operations to process the sales on credit made by the Pinecrest Camera Store for the month of December.

a Open accounts in the general ledger for Accounts Receivable, Sales Tax Payable, Sales, and Sales Returns and Allowances. (Allow four lines for the first account and two lines for the others.) Open customer accounts for Carl Dexter and Mary Holt in the subsidiary ledger. (Allow six lines for each.)

b Record each of the following transactions in the sales journal or in the general journal.

Dec. 6 Sold merchandise for $170 to Mary Holt; Invoice 8965, terms 1/10, n/30; sales tax, $5.10.

7 Accepted merchandise of $20 returned by Mary Holt; Credit Memorandum 347; sales tax, $.60.

16 Sold merchandise for $430 to Carl Dexter; Invoice 8966; terms 2/10, n/30; sales tax, $12.90.

Dec. 17 Issued allowance of $10 to Carl Dexter for imperfect merchandise; Credit Memorandum 348; sales tax $.30.

24 Sold merchandise for $365 to Mary Holt; Invoice 8967; terms 1/10, n/30; sales tax, $10.95.

c Foot and rule the journals.

d Post the entries from the journals to the appropriate ledgers.

e Prepare a schedule of accounts receivable.

TOPIC 4 ■ RECEIVING PAYMENTS
FROM CUSTOMERS

All firms that sell on credit must have some control over their customer accounts. The seller needs to collect the money owed him in order to buy additional goods to resell, to purchase other assets required in operating the business, or to pay expenses. Thus, in order to operate efficiently, a business cannot have too much of its money tied up in accounts receivable for long periods of time. It is also a good policy to attempt to collect accounts promptly so that there will be less danger that the accounts will become uncollectable.

Sales Discounts

As a means of encouraging customers to pay their invoices before the expiration of the credit period, some businesses offer a cash discount. From the viewpoint of the seller, a cash discount is known as a *sales discount*. The customer, on the other hand, regards the cash discount as a purchase discount. In the previous chapter, the procedure for recording purchase discounts was discussed. The procedure the seller follows to record the discount will be discussed in this topic.

Sales discount: cash discount deducted from sales invoice.

The January 7 sales invoice to Wilson's Radio Center for $25 will be used to illustrate how cash receipts from customers are recorded. The terms on this sale are 1/20, n/30. Thus, if Wilson's mails its check on or before January 27 (20 days after January 7) it may deduct 1 percent of $25 ($.25) from the invoice and may pay $24.75 ($25 − $.25). However, if Wilson's does not pay within the discount period, it may wait until February 6 (30 days after January 7). But if it does this, then it must pay the full amount of $25.

Receiving Payments

A sales discount is not recorded at the time the invoice is journalized because the seller does not know whether the customer will pay early or not. Therefore, when the sales invoice is recorded, the customer's account is debited for the full amount of the invoice. The entry to record the sales invoice to Wilson's Radio Center has these effects:

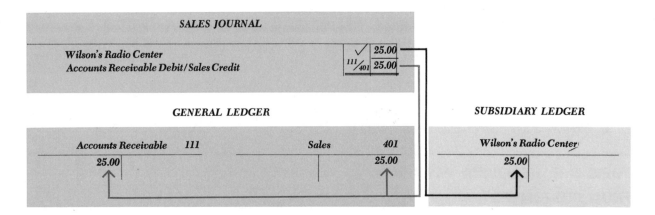

Assume that Wilson's makes payment on February 6, the last day of the credit period. The check then must be for $25, the full amount of the invoice. Since cash is received, the entry is recorded in the cash receipts journal and has the following effects:

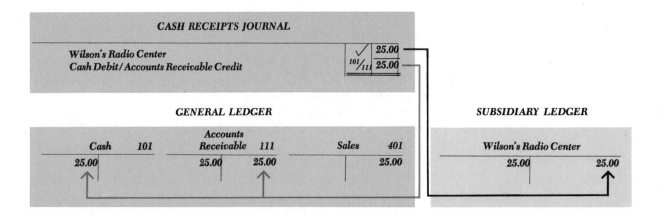

Suppose, however, that Wilson's pays its bill within the discount period. Its check would then be for $24.75. This cash receipt transaction is analyzed as follows:

1 Since the customer's account shows a debit balance of $25, the account must be credited for $25 to show that this amount has been satisfied in full. Regardless of the actual amount of the check, Wilson's account must be credited for $25 to reduce the debit balance to zero.

2 The check amounts to $24.75. Thus the Cash account must be debited for $24.75 because that is the actual amount of cash received.

3 Since the debit and credit amounts must be equal, the cash discount of $.25 must be debited to some account. This discount, in reality, reduces the income from sales and, thereby, decreases owner's equity. For example, the merchandise sold was recorded as income of $25. However, Wilson's paid only $24.75 for it; thus the sales discount reduces the income from the sale of merchandise— by $.25. This reduction in income actually decreases owner's equity.

The debit entry to decrease owner's equity could be to the Sales account. However, it is common accounting practice to record a sales discount in a temporary owner's equity account called Sales Discount. In this way, the owner or manager has a record of all discounts allowed and can readily see what reduction in income is caused by this discount policy.

The illustration below analyzes the entry to record the effects on the accounts when a sales discount of $.25 is given on a $25 purchase.

Rate of cash discount = 1%
1% × $25 = $.25 (amount of discount)
$25 − $.25 = $24.75 (amount of receipt)

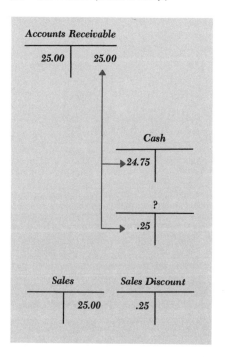

WHAT HAPPENS	ACCOUNTING RULE	ENTRY:
The asset Cash increases by $24.75	*To increase an asset debit the account.*	*Debit: Cash, $24.75.*
The cash discount on sales decreases owner's equity by $.25	*To decrease owner's equity debit the account.*	*Debit: Sales Discounts, $.25.*
The asset Accounts Receivable decreases by $25	*To decrease an asset credit the account.*	*Credit: Accounts Receivable, $25. (also the customer's account)*

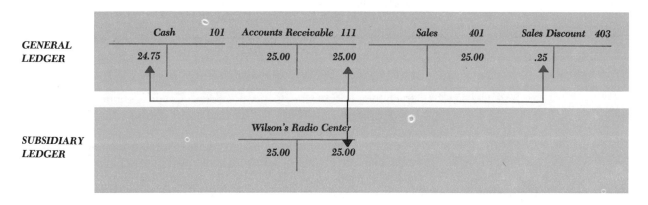

Income from Sales:
Sales. $2,891.00
Less:
Sales Discount. . . . . . $ 30.25
Sales Returns
  and Allowances. . . . 120.00   150.25
Net sales. $2,740.75

CENTRAL SALES COMPANY
CHART OF ACCOUNTS

INCOME
401 Sales
402 Sales Returns and Allowances
403 Sales Discount

To find the net income from sales, subtract the balance of the Sales Discount account from the balance of the Sales account. If the Sales Returns and Allowances account has a balance, that balance must also be subtracted. Because these three accounts are related, they have been assigned numbers 401, 402, and 403 by the Central Sales Company.

Recording Sales Discounts in the Cash Receipts Journal

All cash receipts are recorded in the cash receipts journal. As you have seen from the previous analysis, the entry to record the receipt of cash with a sales discount involves a debit to the Cash account, a debit to the Sales Discount account, and a credit to the Accounts Receivable controlling account (and the individual customer's account). It is impossible to record this type of entry in a one-column cash receipts journal because two debits are involved—Cash and Sales Discount. Thus most businesses adapt the cash receipts journal to their needs by providing the columns shown in the following illustration:

CASH RECEIPTS JOURNAL							Page 3
DATE	ACCOUNT CREDITED	EXPLANATION	POST. REF.	GENERAL LEDGER CREDIT	ACCOUNTS RECEIVABLE CREDIT	SALES DISCOUNT DEBIT	NET CASH DEBIT
19— Jan. 26	Wilson's Radio Center	On account	√		25 00	25	24 75

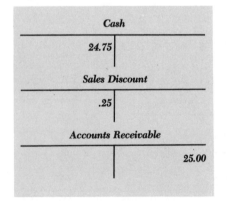

Cash

24.75 |

Sales Discount

.25 |

Accounts Receivable

| 25.00

$24.75 + $.25 = $25.00

The Net Cash Debit column is used to record the total amount of cash received. The Sales Discount Debit column is used to record the amount of the sales discount taken, if any. The Accounts Receivable Credit column is used to record all credits to customers' accounts from receipts. The amount entered in this credit column ($25) must be equal to the total amount of the debits ($24.75 + $.25). This column facilitates the double posting that must be made to the Accounts Receivable controlling account and to the customer's account. The other credit column is the General Ledger Credit column, which is used for credits to any account for which there is no special column.

Posting from the Cash Receipts Journal During the Month

Each amount in the General Ledger Credit column of the cash receipts journal (see 1 in the illustration) is posted individually to the appropriate account in the general ledger. The account numbers in the Posting Reference column indicate that these amounts have been posted to the general ledger. These entries can be posted during the month.

CASH RECEIPTS JOURNAL   Page *3*

DATE	ACCOUNT CREDITED	EXPLANATION	POST. REF.	GENERAL LEDGER CREDIT	ACCOUNTS RECEIVABLE CREDIT	SALES DISCOUNT DEBIT	NET CASH DEBIT
19—							
Jan. 2	*Cash Balance.........*	*$16,200...........*	—				
7	*Sales..............*	*Cash sales for week...*	401	380 00			380 00
9	*Store Equipment......*	*Sold display case.....*	122	50 00			50 00
11	*John Hall, Capital.....*	*Additional investment.*	301	1,000 00			1,000 00
14	*Sales..............*	*Cash sales for week...*	401	290 00			290 00
21	*Sales..............*	*Cash sales for week...*	401	330 00			330 00
24	*Smith & Adams.......*	*On account.........*	√		1,500 00	30 00	1,470 00
26	*Wilson's Radio Center.*	*On account.........*	√		25 00	25	24 75
27	*Jane Miller..........*	*On account.........*	√		80 00		80 00
28	*Sales..............*	*Cash sales for week...*	401	300 00			300 00

1 — Credits posted during the month to accounts in general ledger.

2 — Credits posted during the month to customers' accounts in subsidiary ledger.

3 — Amounts in these two columns are not posted separately during the month.

Each of the three entries in the Accounts Receivable Credit column (see 2 in the illustration) is posted individually to the appropriate customer's account in the subsidiary ledger. A check mark ($\sqrt{}$) in the Posting Reference column indicates that the amount has been posted. Note that the entries for January 24 and 26 involve sales discounts, whereas the entry for January 27 does not. None of the items in the Sales Discount Debit column or the Net Cash Debit column are posted during the month.

ACCOUNTS RECEIVABLE LEDGER

Name   *Jane Miller*   Credit Limit   *$1,000*

Address   *89 Liberty Avenue, Ashley, Ohio 43015*   Telephone   *369-3031*

DATE	EXPLANATION	POST. REF.	DEBIT	CREDIT	BALANCE
19—					
Jan. 11	*Inv. 102................*	*S1*	80 00		80 00
26	*Inv. 106................*	*S1*	160 00		240 00
27	*Cash...................*	*CR3*		80 00	160 00

Name	Smith & Adams				Credit Limit	$4,000
Address	210 Dalmeny Street, St. Paul, Minnesota 55142				Telephone	453-0701

DATE	EXPLANATION	POST. REF.	DEBIT	CREDIT	BALANCE
19—					
Jan. 14	Inv. 103..................	S1	1,600 00		1,600 00
20	Allowance...............	J3		100 00	1,500 00
24	Cash....................	CR3		1,500 00	— 00

Name	Wilson's Radio Center				Credit Limit	$2,000
Address	37 Penton Street, Duluth, Minnesota 55808				Telephone	293-5510

DATE	EXPLANATION	POST. REF.	DEBIT	CREDIT	BALANCE
19—					
Jan. 7	Inv. 101..................	S1	25 00		25 00
15	Inv. 104..................	S1	400 00		425 00
26	Cash....................	CR3		25 00	400 00

Note that the entry of January 24 shows that Smith & Adams has been allowed a sales discount of $30. The original amount of the invoice was $1,600 (Invoice 103 of January 14), but the customer was granted a sales allowance of $100 on January 20 (Credit Memorandum CM-12). Smith & Adams, therefore, was granted a discount on $1,500, the net amount of the invoice ($1,600 − $100).

Posting from the Cash Receipts Journal at the End of the Month

At the end of the month, all the money columns are pencil-footed. A check is made of the equality of the debit and credit totals by adding the two debit totals and then adding the two credit totals; these two sums must be equal. After the equality of the debits and credits has been proved, the journal is totaled and ruled.

Net Cash Debit............	$3,924.75
Sales Discount Debit........	30.25
Total debits...........	$3,955.00
General Ledger Credit.......	$2,350.00
Accounts Receivable Credit...	1,605.00
Total credits...........	$3,955.00

CASH RECEIPTS JOURNAL							Page 3
DATE	ACCOUNT CREDITED	EXPLANATION	POST. REF.	GENERAL LEDGER CREDIT	ACCOUNTS RECEIVABLE CREDIT	SALES DISCOUNT DEBIT	NET CASH DEBIT
19—							
Jan. 28	Sales............	Cash sales for week.......	401	300 00			300 00
31	Totals...........			2,350 00	1,605 00	30 25	3,924 75
				(√)	(111)	(403)	(101)

The total of the General Ledger Credit column is not posted because the amounts in the column were posted individually to accounts in the general ledger. Thus a check mark is placed in the amount column beneath the double rules.

The total of the Accounts Receivable Credit column is posted to the credit side of the controlling account in the general ledger. Each amount in this column is posted to the subsidiary ledger during the month. The account number is written beneath the double rules.

The total of the Sales Discount Debit column is posted as a debit to the Sales Discount account. The total of the Net Cash Debit column is posted as a debit to the Cash account. The account numbers (403 and 101) are written beneath the double rules.

The Statement of Account

In addition to sending an invoice, some businesses also send periodically a statement of the customer's account. The statement of account is prepared from the data in the customer's account in the accounts receivable ledger. Statements may be sent to all customers at the end of each month or may be prepared on a cycle plan. The creditor sends statements to his customers so that both he and the customer can verify their account balances. Also, the statement is a reminder to the customer that a balance is owed.

In its simplest form, the statement of account shows only the balance due at the end of the month. This type of statement is generally used by professional people—those who sell services rather than merchandise (such as doctors and public accountants).

Most merchandising businesses and manufacturers use a descriptive or nondescriptive statement that lists all the customer's transactions during the month. The nondescriptive statement sent by Central Sales Company to Smith & Adams on January 31 is prepared from the data in the customer's account. When Smith & Adams receives the statement, their accounting clerk should compare it with the account he maintains in the accounts payable ledger for Central Sales Company. Any differences should be promptly investigated.

Statement of Account	J. Thomas Fisher, M.D. 962-2578
	911 Medical Plaza
	Houston, Texas 77018

Mary J. O'Neill
88 South Gulf Street
Houston, Texas 77021   June 30, 19—

For professional services

June 12, 19— $15.00

CENTRAL SALES COMPANY STATEMENT OF ACCOUNT
423 Vernon Avenue
St. Paul, Minnesota 55108

Smith & Adams   Date January 31, 19—
210 Dalmeny Street
St. Paul, Minnesota 55542   Amount
Please return this stub with your check   Enclosed $_____

Date	Reference	Charges	Credits	Balance
Balance Forwarded				.00
Jan. 14	103	1,600.00		1,600.00
20	Allowance		100.00	1,500.00
24	Cash		1,500.00	.00
30	108	200.00		200.00

ACCOUNTS RECEIVABLE LEDGER

Name Smith & Adams   Credit Limit $4,000
Address 210 Dalmeny Street, St. Paul, Minnesota 55142   Telephone 453-0701

DATE	EXPLANATION	POST. REF.	DEBIT	CREDIT	BALANCE
19—					
Jan. 14	Inv. 103	S1	1,600 00		1,600 00
20	Allowance, CM-12	J3		100 00	1,500 00
24	Cash	CR3		1,500 00	—00
30	Inv. 108	S1	200 00		200 00

Summary of Transactions Involving Sales

The following chart summarizes the various types of transactions involved with the function of sales. In each case, the chart shows how the transaction should be recorded.

RECORDING THE TRANSACTIONS INVOLVING SALES

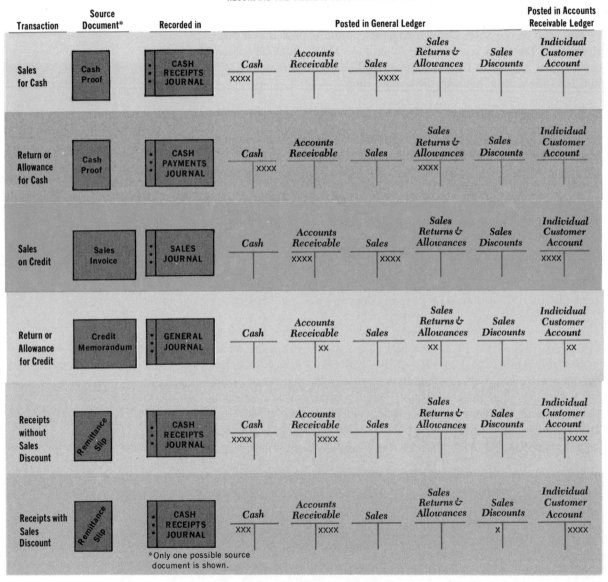

Transaction	Source Document*	Recorded in	Posted in General Ledger					Posted in Accounts Receivable Ledger
			Cash	Accounts Receivable	Sales	Sales Returns & Allowances	Sales Discounts	Individual Customer Account
Sales for Cash	Cash Proof	CASH RECEIPTS JOURNAL	XXXX		XXXX			
Return or Allowance for Cash	Cash Proof	CASH PAYMENTS JOURNAL	XXXX			XXXX		
Sales on Credit	Sales Invoice	SALES JOURNAL		XXXX	XXXX			XXXX
Return or Allowance for Credit	Credit Memorandum	GENERAL JOURNAL		XX		XX		XX
Receipts without Sales Discount	Remittance Slip	CASH RECEIPTS JOURNAL	XXXX	XXXX				XXXX
Receipts with Sales Discount	Remittance Slip	CASH RECEIPTS JOURNAL	XXX	XXXX			X	XXXX

*Only one possible source document is shown.

Sales Taxes and Sales Discount

Sales discounts are granted on the net sales price of the merchandise sold—not on any sales taxes charged. For example, on a sale of $80 with the terms of 2/10, n/30, the sales tax of 3 percent charged to the customer would be $2.40. If this invoice is paid within the discount period, a sales discount is allowed on the $80 only—not on the $2.40. Thus the sales discount would be $1.60 (2% × $80). The customer would have to remit $80.80 ($80 + $2.40 − $1.60).

Amount of invoice = $80 + $2.40 = $82.40
Rate of cash discount = 2%
2% × $80 = $1.60 (amount of discount)
$82.40 − $1.60 = $80.80 (amount of receipt)

TOPIC 4 ■ PROBLEMS

41 Answer the following questions about the cash receipts journals shown on pages 249 and 250.

a What accounts were debited and credited in the entry of January 26? What amounts were debited? credited?

b Why is a check mark in the Posting Reference column of the journal for the January 26 entry?

c Why are two debit entries needed in the journal entry of January 26?

d When the January 26 journal entry is posted to the subsidiary ledger, is $.25 posted as a debit to Sales Discount at the same time? Is $24.75 posted as a debit to Cash at the same time?

e When will the discount of $.25 and the cash receipts of $24.75 be posted into the Sales Discount account and the Cash account?

f What account was credited in the entry of January 9?

g When the January 9 credit is posted from the cash receipts journal, is a $50 debit posted to the Cash account at that time? Why or why not?

h When is the January 27 receipt posted to the Accounts Receivable account?

i When the Sales Discount column total is posted on January 31, is any other account credited for $30.25 at that time? Why or why not?

j What account is credited for $2,350 on January 31?

k Is there any way to prove that the total debits equal the total credits in the cash receipts journal? How?

42 Perform the following operations to process the transactions involving sales and cash receipts for Gordon's Supply Store during the month of June.

a Open general ledger accounts for Cash; Accounts Receivable; Fred Gordon, Capital; Sales; and Sales Discount. Open accounts receivable ledger accounts for Jane Gold and Earl Griffin. Allow two lines for each general ledger account and twelve lines for each accounts receivable account.

b Record each of the following transactions in a sales journal or a cash receipts journal.

June 2 Sold merchandise for $420 to Earl Griffin; Invoice 627; terms 2/10, n/30.

4 Sold merchandise for $330 to Jane Gold; Invoice 628; terms 1/10, n/30.

5 Fred Gordon invested an additional $2,500.

9 Sold merchandise for $210 to Earl Griffin; Invoice 629; terms 2/10, n/30.

June 11 Received $411.60 in cash from Earl Griffin in payment of Invoice 627 of June 2, less discount.

13 Sold merchandise for $170 to Jane Gold; Invoice 630; terms 1/10, n/30.

14 Received cash from Jane Gold in payment of Invoice 628 of June 4, less discount.

June 18 Sold merchandise for $80 to Earl Griffin; Invoice 631; terms 2/10, n/30.

    23 Sold merchandise for $165 to Earl Griffin; Invoice 632; terms 2/10, n/30.

June 27 Received cash from Earl Griffin in payment of Invoice 631 of June 18, less discount.

    30 Received cash from Earl Griffin in payment of Invoice 629 of June 9.

c Foot and rule the journals.
d Post the entries from the journals to the ledgers.
e Prepare a schedule of accounts receivable.
f Prepare a trial balance.

NOTE: Save your working papers for use in Problem 43.

43 Using the working papers from Problem 42, perform the following operations.
a Record these transactions in the sales journal or the cash receipts journal.

July 2 Received cash from Earl Griffin in payment of Invoice 632 of June 23, less discount.

    5 Sold merchandise for $380 to Earl Griffin; Invoice 633; terms 2/10, n/30.

    8 Sold merchandise for $75 to Jane Gold; Invoice No. 634; terms 1/10, n/30.

    13 Received cash from Jane Gold in payment of full amount of Invoice 630 of June 13.

    14 Fred Gordon invested an additional $2,000 in the business.

July 15 Received cash from Earl Griffin in payment of Invoice 633 of July 5, less discount.

    18 Received cash from Jane Gold in payment of Invoice 634 of July 8, less discount.

    21 Sold merchandise for $400 to Earl Griffin; Invoice 635; terms 2/10, n/30.

    26 Sold merchandise for $110 to Earl Griffin; Invoice 636; terms 2/10, n/30.

    30 Sold merchandise for $160 to Jane Gold; Invoice 637; terms 1/10, n/30.

b Foot and rule the journals.
c Post the journal entries to the ledgers.
d Prepare a schedule of accounts receivable.
e Prepare a trial balance.

The Language of Business

The following terms are important. Do you understand the meaning of each? Can you define each term and use it in an original sentence?

sales order	sales journal	Accounts Receivable account
shipping order	sales tax	schedule of accounts receivable
back order	Sales Tax Payable	sales returns and allowances
packing slip	accounts receivable ledger	sales discount
sales invoice	standard ledger form	statement of account
periodic billing	balance ledger form	nondescriptive statement

Chapter Questions

1 Name and describe the three operations of a system for the control of sales on credit.

2 The shipping order in this chapter was prepared in seven copies. How does the use of this multicopy form save time?

3 In what way does the credit department have a powerful control over the sales department? On what department does the credit department depend heavily for its information? Why?

4 List and explain the advantages of a special sales journal. Describe the procedure in posting from the sales journal.

5 How do the standard ledger form and the balance ledger form differ? What are the advantages of each one?

6 What advantage is there in using a separate account for sales returns and allowances? When this is done, how is the net income from sales computed?

7 Describe the procedure followed in posting the individual amounts and the totals in the four-column cash receipts journal.

8 When a sales tax is collected from a customer, why is it credited to a liability account?

9 A sale on credit to the Jay Stores was journalized correctly as $89. The amount, however, was posted as $98 in the customer's account. When should this error be discovered? How might the customer detect the error?

Management Cases

Returned Merchandise It is expensive for a business to handle merchandise returned. First, many expenses are incurred in selling the goods: salaries to salesmen, and expenses for wrapping the merchandise, recording the transaction, and delivering the merchandise. Moreover, additional costs are incurred when goods are returned, such as the costs of handling the complaint, inspecting the merchandise, recording the transaction, and placing the merchandise back in stock for resale.

Expenses are reflected in higher prices. A store with a policy of "All Sales Final—No Returns" eliminates the expense of sales returns and is able to sell at a lower price.

Case M-10

The accountant set up one income account for the Greenvale Furniture Store. This account is credited for all sales and debited for all sales returns. In this way, only the balance of the Sales account is shown on the income statement. The manager of the store, however, wants to know more than the amount of net sales; he wants to know the amount of the sales and also the amount of the sales returned.

a Why would a store manager want to know the total of the sales returns?

b How could the accountant arrange the records to provide this information?

c How would you suggest that the information be shown on the income statement?

d The store's gross sales for the year were $245,000 and the sales returns totaled $56,500. In your judgment, were the sales returns too high? How could the store manager determine if they were excessive? What steps could he take to reduce the amount of returned goods?

Case M-11

Eric Burns owns a shoe store. His net sales (gross sales less sales returned) were $220,000. His gross profit on sales for the year ($88,000) was 40 percent of net sales.

Mr. Burns estimates that the expenses of handling returned items costs the store $11,000 a year. He is considering the possibility of adopting a policy of "All Sales Final—No Returns" and reducing the selling price of his shoes.

a What percent of the gross profit was the $11,000 for handling returned items?

b He has a line of shoes that sells for $16 a pair. If he allows no sales returns, what price would he have to charge for each pair of shoes to maintain the same net income?

c In addition to reducing the selling price, what other factors should Mr. Burns consider before adopting the policy of "All Sales Final—No Returns"?

d Is it possible that Mr. Burns might establish a policy of "All Sales Final" yet find that he actually has to increase the selling price of his shoes? How could this happen?

Case M-12

Mr. Pendleton, a house painter, purchased 20 gallons of paint from the Durex Paint Store at a price of $4.50 per gallon. The terms of the sale were 2/10, n/30. Before the end of the discount period, he paid the invoice by writing a check for $88.20.

At a later date he returned four gallons to the Paint Store and asked for a cash refund. When the cashier offered to refund $17.64 to him, Mr. Pendleton protested. Mr. Pendleton claimed that the price of the paint was $4.50 a gallon. Since the paint had been billed to him at $4.50 a gallon, he thought he was entitled to a refund of $18.00. He stated that if he did not receive the full refund, he would take his business elsewhere.

a What amount should have been refunded to Mr. Pendleton?

b How would you have handled the situation?

Working Hint

Approximating Sales Discounts

1% × $456.20 = $4.5620 = $4.56
1% × $84.65 = $.8465 = $.85

It is quite easy to calculate 1 percent of a number mentally. 1 percent means 1/100. Merely move the decimal point two places to the left to obtain 1 percent of any number.

2% × $845.15 = ?
1% × $845.15 = $8.4515
2 × $8.4515 = $16.90

To calculate a 2 percent discount quickly, simply compute the 1 percent discount and double it.

$845.15 rounded = $800.00
2% × $800 = $16.00

The incorrect placement of the decimal point will produce a discount a great deal more or less than the correct answer. This error might be avoided by applying the approximation test to your answer (determining whether the answer is approximately correct). An approximate answer can be easily obtained by rounding the amount. If the amount obtained in the example was a great deal more or less than $16, the answer obviously would be incorrect.

Chapter 5
Adjusting
and Closing
the Books

In this chapter, the entire accounting cycle will be covered for a merchandising business. The emphasis will be placed upon the special problems and procedures related to completing the records for a merchandising business at the end of the accounting period.

TOPIC 1 ■ BEGINNING THE ACCOUNTING CYCLE

A transaction is a financial event that affects one or more of the asset, liability, or owner's equity accounts. The data from all the transactions during an accounting period is processed through the accounting system, and the results are reported on financial statements. Although the procedures followed in a system vary according to the size and nature of the business, every accounting system begins with collecting the data from the transactions to be processed.

Starting Point—Origination of Data

The original record of each business transaction is a source document. Some examples of source documents are cash register tapes, sales slips, remittance slips, check stubs, purchase invoices, sales invoices, and credit memorandums. The data is "captured" on these source documents at the time the transaction occurs.

The source documents may be handwritten, typewritten, or prepared by other means, such as the cash register. Regardless of the method used, the data must be captured efficiently and accurately. The accuracy of the information on the financial statements depends upon how accurately the data is recorded at this point of origin. Source documents are important to the accountant because they provide evidence of what was involved in the transaction. Furthermore, they provide the basis for journalizing the transaction.

Step 1—Journalizing

Once the data has been recorded on the source documents it is ready to be put into the accounting records. The transaction must be analyzed according to account titles. For example, the accounting clerk receives a cash register tape for cash sales of $100. He analyzes this transaction as a debit to Cash and a credit to Sales and then records it in the cash receipts journal. This procedure of analyzing and recording the transaction in the journal (the book of original entry) is known as journalizing.

All transactions may be journalized in the general journal. In many businesses, however, a number of special journals are used to save time, to divide the work, and to increase accuracy. The special journals most frequently used are the cash receipts journal, the cash payments journal, the purchases journal (for merchandise purchased on credit), and the sales journal (for merchandise sold on credit). Other special journals may be used to fill the needs of certain businesses.

Step 2—Posting

Every journal entry is transferred to a ledger (the book of final entry). A small business may need only a general ledger. A larger business usually needs subsidiary ledgers as well. It may use a *general ledger* for asset, liability, and temporary and permanent owner's equity accounts; an *accounts payable ledger* for accounts with creditors; and an *accounts receivable ledger* for accounts with customers.

When subsidiary ledgers are used, an Accounts Payable controlling account and an Accounts Receivable controlling account are maintained in the general ledger. The balance of the Accounts Payable controlling account must equal the total of all the individual account balances in the accounts payable ledger. The balance of the Accounts Receivable controlling account must equal the total of all the individual account balances in the accounts receivable ledger.

Step 3—Proving the Ledger

After all the entries have been posted in the journals, a proof must be made of the accuracy of the postings. First, a schedule of accounts receivable (listing the name of each charge customer and the amount he owes) is made from the accounts receivable ledger. The total on this schedule is compared with the balance of the Accounts Receivable controlling account in the general ledger to prove the accuracy of the postings to the accounts receivable ledger. A similar schedule is prepared for accounts payable, and the total is compared with the balance in the Accounts Payable controlling account.

A trial balance is then taken of the general ledger accounts to show that the total of the debit balances equals the total of the credit balances.

Central Sales Company
Trial Balance
March 31, 19—

ACCOUNT TITLE	ACCT. NO.	DEBIT	CREDIT
Cash	101	9,600 00	
Accounts Receivable	111	3,300 00	
Merchandise Inventory	112	5,000 00	
Prepaid Insurance	113	360 00	
Supplies on Hand	114	400 00	
Office Equipment	121	7,200 00	
Stockroom Equipment	122	12,100 00	
Accounts Payable	211		4,600 00
John Hall, Capital	301		32,000 00
John Hall, Drawing	302	400 00	
Sales	401		9,260 00
Sales Returns and Allowances	402	160 00	
Sales Discount	403	37 00	
Purchases	501	4,955 00	
Purchases Returns and Allowances	502		125 00
Purchases Discount	503		50 00
Cash Short and Over	511	8 00	
Miscellaneous Expense	513	15 00	
Rent Expense	514	310 00	
Salaries Expense	515	2,100 00	
Utilities Expense	517	90 00	
		46,035 00	46,035 00

Central Sales Company
Schedule of Accounts Receivable
March 31, 19—

Jane Miller	$ 650.00
Smith & Adams	1,280.00
Wilson's Radio Center	785.00
Winston, Inc.	585.00
Total Accounts Receivable	$3,300.00

Central Sales Company
Schedule of Accounts Payable
March 31, 19—

Dixon & Hicks	$1,260.00
Todd Electronics	1,970.00
Vista Corporation	990.00
George Young	380.00
Total Accounts Payable	$4,600.00

Note that this trial balance for the Central Sales Company contains four new accounts: Merchandise Inventory (112), Prepaid Insurance (113), Supplies on Hand (114), and John Hall, Drawing (302). Beginning with the drawing account, each account will be explained.

Drawing Account Since the owner of a single proprietorship does not receive a salary, he customarily withdraws cash and other assets from the business for his personal use. He makes these withdrawals against the net income he anticipates having at the end of the accounting period. In previous chapters, all withdrawals were deducted from the owner's capital account. Generally, however, withdrawals against anticipated profits are recorded in a separate owner's equity account known as a *drawing account*. When a drawing account is established, the capital account can be used only to record the following: (1) the original investment, (2) additional investments, and (3) permanent withdrawals of investment. The entry for an additional investment is credited to the capital account. The entry for a permanent withdrawal of investment is debited to the capital account, but the entry for a personal withdrawal is debited to the drawing account.

CENTRAL SALES COMPANY CHART OF ACCOUNTS

ASSETS

112 Merchandise Inventory
113 Prepaid Insurance
114 Supplies on Hand

OWNER'S EQUITY

302 John Hall, Drawing

The entry required to show an additional investment of $1,000 in the Central Sales Company by John Hall is recorded in the cash receipts journal because cash is received. The Cash account is debited to reflect the increase in the assets, and the Capital account is credited to reflect the increase in the owner's investment.

CASH RECEIPTS JOURNAL — Page 5

DATE	ACCOUNT CREDITED	EXPLANATION	POST. REF.	GENERAL LEDGER CREDIT	ACCOUNTS RECEIVABLE CREDIT	SALES DISCOUNT DEBIT	NET CASH DEBIT
19— Mar. 2	John Hall, Capital	Additional investment	301	1,000 00			1,000 00

John Hall, Capital — Account No. 301

DATE	EXPLANATION	POST. REF.	DEBIT	DATE	EXPLANATION	POST. REF.	CREDIT
				19— Mar. 1 2	Balance	√ CR5	31,000 00 1,000 00

When John Hall withdraws $400 in cash for personal use, the transaction is recorded in the cash payments journal because cash is paid out. The Cash account is credited to show a decrease in assets; the Drawing account is debited to show a decrease in owner's equity.

CASH PAYMENTS JOURNAL — Page 5

DATE	ACCOUNT DEBITED	EXPLANATION	CHECK NO.	POST. REF.	GENERAL LEDGER DEBIT	ACCOUNTS PAYABLE DEBIT	PURCHASES DISCOUNT CREDIT	NET CASH CREDIT
19— Mar. 23	John Hall, Drawing	Withdrawal	331	302	400 00			400 00

John Hall, Drawing — Account No. 302

DATE	EXPLANATION	POST. REF.	DEBIT	DATE	EXPLANATION	POST. REF.	CREDIT
19— Mar. 23	Withdrawal	CP5	400 00				

In this transaction involving the Drawing account, the owner made a withdrawal against anticipated net income. If, however, the owner planned to permanently reduce the amount of his investment in the business, this reduction would be debited against the Capital account (and not the Drawing account). The drawing account, like the income and expense accounts, is a temporary account and helps to distinguish temporary changes in owner's equity from the owner's permanent investment.

Merchandise Inventory Account

The Merchandise Inventory account shows the cost of the merchandise on hand at the beginning of the accounting period. This merchandise is owned by the business; thus it is an asset. The Central Sales Company, for example, owns merchandise of $5,000 on March 1, the beginning of the accounting period. This amount would be shown as an asset on a balance sheet prepared at that time.

Central Sales Company				
Balance Sheet				
March 1, 19—				
Assets		*Liabilities*		
Cash	8,700 00	*Accounts Payable*	4,000 00	
Accounts Receivable	2,000 00			
Merchandise Inventory	5,000 00	*Owner's Equity*		
Office Equipment	7,200 00	*John Hall, Capital*	31,000 00	
Stockroom Equipment	12,100 00			
Total	35,000 00	*Total*	35,000 00	

As you will recall, additional merchandise purchased during the accounting period is debited to the Purchases account. If the cost of these purchases is reduced by returning some items or receiving an allowance, the Purchases Returns and Allowances account is credited to offset the debit to the Purchases account. In addition, the cash discounts that are taken during the period are credited to the Purchases Discount account. These three accounts are temporary owner's equity accounts and are used to accumulate the data regarding the merchandise purchased *during* the accounting period.

During the accounting period, the Central Sales Company purchased merchandise costing $4,955. However, it had purchases returns and allowances of $125; and it took purchases discounts of $50. The net purchases during March was $4,780 ($4,955 − $125 − $50).

At no time during the accounting period was an entry made to the Merchandise Inventory account; all entries were made to these temporary cost accounts. As a result, at the end of the accounting

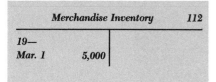

Beginning of Period

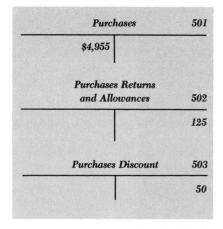

During Period

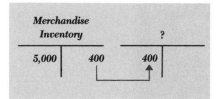

period the Merchandise Inventory account still shows the inventory for the beginning of the period ($5,000). It is necessary, therefore, to change this amount to the amount of the inventory at the end of the period. This is done by making an adjusting entry.

In order to determine how much merchandise remains unsold at the end of the accounting period, it is necessary to take a physical inventory (actual count). The physical inventory for the Central Sales Company on March 31 shows the total cost of the unsold merchandise to be $4,600. Obviously, the $5,000 shown in the Merchandise Inventory is incorrect. Therefore, the account must be adjusted to show the actual inventory on March 31, the end of the period.

In order to decrease this debit balance from $5,000 to $4,600, the Merchandise Inventory account must be credited for $400. What account, however, should be debited?

At the end of the period, Central Sales Company has $400 less merchandise on hand than it had at the beginning of the period. This means that $400 more merchandise was sold than was purchased during the period. The entry to record the cost of this merchandise sold from the inventory could be made by debiting the Purchases account. However, it is better practice not to distort the data in the Purchases account. Therefore, the Income and Expense Summary account is used.

To understand why the Income and Expense Summary account is used, remember that at the end of the accounting period the temporary owner's equity accounts are closed into the Income and Expense Summary account. Thus, the balances of the Purchases, Purchases Returns and Allowances, and Purchases Discount accounts will be transferred to the appropriate side of the Income and Expense Summary account.

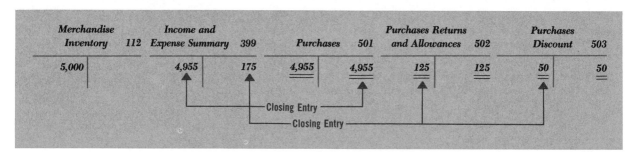

This additional cost of $400 is, therefore, transferred directly from the Merchandise Inventory account to the Income and Expense Summary account.

Thus the Income and Expense Summary account contains all the data regarding the cost of the goods sold. On the debit side are the costs due to (1) purchases during the month and (2) reduction in the inventory. On the credit side are reductions in the cost due to (3) returns, allowances, and discounts. Therefore, the cost of the goods sold during the period is $5,180 ($4,955 + $400 − $175).

ACCOUNTS PAYABLE DEBIT	GENERAL LEDGER DEBIT	DATE	ACCOUNT TITLE AND EXPLANATION	POST. REF.	GENERAL LEDGER CREDIT	ACCOUNTS RECEIVABLE CREDIT
	400 00	19— Mar. 31	Income & Expense Summary Merchandise Inventory	399 112	400 00	

GENERAL JOURNAL — Page 6

In March, the Central Sales Company sold more merchandise than it purchased. As a result, the merchandise inventory decreased by $400 at the end of the month. The merchandise counted on the last day of the accounting period is the same merchandise in inventory on the first day of the next period. Thus, on April 1, the balance of the Merchandise Inventory account is $4,600. Suppose the business has purchases of $6,000 during April and has an ending inventory of $5,200. Since the ending inventory ($5,200) is $600 more than the beginning inventory ($4,600), more merchandise was purchased than was sold. Thus, an adjusting entry must be made to increase the merchandise inventory account by $600.

April 30: Adjusting entry to increase the Merchandise Inventory account by $600.

WHAT HAPPENS	ACCOUNTING RULE	ENTRY
The asset Merchandise Inventory *increases* by $600.	To increase an asset, debit the account.	Debit: Merchandise Inventory, $600.
The reduction in the cost of merchandise increases owner's equity by $600.	To increase owner's equity, credit the account.	Credit: Income and Expense Summary, $600.

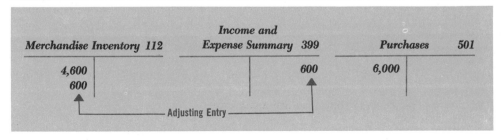

When the closing entries are made, all temporary owner's equity accounts will be closed into the Income and Expense Summary account. The credit of $600 to owner's equity can therefore be posted directly to this temporary summary account. As a result, the Merchandise Inventory account will show the cost of the merchandise in inventory at the end of the period ($5,200). The cost of the merchandise that has been sold during the month is shown in the Income and Expense Summary ($6,000 − $600 = $5,400).

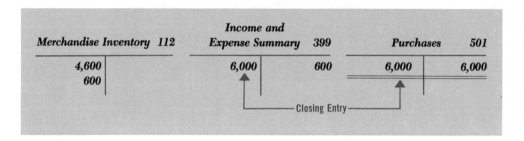

Merchandise Inventory Decreased	Merchandise Inventory Increased
Ending inventory less than beginning inventory.	*Ending inventory more than beginning inventory.*
Sold more merchandise than purchased.	*Sold less merchandise than purchased.*
Decrease *Merchandise Inventory account balance.*	Increase *Merchandise Inventory account balance.*
Adjusting entry for amount of decrease:	*Adjusting entry for amount of increase:*

Income and Expense Summary	xxx		Merchandise Inventory	xxx	
Merchandise Inventory		xxx	Income and Expense Summary		xxx

Supplies on Hand Account   Some business transactions affect more than one accounting period. For example, a business usually buys enough office supplies at one time to last for several months. Therefore, if the income statement is prepared on a monthly basis, it would not be accurate to show the entire expense for supplies in March and no expense in April. The expense of only those supplies actually used during the accounting period should be considered as an expense for that period. Unused supplies will not become an expense until some future accounting period.

The cost of goods and services that are bought to be used in operating the business but that remain unused at the end of the accounting period are called *prepaid expenses*. Prepaid expenses include such items as supplies on hand and prepaid insurance.

Prepaid expenses: cost of goods or services that remain unused at the end of the accounting period.

Deferred charge: prepaid expense.

At the time supplies are bought, they are considered assets. When these supplies are used in the normal operations of the business, however, they become expenses. Since these supplies are paid for before they are used, they are called a prepaid expense. The cost of these items is sometimes called a *deferred charge* because the expense is deferred (put off) until a later period.

The general procedure for processing expenses for supplies is as follows: (1) When the supplies are purchased, they are debited to an appropriate asset account called Supplies on Hand. (2) At the end of the accounting period, the actual supplies on hand are counted. (3) The amount of the supplies used in the accounting period is transferred from the asset account to an expense account. Thus, the asset account is decreased for the amount of supplies used.

March 3: The Central Sales Company draws a check for $400 to pay for supplies to last for several months.

WHAT HAPPENS	ACCOUNTING RULE	ENTRY
The asset Supplies on Hand increases by $400.	*To increase an asset, debit the account.*	*Debit: Supplies on Hand, $400.*
The asset Cash decreases by $400.	*To decrease an asset, credit the account.*	*Credit: Cash, $400.*

To record prepaid expenses:

1. Debit asset account when items are purchased.
2. Determine unused portion at end of period.
3. Debit expense account for portion used.

Credit asset account for portion used.

Cash	101	Supplies on Hand	114
	400	400	

At the end of the accounting period on March 31, the supplies on hand were counted. This physical inventory showed that there were $300 of supplies on hand, meaning that supplies of $100 ($400 − $300) were used during March. Therefore, an adjusting entry must be made to transfer the amount of the used supplies ($100) from the asset account to the Supplies Expense account.

Supplies Available	*$400*
Less: Supplies on Hand	*300*
Supplies Used	*$100*

March 31: A physical count of the supplies on hand showed that unused supplies amounted to $300.

WHAT HAPPENS	ACCOUNTING RULE	ENTRY
Expenses decrease owner's equity by $100.	*To decrease owner's equity, debit the account.*	*Debit: Supplies Expense, $100.*
The asset Supplies on Hand decreases by $100.	*To decrease an asset, credit the account.*	*Credit: Supplies on Hand, $100.*

Cash	101	Supplies on Hand	114	Supplies Expense	516
	400	400	100	100	

**CENTRAL SALES COMPANY
CHART OF ACCOUNTS**

ASSETS

114   *Supplies on Hand*

COSTS & EXPENSES

516   *Supplies Expense*

The effect of this adjusting entry is that the Supplies on Hand account now has a balance of $300, the amount of the asset to be shown on the balance sheet. In addition, the Supplies Expense account shows a debit balance of $100, the amount of the supplies used during the accounting period. Thus the financial statements reveal the accurate amounts for the asset and the expenses.

The Prepaid Insurance Account   Many assets of a business, such as equipment and buildings, are usually insured against loss through theft, fire, flood, or storm.   The premium on an insurance policy is paid at the beginning of the insurance period; thus it is paid in advance.

If a policy is in force for more than one accounting period, the insurance premium is a prepaid expense. When the premium is paid, the amount is debited to the asset account Prepaid Insurance. When each portion of the insurance premium expires, it becomes an expense.

March 1:   The Central Sales Company issues a check for $360 to pay the annual premium for fire insurance covering its equipment and furniture.

WHAT HAPPENS	ACCOUNTING RULE	ENTRY
The asset **Prepaid Insurance** *increases by $360.*	*To increase an asset, debit the account.*	*Debit:* **Prepaid Insurance**, *$360.*
The asset **Cash** *decreases by $360.*	*To decrease an asset, credit the account.*	*Credit:* **Cash**, *$360.*

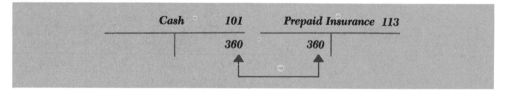

The premium of $360 provides a year's coverage of fire insurance. Since it is paid in advance, the premium is a prepaid expense. Thus each accounting period throughout the year must be charged for the portion of the premium that expires during that period. Therefore, if the company has an accounting period of one month, the cost of the insurance for the month of March would be one-twelfth of the annual premium of $360, or $30. At the end of March, an entry would be made to transfer one month's insurance ($30) from the Prepaid Insurance account to the Insurance Expense account.

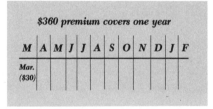

March 31:   Record the amount of insurance expired during the month of March.

WHAT HAPPENS	ACCOUNTING RULE	ENTRY
Expenses decrease owner's equity by $30.	*To decrease owner's equity, debit the account.*	*Debit:* **Insurance Expense**, *$30.*
The asset **Prepaid Insurance** *decreases by $30.*	*To decrease an asset, credit the account.*	*Credit:* **Prepaid Insurance**, *$30.*

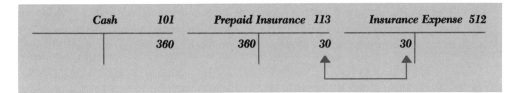

The balance of the Prepaid Insurance account on April 1 will be $330. This represents eleven months' insurance that has not expired ($30 × 11 = $330). Through this adjusting entry at the end of each accounting period, the asset Prepaid Insurance will contain the amount of the unexpired insurance and the Insurance Expense account will contain the amount of the insurance that expired during the accounting period.

Other Prepaid Expense Accounts In addition to the supplies on hand and prepaid insurance, a business may have other prepaid expenses that require adjusting at the end of the accounting period. The basic principle for all adjustments for prepaid items is the same: (1) Record the prepaid expense amount in the appropriate asset account. (2) At the end of the period, determine the amount of the asset that has been used during that accounting period. (3) Transfer the amount of the expense from the asset account to the appropriate expense account.

The steps in the accounting cycle will be resumed in the next topic. At that time, the adjusting entries will be discussed in detail.

> **CENTRAL SALES COMPANY**
> **CHART OF ACCOUNTS**
> ───────────────────────
> **ASSETS**
>
> **113 Prepaid Insurance**
>
> **COSTS & EXPENSES**
>
> **512 Insurance Expense**

TOPIC 1 ■ PROBLEMS

44 Answer the following questions about the entries in the cash receipts journal and the cash payments journal on page 260.

    a What account was credited in the entry of March 2? Why?
    b What account was debited in the entry of March 23? Why?

    c If the withdrawal on March 23 had been considered a permanent withdrawal of investment, what account would have been debited?

Answer the following questions about the general journal and general ledger accounts shown on page 263.

    d Why was the Merchandise Inventory account credited for $400?
    e What effect does the $400 adjustment have on the owner's equity?

    f If on March 31 the merchandise inventory had been larger than on March 1, what adjusting entry would have been required?

Answer the following questions about the transaction analysis and accounts shown on page 265.

    g Why was it necessary to adjust the Supplies on Hand account on March 31?
    h What effect does the $100 credit to the Supplies on Hand account have on the total assets of the business?

    i When the Supplies on Hand account was credited for $100, what account was debited?
    j What is the effect upon the owner's equity of the debit to the Supplies Expense account?

45 From this data make adjusting entries in a general journal on April 30.

a Merchandise inventory at beginning of the accounting period: $8,460. Merchandise inventory at end of the accounting period: $9,685.

b Supplies on hand at beginning of the accounting period: $110. Supplies on hand at end of the period: $85.

c Value of prepaid insurance at beginning of period: $480. Value of prepaid insurance at end of period: $360.

46 From this data make adjusting entries in a general journal on July 31.

a Merchandise inventory at the beginning of the accounting period: $10,280. Merchandise inventory at the end of the period: $7,170.

b Supplies on hand at the beginning of the accounting period: $30.

Supplies purchased during the period: $25. Supplies on hand at the end of the period: $20.

c Prepaid insurance at the beginning of the period: $180. Insurance that expired during the period: $45.

TOPIC 2 ■ COMPLETING THE WORKSHEET

When the trial balance shows the correct balances of all accounts, the financial statements can be prepared directly from the trial balance. However, if the balances must be adjusted before statements are prepared, accountants prefer to prepare the trial balance on a worksheet that can also be used to compute the adjustments.

The Worksheet

Worksheet: expanded trial balance for computing, classifying, and sorting account balances before preparing financial statements.

Ten-column worksheet sections:

Trial Balance
Adjustments
Adjusted Trial Balance
Income Statement
Balance Sheet

Central Sales Company
Worksheet
For the Month Ended March 31, 19—

The worksheet is a columnar form that resembles the trial balance form used earlier. However, additional columns are included to assist the accountant in computing the amounts of the adjustments and in sorting and classifying the account balances in terms of the financial statements on which the accounts will appear. The worksheet presented in this chapter is a ten-column worksheet that consists of five main sections: (1) the Trial Balance section, (2) the Adjustments section, (3) the Adjusted Trial Balance section, (4) the Income Statement section, and (5) the Balance Sheet section.

The worksheet is an expanded trial balance that is the accountant's *working tool;* it is *not a statement.* The worksheet is prepared in pencil so that figures can be erased and changed. It is designed so that proofs are provided for each part of the work.

The worksheet prepared for the Central Sales Company on March 31 will be used to illustrate how the worksheet is prepared and used in the accounting cycle.

The heading of the worksheet presents who (the name of the business), what (worksheet), and when (the accounting period). The worksheet covers the accounting period because it is used to compute the net income for the period. After the heading has been completed, the following procedures should be used to complete the five sections of the worksheet.

Step 3a: Completing the Trial Balance Section   The trial balance may be prepared directly on the worksheet. Each account with a balance is listed in numerical order, just as it appears in the ledger. The account title and number are listed, and the account balance is entered in the appropriate Debit or Credit money column of the Trial Balance section. After all the account balances are entered, a single rule is drawn across both money columns and the figures are totaled. If the trial balance is in balance, double rules are drawn across both money columns. If the trial balance is out of balance, the error must be located and corrected before continuing the work.

Central Sales Company
Worksheet
For the Month Ended March 31, 19—

	ACCOUNT TITLE	ACCT. NO.	TRIAL BALANCE		ADJUSTMENTS		ADJUSTED TRIAL BALANCE		INCOME STATEMENT		BALANCE SHEET		
			DEBIT	CREDIT	DEBIT	CREDIT	DEBIT	CREDIT	DEBIT	CREDIT	DEBIT	CREDIT	
1	Cash	101	9,600										1
2	Accounts Receivable	111	3,300										2
3	Merchandise Inventory	112	5,000										3
4	Prepaid Insurance	113	360										4
5	Supplies on Hand	114	400										5
6	Office Equipment	121	7,200										6
7	Stockroom Equipment	122	12,100										7
8	Accounts Payable	211		4,600									8
9	John Hall, Capital	301		32,000									9
10	John Hall, Drawing	302	400										10
11	Sales	401		9,260									11
12	Sales Returns and Allowances	402	160										12
13	Sales Discount	403	37										13
14	Purchases	501	4,955										14
15	Purchases Returns and Allowances	502		125									15
16	Purchases Discount	503		50									16
17	Cash Short and Over	511	8										17
18	Miscellaneous Expense	513	15										18
19	Rent Expense	514	310										19
20	Salaries Expense	515	2,100										20
21	Utilities Expense	517	90										21
22			46,035	46,035									22
23													23
24													24

NOTE: *The cents columns have been omitted in order to show the entire worksheet.*

Step 3b: Completing the Adjustments Section   The balances of some of the accounts shown on the trial balance must be adjusted to show the correct balances. As shown in the previous topic, three accounts need to be adjusted on March 31 for the Central Sales Company: the Merchandise Inventory account, the Prepaid Insurance account, and the Supplies on Hand account. In actual practice, these adjustments would be computed on the worksheet before they are journalized and posted to the accounts.

Adjustments: computed on worksheet before journalized.

(a) *Adjustment for Merchandise Inventory.* The beginning inventory was $5,000 (as shown on the trial balance). The ending inventory is $4,600 (as determined by the physical inventory on March 31). Therefore, the Merchandise Inventory account must be decreased by $400 ($5,000 − $4,600). Since the Merchandise Inventory account has a debit balance, this account must be credited to decrease the balance. Thus $400 is entered in the Credit column of the Adjustments section on the same line as the Merchandise Inventory (line 3). The debit and credit amounts for each adjustment are identified by a letter such as (a), (b), or (c), so that the complete entry can be identified for journalizing. This amount is transferred to the debit side of the Income and Expense Summary account. Since the Income and Expense Summary account had no balance when the trial balance was prepared on the worksheet, the account was not listed. Therefore, on the first line beneath the trial balance totals (line 23), the title and number of the Income and Expense Summary account are written. The $400 is then entered in the Debit column of the Adjustments section and is identified with the letter (a).

(b) *Adjustment for Expired Insurance.* The balance of $360 in the Prepaid Insurance account shown on the trial balance represents the payment for insurance providing coverage for one year. Since one twelfth of this amount has expired, $30 ($\frac{1}{12} \times$ $360) needs to be transferred from the asset account (Prepaid Insurance account) to the expense account (Insurance Expense). Thus $30 is entered in the Credit column of the Adjustments section for Prepaid Insurance, item (b). Since the Insurance Expense account does not appear on the trial balance, the account title is written on the first available line beneath the trial balance totals (line 24). In the Debit column of the Adjustments section for Insurance Expense, $30 is entered to record the expense.

(c) *Adjustment for Supplies Used.* The trial balance shows a balance of $400 for Supplies on Hand. When the supplies on hand were counted on March 31, however, only $300 of the supplies were unused. Therefore, the Supplies on Hand account must be decreased by a credit of $100 ($400 − $300). The expense for the supplies used is transferred as a debit to the Supplies Expense account. Since the Supplies Expense account was not listed in the trial balance, the account title and number are entered on the first available line (line 25). The amount is entered in the Debit column of the Adjustments section and is identified as adjustment (c).

Totaling the Adjustment Columns. After all the adjustments have been entered, a single rule is drawn across the money columns and the columns are totaled. The two totals must equal to prove the equality of the debit and credit entries. If an error was made in one of the amounts, the worksheet could not be completed accurately. When the two amounts agree, draw double rules beneath the totals.

Step 3c: Completing the Adjusted Trial Balance Section The new balances for the accounts that have been adjusted are obtained by

Central Sales Company
Worksheet
For the Month Ended March 31, 19—

	ACCOUNT TITLE	ACCT. NO.	TRIAL BALANCE		ADJUSTMENTS		ADJUSTED TRIAL BALANCE		INCOME STATEMENT		BALANCE SHEET		
			DEBIT	CREDIT	DEBIT	CREDIT	DEBIT	CREDIT	DEBIT	CREDIT	DEBIT	CREDIT	
1	Cash.........................	101	9,600				9,600						1
2	Accounts Receivable............	111	3,300				3,300						2
3	Merchandise Inventory.........	112	5,000			(a) 400	4,600						3
4	Prepaid Insurance..............	113	360			(b) 30	330						4
5	Supplies on Hand..............	114	400			(c) 100	300						5
6	Office Equipment..............	121	7,200				7,200						6
7	Stockroom Equipment...........	122	12,100				12,100						7
8	Accounts Payable..............	211		4,600				4,600					8
9	John Hall, Capital.............	301		32,000				32,000					9
10	John Hall, Drawing............	302	400				400						10
11	Sales........................	401		9,260				9,260					11
12	Sales Returns and Allowances......	402	160				160						12
13	Sales Discount.................	403	37				37						13
14	Purchases....................	501	4,955				4,955						14
15	Purchases Returns and Allowances..	502		125				125					15
16	Purchases Discount.............	503		50				50					16
17	Cash Short and Over...........	511	8				8						17
18	Miscellaneous Expense..........	513	15				15						18
19	Rent Expense..................	514	310				310						19
20	Salaries Expense..............	515	2,100				2,100						20
21	Utilities Expense..............	517	90				90						21
22			46,035	46,035									22
23	Income and Expense Summary....	399			(a) 400		400						23
24	Insurance Expense..............	512			(b) 30		30						24
25	Supplies Expense..............	516			(c) 100		100						25
26					530	530	46,035	46,035					26

NOTE: *The cents columns have been omitted in order to show the entire worksheet.*

completing the Adjusted Trial Balance section of the worksheet. Each account balance in the Trial Balance section is combined with its adjustment, if any, in the Adjustments section. The new balance is extended to the Adjusted Trial Balance section. This crossfooting procedure requires either adding the adjustment or subtracting the adjustment from the balance.

For any account in which there is no adjustment, the balance shown in the Trial Balance section is extended directly to the Adjusted Trial Balance section. For example, the first two accounts (Cash and Accounts Receivable) were not adjusted, so the balances extended to the Debit column of the Adjusted Trial Balance section are exactly the same as those shown in the Trial Balance section. However, Merchandise Inventory (line 3) was adjusted. The trial balance shows a debit of $5,000. There is, however, a credit adjustment of $400. The new balance is obtained by subtracting the $400 credit from the

$5,000 debit. Since the debits are larger, there is a debit balance of $4,600. This adjusted balance is then entered in the Debit column of the Adjusted Trial Balance section. The same procedure is followed for Prepaid Insurance and Supplies on Hand.

The Income and Expense Summary account had no balance in the Trial Balance section. However, there was a $400 debit in the Adjustments section. The balance carried over to the Adjusted Trial Balance section is, therefore, a debit balance of $400. The same procedure is followed for Insurance Expense and Supplies Expense.

After all the account balances have been entered in the Adjusted Trial Balance section, the columns are totaled. If the total debits equal the total credits, the columns are ruled, and the accountant assumes that he has made no arithmetical error. This adjusted trial balance is actually the second trial balance prepared. It is used to check the equality of the debit and credit balances of the accounts after the adjustments are made.

Step 3d: Completing the Statement Section   Each balance in the Adjusted Trial Balance column is extended into one, but only one, of the remaining four columns. The balances of the assets, liabilities, and the owner's capital and drawing accounts are extended to the appropriate Debit or Credit columns in the Balance Sheet section. For example, Cash, the first account, has a debit balance of $9,600. Since Cash is an asset, the balance of the account must be extended to the balance sheet. The adjusted trial balance amount of $9,600 is extended into the Debit column of the Balance Sheet section. Likewise, the next six accounts on the adjusted trial balance are assets. Therefore, these balances are extended to the Debit column of the Balance Sheet section. The amounts of the Accounts Payable and John Hall, Capital accounts are both extended to the Credit column of the Balance Sheet section. The John Hall, Drawing account has a debit balance, and the amount is, therefore, recorded in the Debit column of the Balance Sheet section.

Balances of the cost, expense, and income accounts (including the Income and Expense Summary account) are extended to the appropriate Debit or Credit columns in the Income Statement section. For example, sales is an income account and has a credit balance. Since it appears on the income statement, the balance of $9,260 is extended to the Credit column of the Income Statement section. The remainder of the account balances are extended to the appropriate columns of the Income Statement section.

The worksheet not only helps the accountant obtain the adjusted balances, but also acts as a sorting device to help the accountant classify the various accounts according to the statement on which they will appear. The financial statements then can be made easily from the worksheet.

Determining the Net Income or Net Loss   After each account balance has been extended into one of the columns in either the Income Statement section or the Balance Sheet section, a single line is

Central Sales Company
Worksheet
For the Month Ended March 31, 19—

	ACCOUNT TITLE	ACCT. NO.	TRIAL BALANCE		ADJUSTMENTS		ADJUSTED TRIAL BALANCE		INCOME STATEMENT		BALANCE SHEET		
			DEBIT	CREDIT	DEBIT	CREDIT	DEBIT	CREDIT	DEBIT	CREDIT	DEBIT	CREDIT	
1	Cash.........................	101	9,600				9,600				9,600		1
2	Accounts Receivable.............	111	3,300				3,300				3,300		2
3	Merchandise Inventory...........	112	5,000			(a) 400	4,600				4,600		3
4	Prepaid Insurance................	113	360			(b) 30	330				330		4
5	Supplies on Hand................	114	400			(c) 100	300				300		5
6	Office Equipment................	121	7,200				7,200				7,200		6
7	Stockroom Equipment............	122	12,100				12,100				12,100		7
8	Accounts Payable................	211		4,600				4,600				4,600	8
9	John Hall, Capital...............	301		32,000				32,000				32,000	9
10	John Hall, Drawing..............	302	400				400				400		10
11	Sales.........................	401		9,260				9,260		9,260			11
12	Sales Returns and Allowances......	402	160				160		160				12
13	Sales Discount..................	403	37				37		37				13
14	Purchases......................	501	4,955				4,955		4,955				14
15	Purchases Returns and Allowances..	502		125				125		125			15
16	Purchases Discount..............	503		50				50		50			16
17	Cash Short and Over.............	511	8				8		8				17
18	Miscellaneous Expense...........	513	15				15		15				18
19	Rent Expense...................	514	310				310		310				19
20	Salaries Expense................	515	2,100				2,100		2,100				20
21	Utilities Expense...............	517	90				90		90				21
22			46,035	46,035									22
23	Income and Expense Summary.....	399			(a) 400		400		400				23
24	Insurance Expense...............	512			(b) 30		30		30				24
25	Supplies Expense................	516			(c) 100		100		100				25
26					530	530	46,035	46,035	8,205	9,435	37,830	36,600	26
27									8,205				27
28	Net Income....................								1,230			1,230	28
29											37,830	37,830	29

NOTE: *The cents columns have been omitted in order to show the entire worksheet.*

drawn across all money columns, and the figures are totaled. At this point, however, the total debits on the Income Statement section do not equal the total credits. These two totals do not agree because the company has earned a *net income* (income is greater than expenses) or has suffered a *net loss* (expenses are greater than income).

The two columns for the Balance Sheet section do not agree for the same reason. If the company has made a net income, this amount has not been entered in the owner's equity account (this is not done until the closing entry transfers the balance of the Income and Expense Summary account to the owner's equity account). Thus the difference between the Debit column and the Credit column is the amount of the net income or net loss.

Net Income

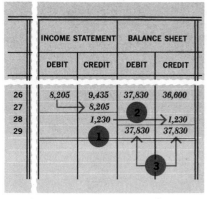

	INCOME STATEMENT		BALANCE SHEET	
	DEBIT	CREDIT	DEBIT	CREDIT
26	8,205	9,435	37,830	36,600
27		8,205		
28		1,230		1,230
29			37,830	37,830

To obtain the net income, or net loss, begin with the Income Statement section. If the total of the Credit column is greater than the total of the Debit column, then a net income will result. To obtain this amount, follow this procedure:

1 Place the total of the Debit column beneath the total of the Credit column and subtract. The amounts entered in the Debit column of the Income Statement section represent decreases to owner's equity; the amounts entered in the Credit column represent increases to owner's equity. Since the increases to owner's equity (credits) are greater than the decreases (debits), the difference between the two totals is a net income.

2 Extend the amount of the net income to the Credit column of the Balance Sheet section. This is done because a net income increases owner's equity, and owner's equity is increased on the credit side. Thus the net income is now available to be shown on the balance sheet.

3 Add the net income to the total of the Credit column because a net income increases owner's equity. If all computations are correct on the worksheet, the total of the Credit column must now equal the total of the Debit column in the Balance Sheet section. These amounts must be equal after the net income has been transferred to the capital account because this is the fundamental equation.

Total Assets = Total Liabilities + Owner's Equity

Complete the worksheet by drawing double rules as shown in the illustration.

If these totals do not agree, then recheck all the figures until the error is found. If the adjusted trial balance was correct, then the error was made either in extending the amounts or in computing the totals.

If the total of the Debit column of the Income Statement section is greater than the Credit column, then the business has suffered a loss. In this case, follow this procedure:

1 Move the total of the Credit column under the total of the Debit column and subtract. The difference is the net loss.

2 Extend the amount of the net loss to the Debit column of the Balance Sheet section. This is done because a net loss decreases owner's equity and owner's equity is decreased on the debit side.

3 Add the net loss to the total of the Debit column. If no errors were made, the total of the Debit column must equal the total of the Credit column.

Net Loss

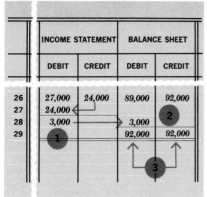

	INCOME STATEMENT		BALANCE SHEET	
	DEBIT	CREDIT	DEBIT	CREDIT
26	27,000	24,000	89,000	92,000
27	24,000			
28	3,000		3,000	
29			92,000	92,000

Summary of Step 3—Proving the Ledger and Completing the Worksheet

Because of the complexities that arise in adjusting the books and preparing the financial statement, most accountants prefer to prepare a worksheet. The third step of the accounting cycle, then, can be generally stated as proving the ledger and preparing the worksheet.

TOPIC 2 ■ PROBLEMS

47   Answer the following questions about the completed worksheet on page 273.

a   Is every amount in the Trial Balance section extended to the Adjusted Trial Balance section? If so, are the balances for the same account always the same? Why or why not?

b   When Merchandise Inventory was credited for $400 in the Adjustments section, what account was debited? Why was this entry made?

c   Prepaid Insurance was credited for $30 and Supplies on Hand was credited for $100. What accounts were debited? Why were the entries made?

d   What is the purpose of the small letters in the Adjustments section?

e   What is the amount of the net income? How is it determined?

f   Why was the $1,230 net income added to the total of the credit column of the Balance Sheet section?

g   Does the amount of net income in the Income Statement section always have to be the same as the amount of net income in the Balance Sheet section? Why, or why not?

h   How can you tell that the $1,230 is net income and not net loss?

i   Why was the $5,000 for Merchandise Inventory not extended to the Balance Sheet section?

48   The accounts in the general ledger of the Towne Men's Shop showed the following balances on June 30. The physical inventory on June 30 showed (1) merchandise on hand of $9,830 and (2) unused supplies of $120. The amount of unexpired insurance as of June 30 is $450. Complete a worksheet for the shop. The information for the trial balance is as follows:

Account	Acct. No.	Debit Balance	Credit Balance
Cash	101	8,240	
Accounts Receivable	102	3,875	
Merchandise Inventory	103	12,653	
Equipment	104	2,940	
Prepaid Insurance	105	540	
Supplies on Hand	106	160	
Accounts Payable	201		1,384
Gerald Baxter, Capital	301		21,948
Gerald Baxter, Drawing	302	450	
Sales	401		9,846
Sales Returns and Allowances	402	138	
Sales Discount	403	183	
Purchases	501	3,810	
Purchases Returns and Allowances	502		87
Purchases Discount	503		76
Miscellaneous Expense	504	80	
Rent Expense	505	240	
Telephone Expense	506	32	

NOTE: Save this worksheet for use in Problem 53.

49 The accounts in the general ledger of the Golden Record Store showed the following balances on December 31. The physical inventory on December 31 showed merchandise on hand of $7,323. The cost of the supplies used was $15, and the amount of expired insurance as of December 31 is $75. Complete a worksheet for the store. The data for the trial balance is as follows:

Account	Acct. No.	Debit Footing	Credit Footing
Cash	101	4,325	804
Accounts Receivable	102	1,868	750
Merchandise Inventory	103	6,213	
Equipment	104	2,489	60
Prepaid Insurance	105	300	
Supplies on Hand	106	45	
Accounts Payable	201	610	938
Thomas Lyle, Capital	301		14,696
Thomas Lyle, Drawing	302	140	
Sales	401		4,824
Sales Returns and Allowances	402	90	
Sales Discount	403	70	
Purchases	501	5,701	
Purchases Returns and Allowances	502		35
Purchases Discount	503		114
Advertising Expense	504	140	
Miscellaneous Expense	505	60	
Rent Expense	506	170	

NOTE: Save this worksheet for use in Problem 54.

TOPIC 3 ■ COMPLETING THE ACCOUNTING CYCLE

On the worksheet, the data has been sorted according to the statements on which it appears and the net income (or net loss) has been computed. Therefore, it is easy to prepare the financial statements, the next step in the cycle after the worksheet has been prepared.

Step 4a: Preparing the Income Statement

The income statement reports the results of the operations during the accounting period. The net income for a service business is determined by deducting the expenses from the income. Thus the income statement for a service business generally contains three sections: (1) the income, (2) the expenses, and (3) the net income or the net loss. A typical income statement for a service business is shown in the margin.

The income statement for a merchandising business, however, is somewhat more complicated. Its net income is determined by

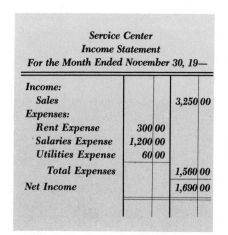

Service Center Income Statement For the Month Ended November 30, 19—		
Income:		
Sales		3,250 00
Expenses:		
Rent Expense	300 00	
Salaries Expense	1,200 00	
Utilities Expense	60 00	
Total Expenses		1,560 00
Net Income		1,690 00

deducting not only the expenses of operating the business but also the cost of the merchandise sold. The income statement for a merchandising business, therefore, contains five sections: (1) the income, (2) the cost of the goods sold, (3) the gross profit, (4) the operating expenses, and (5) the net income or the net loss.

The income statement for a merchandising business would be similar to the income statement prepared for the Central Sales Company for the month of March. The amounts of the income, operating expenses, and net income are obtained directly from the income statement section of the worksheet. However, the cost of goods sold and the gross profit must be computed.

Income statement
for merchandising
business:

Income
Cost of Goods Sold
Gross Profit
Operating Expenses
Net Income

Central Sales Company
Worksheet
For the Month Ended March 31, 19—

ACCOUNT TITLE	INCOME STATEMENT	
	DEBIT	CREDIT
Sales		9,260
Sales Ret. and Allow.	160	
Sales Discount	37	
Purchases	4,955	
Purchas Ret. and Allow.		125
Purchases Discount		50
Cash Short and Over	8	
Miscellaneous Expense	15	
Rent Expense	310	
Salaries Expense	2,100	
Utilities Expense	90	
I. & E. Summary	400	
Insurance Expense	30	
Supplies Expense	100	
	8,205	9,435
		8,205
Net Income		1,230

Central Sales Company
Income Statement
For the Month Ended March 31, 19—

Income from Sales:				
Sales			9,260 00	
Less: Sales Returns and Allowances		$160.00		
Sales Discounts		37.00	197 00	
Net Sales				9,063 00
Cost of Goods Sold:				
Merchandise Inventory, March 1			5,000 00	
Purchases		$4,955.00		
Less: Purchases Ret. and Allowances	$125.00			
Purchases Discount	50.00	175.00		
Net Purchases			4,780 00	
Cost of Goods Available for Sale			9,780 00	
Less: Merchandise Inventory, March 31			4,600 00	
Cost of Goods Sold				5,180 00
Gross Profit on Sales				3,883 00
Operating Expenses:				
Cash Short and Over			8 00	
Insurance Expense			30 00	
Miscellaneous Expense			15 00	
Rent Expense			310 00	
Salaries Expense			2,100 00	
Supplies Expense			100 00	
Utilities Expense			90 00	
Total Operating Expenses				2,653 00
Net Income				1,230 00

Income from Sales   The total sales for the month ($9,260) are reported as shown in the Income Statement section of the worksheet. From this amount, the sales returns and allowances ($160) and sales discounts ($37) are deducted to obtain the net sales ($9,063).

Cost of Goods Sold   The details of the cost of goods sold amount are shown on the income statement. However, the cost of goods sold is usually treated as a schedule that supplements the income statement. This latter plan will be followed in the remainder of this discussion.

Income from Sales:			
Sales			9,260
Less: Sales Returns and			
Allowances		160	
Sales Discount		37	197
Net Sales			9,063

*Schedule of cost
of goods sold:
supports income
statement.*

Cost of Goods Sold	5,180

*Data needed:
Beginning inventory
Net purchases
Ending inventory*

When a schedule of cost of goods sold is used to support the income statement, only one amount appears on the income statement —the cost of goods sold. Therefore, the schedule is prepared before the income statement because the amount of the cost of goods sold is needed to complete the income statement.

To compute the cost of goods sold, the accountant must have the following data:

1 The cost of the merchandise on hand at the beginning of the accounting period. (This amount is called the *beginning inventory*.)

2 The net cost of the purchases made during the period.

3 The cost of the merchandise remaining unsold at the end of the period. (This amount is called the *ending inventory*.)

Here is the schedule of cost of goods sold computed for the Central Sales Company for the month of March. Note that the heading indicates that the schedule covers a period of time.

Central Sales Company
Schedule of Cost of Goods Sold
For the Month Ended March 31, 19—

Merchandise Inventory, March 1.....................			5,000 00	← 1
Purchases..		4,955 00	
Less: Purchases Returns and Allowances........ $125.00			
Purchases Discount................... 50.00		175 00	
Net Purchases....................................			4,780 00	← 2
Cost of Goods Available for Sale....................			9,780 00	← 3
Less: Merchandise Inventory, March 31.............			4,600 00	← 4
Cost of Goods Sold...............................			5,180 00	← 5

1 Beginning Inventory. The inventory at the beginning of the accounting period shows the amount on the first day of the period (in this case, March 1). This amount ($5,000) is obtained from the Trial Balance section of the worksheet.

2 Net Purchases. The data to determine the net purchases is obtained from the Income Statement section of the worksheet. During the month of March, the Central Sales Company purchased $4,955 worth of merchandise for resale. During the month, the business returned merchandise costing $125 and also took advantage of cash discounts of $50 offered by the suppliers. These amounts reduced the net cost of the merchandise by $175 ($125 + $50). Therefore, net purchases were $4,780 ($4,955 − $175).

3 Cost of Goods Available for Sale. The merchandise available for sale during the month is not only the merchandise purchased during the month but also the merchandise that remained unsold from the previous period. Thus, the cost of goods available for sale by the

Central Sales Company during March is $9,780 ($4,780 purchased during the period and $5,000 carried over from the previous period).

4 *Ending Inventory.* The physical inventory on March 31 revealed unsold merchandise costing $4,600. This amount is the Merchandise Inventory shown in the Adjusted Trial Balance section of the worksheet.

5 *Cost of Goods Sold.* The cost of the merchandise inventory at the end of the period is subtracted from the cost of the goods available for sale during the period. The difference between the two is the cost of goods sold. The Central Sales Company had merchandise costing $9,780 available for sale during the period. Since all except $4,600 of the merchandise was sold, the cost of goods sold is $5,180 ($9,780 − $4,600). The cost of goods sold is obtained by using this formula:

Beginning Inventory		*Net Purchases*		*Cost of Goods Available for Sale*		*Ending Inventory*		*Cost of Goods Sold*
$5,000	+	$4,780	=	$9,780	−	$4,600	=	$5,180

The amount of the Income and Expense Summary account is the only amount in the Income Statement section of the worksheet that is not shown directly on the income statement or schedule of cost of goods sold. This amount of $400 is, as you will recall, the difference between the beginning inventory ($5,000) and the ending inventory ($4,600). So that the owner or managers will have complete information about the business, the accountant shows the amounts of the inventories rather than just the decrease of $400 ($5,000 − $4,600).

The amount of the cost of goods sold is transferred from the schedule to the income statement. The income statement for the month of March prepared for the Central Sales Company is below.

Central Sales Company
Income Statement
For the Month Ended March 31, 19—

Income from Sales:..........			
Sales.......................		9,260 00	
Less: Sales Returns and Allowances............... $160.00			
Sales Discounts........................ 37.00		197 00	
Net Sales...............			9,063 00
Cost of Goods Sold (see schedule)................			5,180 00
Gross Profit on Sales................			3,883 00
Operating Expenses:			
Total Operating Expenses..........			2,653 00
Net Income.................			1,230 00

Income from Sales	$9,063
Cost of Goods Sold	− 5,180
Gross Profit on Sales	$3,883

Gross Profit on Sales In a merchandising business, a gross profit on sales is made by selling merchandise for a higher price than the business paid for it. The amount of gross profit on sales is found by subtracting the cost of the goods sold from the amount of net sales. The Central Sales Company, for example, had net sales of $9,063. However, it had to pay $5,180 for the merchandise it sold. Therefore, it has a gross profit on its sales of $3,883 ($9,063 − $5,180).

Operating expenses: expenses incurred in operating the business.

Operating Expenses The expenses of operating the business are obtained from the Income Statement section of the worksheet.

Net Income The net income is the amount of the gross profit that remains after the total of the operating expense is deducted from the gross profit on sales. However, if the expenses are greater than the gross profit on sales, then a net loss would occur. During March, Central Sales had a gross profit on sales of $3,883. However, it incurred expenses of $2,653 to operate the business during that month. Thus it has a net income of $1,230 ($3,883 − $2,653). This amount is the same as the net income computed on the worksheet.

Gross Profit on Sales	$3,883
Operating Expenses	− 2,653
Net Income	$1,230

Step 4b: Preparing the Balance Sheet and the Statement of Owner's Equity

The balance sheet shows the financial condition of the business at the end of the accounting period. The data to prepare the balance sheet is obtained from the Balance Sheet section of the worksheet. Here is a balance sheet for March 31, 19—, prepared for Central Sales.

ACCOUNT TITLE	BALANCE SHEET DEBIT	BALANCE SHEET CREDIT
Cash.................	9,600	
Accounts Receivable..	3,300	
Merchandise Inventory	4,600	
Prepaid Insurance....	330	
Supplies on Hand....	300	
Office Equipment....	7,200	
Stockroom Equipment.	12,100	
Accounts Payable....		4,600
John Hall, Capital....		32,000
John Hall, Drawing...	400	
Net Income.........		1,230
	37,830	37,830

Central Sales Company
Balance Sheet
March 31, 19—

Assets		
Cash..........................	9,600 00	
Accounts Receivable...........	3,300 00	
Merchandise Inventory.........	4,600 00	
Prepaid Insurance.............	330 00	
Supplies on Hand.............	300 00	
Office Equipment.............	7,200 00	
Stockroom Equipment.........	12,100 00	
Total Assets.............		37,430 00

Liabilities		
Accounts Payable.............		4,600 00

Owner's Equity		
John Hall, Capital.............		32,000 00
Net Income............ $1,230 00		
Less: Withdrawals...... 400.00	830 00	
Total Owner's Equity...........		32,830 00
Total Liabilities and Owner's Equity..........		37,430 00

Frequently, however, the owner desires more detailed information about the changes in his owner's equity during the accounting period than is shown on the balance sheet. In this case, another statement, *the statement of owner's equity*, is prepared to report his investments and withdrawals for the period as well as net income or net loss for the period. When this is issued, it is prepared before the balance sheet. The heading indicates the period of time covered by the statement.

Statement of owner's equity: reports changes in owner's equity for period.

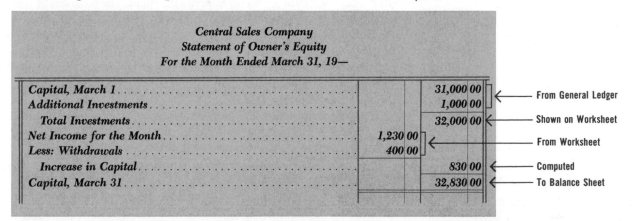

The owner's equity on March 1, the beginning of the accounting period, was $31,000. On March 31, the end of the accounting period, the owner's capital increased to $32,830. This increase of $1,830 was caused by an additional investment of $1,000 and the net income of $1,230, less withdrawals of $400.

If a separate statement of owner's equity is prepared, the owner's capital at the end of the period is the only amount shown in the owner's equity section of the balance sheet. Thus the balance sheet prepared for the Central Sales Company on March 31 would report just one amount in the owner's equity section.

Suppose the Central Sales Company had suffered a net loss instead of earning a net income. Then a decrease in capital would be shown on the statement. For example, if there were a net loss of $1,500 for March, then the capital would decrease by $1,900 (net loss of $1,500 plus withdrawals of $400).

Not all the information needed to prepare the statement of owner's equity is contained on the worksheet. The balance of the capital account at the beginning of the accounting period and the amount of additional investment are obtained from the owner's capital account in the general ledger. The amount of the withdrawals and the net income (or net loss) for the period, of course, are obtained from the Balance Sheet section of the worksheet.

The statement of owner's equity reports the changes in the equity of the owner of a single proprietorship. Partnerships and corporations report this information in similar statements. A partnership issues a statement of partners' equity. A corporation reports the information in a statement of retained earnings.

Liabilities	
Accounts Payable	4,600.00
Owner's Equity	
John Hall, Capital	32,830.00
Total Liabilities and O.E.	37,430.00

Total Investment		$32,000
Net Loss for the Month	$1,500	
Plus Withdrawals	400	
Decrease in Capital		1,900
Capital, March 31		$30,100

Partnership: statement of partners' equity.

Corporation: statement of retained earnings.

Step 5a: Making the Adjusting Entries

After the financial statements have been prepared, the adjusting entries are journalized and posted. The adjustments have been computed on the worksheet to provide the correct account balances to be shown on the statements. In the example of the Central Sales Company, adjustments were needed for (a) Merchandise Inventory, (b) Prepaid Insurance, and (c) Supplies on Hand. The balances of these accounts in the general ledger, however, still show the incorrect figures. It is necessary, therefore, to journalize these adjustments in the general journal and to post the entries to the ledger. Then the balances of the accounts in the general ledger will agree with amounts shown on the statements and will show the correct amounts for the next accounting period.

The information for the adjusting entries is obtained from the Adjustments section of the worksheet.

GENERAL JOURNAL   Page 6

ACCOUNTS PAYABLE DEBIT	GENERAL LEDGER DEBIT	DATE	ACCOUNT TITLE AND EXPLANATION	POST. REF.	GENERAL LEDGER CREDIT	ACCOUNTS RECEIVABLE CREDIT
		19—				
	400 00	Mar. 31	Income and Expense Summary	399		
			Merchandise Inventory	112	400 00	
			To adjust inventory.			
	30 00	31	Insurance Expense	512		
			Prepaid Insurance	113	30 00	
			To record expired insurance.			
	100 00	31	Supplies Expense	516		
			Supplies on Hand	114	100 00	
			To record supplies used.			

Merchandise Inventory   Account No. 112

DATE	EXPLANATION	POST. REF.	DEBIT	DATE	EXPLANATION	POST. REF.	CREDIT
19— Mar. 1	Balance	√	5,000 00	19— Mar. 31	Adjustment	J6	400 00

Prepaid Insurance   Account No. 113

DATE	EXPLANATION	POST. REF.	DEBIT	DATE	EXPLANATION	POST. REF.	CREDIT
19— Mar. 1		CP6	360 00	19— Mar. 31	Expired	J6	30 00

Supplies on Hand   Account No. 114

DATE	EXPLANATION	POST. REF.	DEBIT	DATE	EXPLANATION	POST. REF.	CREDIT
19— Mar. 3		CP6	400 00	19— Mar. 31	Used	J6	100 00

Income and Expense Summary   Account No. 399

DATE	EXPLANATION	POST. REF.	DEBIT	DATE	EXPLANATION	POST. REF.	CREDIT
19— Mar. 31	Inv. adj.	J6	400 00				

		Insurance Expense					Account No. 512	
DATE	EXPLANATION	POST REF.	DEBIT	DATE	EXPLANATION	POST REF.	CREDIT	
19— Mar. 31		J6	30 00					

		Supplies Expense					Account No. 516	
DATE	EXPLANATION	POST REF.	DEBIT	DATE	EXPLANATION	POST REF.	CREDIT	
19— Mar. 31		J6	100 00					

Step 5b: Making Closing Entries

After the adjusting entries have been made, all temporary owner's equity accounts—income, cost and expense, summary, and drawing accounts have to be closed. This is done by transferring their balances to other accounts. The temporary accounts will then have zero balances and will be ready to accumulate the income and expense data for the next accounting period. Four journal entries are made to close the accounts.

1 Close all the income and the cost accounts listed in the Credit column of the Income Statement section of the worksheet. These balances are transferred to the Income and Expense Summary account by debiting the individual accounts for the amount of their balances and crediting the Income and Expense Summary account for the total of these balances.

1. Transfer temporary accounts with credit balances in Income Statement section to the Income and Expense Summary account.

ACCOUNTS PAYABLE DEBIT	GENERAL LEDGER DEBIT	DATE	ACCOUNT TITLE AND EXPLANATION	POST REF.	GENERAL LEDGER CREDIT	ACCOUNTS RECEIVABLE CREDIT
			GENERAL JOURNAL Page 6			
		19— Mar. 31	Sales	401		
	9,260 00					
	125 00		Purchases Ret. and Allow. .	502		
	50 00		Purchases Discount	503		
			I. & E. Summary	399	9,435 00	
			To close accounts			
			with credit			
			balances.			

Central Sales Company
Worksheet
For the Month Ended March 31, 19—

ACCOUNT TITLE	INCOME STATEMENT	
	DEBIT	CREDIT
Sales		9,260
Purchases Ret. and Allow		125
Purchases Discount		50
		9,435

2 Close all the accounts (except the Income and Expense Summary account) listed in the Debit column of the Income Statement section of the worksheet. These balances are transferred by crediting the individual accounts for the amount of their balances and debiting the Income and Expense Summary account for the total of these balances. (The amount of the debit to the Income and Expense Summary is not transferred because it already appears in the Income and Expense Summary account.)

2. Transfer temporary accounts with debit balances in Income Statement section to the Income and Expense Summary account.

Central Sales Company
Worksheet
For the Month Ended March 31, 19—

ACCOUNT TITLE	INCOME STATEMENT	
	DEBIT	CREDIT
Sales Ret. and Allow. . .	160	
Sales Discount	37	
Purchases	4,955	
Cash Short and Over	8	
Miscellaneous Expense . .	15	
Rent Expense	310	
Salaries Expense	2,100	
Utilities Expense	90	
I. & E. Summary	400	
Insurance Expense	30	
Supplies Expense	100	
Not	8,205	9,435
Transferred		8,205
Net Income		1,230

GENERAL JOURNAL   Page 6

ACCOUNTS PAYABLE DEBIT	GENERAL LEDGER DEBIT	DATE	ACCOUNT TITLE AND EXPLANATION	POST. REF.	GENERAL LEDGER CREDIT	ACCOUNTS RECEIVABLE CREDIT
		19—				
	7,805 00	Mar. 31	I. & E. Summary	399		
			Sales Ret. and Allow. . . .	402	160 00	
			Sales Discount	403	37 00	
			Purchases	501	4,955 00	
			Cash Short and Over . . .	511	8 00	
			Insurance Expense	512	30 00	
			Miscellaneous Expense . .	513	15 00	
			Rent Expense	514	310 00	
			Salaries Expense	515	2,100 00	
			Supplies Expense	516	100 00	
			Utilities Expense	517	90 00	
			To close accounts with debit balances.			

Income and Expense Summary   Account No. 399

DATE	EXPLANATION	POST. REF.	DEBIT	DATE	EXPLANATION	POST. REF.	CREDIT
19—				19—			
Mar. 31	Inv. adjust.	J6	400 00	Mar. 31	Closing entry	J6	9,435 00
31	Closing entry	J6	7,805 00			1,230.00	
			8,205 00				

Equals total of Debit column of Income Statement section.

Balance is net income.

Equals total of Credit column of Income Statement section.

3 Close the Income and Expense Summary account. After the first two closing entries are posted, the balance of the Income and Expense Summary account will be the net income (or net loss). This balance is transferred to the drawing account so that the withdrawals by the owner can be offset against this net income (or net loss). A net income is transferred to the drawing account by debiting the Income and Expense Summary account for the amount of the net income and crediting the drawing account for a like amount. A net loss is transferred to the drawing account by debiting the drawing account for the amount of the loss and crediting the Income and Expense Summary for the same amount.

3. Transfer Income and Expense Summary account balance to drawing account.

ACCOUNTS PAYABLE DEBIT	GENERAL LEDGER DEBIT	DATE	ACCOUNT TITLE AND EXPLANATION	POST. REF.	GENERAL LEDGER CREDIT	ACCOUNTS RECEIVABLE CREDIT
			GENERAL JOURNAL			**Page 6**
	1,230 00	19— Mar. 31	Income and Expense Summary..........	399		
			John Hall, Drawing....	302	1,230 00	
			To transfer net income.			

Central Sales Company
Worksheet
For the Month Ended March 31, 19—

ACCOUNT TITLE	INCOME STATEMENT	
	DEBIT	CREDIT
	8,205	9,435
	→8,205	
Net Income...........		1,230

John Hall, Drawing   Account No. 302

DATE	EXPLANATION	POST. REF.	DEBIT	DATE	EXPLANATION	POST. REF.	CREDIT
19— Mar. 23	Withdrawal	CP5	400 00	19— Mar. 31	Net income	J6	1,230 00

Income and Expense Summary   Account No. 399

DATE	EXPLANATION	POST. REF.	DEBIT	DATE	EXPLANATION	POST. REF.	CREDIT
19— Mar. 31	Merchandise adj.	J6	400 00	19— Mar. 31	Closing entry	J6	9,435 00
	31 Closing entry	J6	7,805 00 8,205 00				
	31 Trans. net income	J6	1,230 00				

4 Close the drawing account. At the time the owner makes withdrawals against anticipated net income, the amounts are debited to the drawing account.

At the end of the accounting period, net income is transferred to the drawing account. As a result, the balance of the drawing account is now the amount of net income the owner has not withdrawn from the business (net income — withdrawal). This amount is treated as additional investment and is transferred to the capital account.

If the drawing account has a credit balance after the net income has been transferred to it, then the net income is greater than the withdrawals. The drawing account for John Hall, for example, had a debit balance of $400 on the worksheet. The net income of $1,230 was credited to the account. Thus the drawing account now has a credit balance of $830 ($1,230 — $400). Since the owner has not withdrawn this amount, the $830 is treated as an additional investment and is transferred to the credit side of the capital account. (The data is obtained from the Balance Sheet section of the worksheet.)

4. Transfer Drawing account balance to capital account.

ACCOUNTS PAYABLE DEBIT	GENERAL LEDGER DEBIT	DATE	ACCOUNT TITLE AND EXPLANATION	POST. REF.	GENERAL LEDGER CREDIT	ACCOUNTS RECEIVABLE CREDIT
			GENERAL JOURNAL			**Page 6**
	830 00	19— Mar. 31	John Hall, Drawing......	302		
			John Hall, Capital.....	301	830 00	
			Transfer to Capital.			

Central Sales Company
Worksheet
For the Month Ended March 31, 19—

ACCOUNT TITLE	BALANCE SHEET	
	DEBIT	CREDIT
John Hall, Drawing ...	400	
Net Income.........		1,230

				John Hall, Capital			Account No. 301
DATE	EXPLANATION	POST. REF.	DEBIT	DATE	EXPLANATION	POST. REF.	CREDIT
				19— Mar. 1	Balance	√	31,000 00
				2	Add. invest.	CR5	1,000 00
				31	Trans. fr. Draw.	J6	830 00

				John Hall, Drawing			Account No. 302
DATE	EXPLANATION	POST. REF.	DEBIT	DATE	EXPLANATION	POST. REF.	CREDIT
19— Mar. 23	Withdrawal	CP5	400 00	19— Mar. 31	Net income	J6	1,230 00
31	Trans. to Cap.	J6	830 00				

If the drawing account has a debit balance after the net income has been transferred to it, then the withdrawals are greater than the net income. In this case the balance would be transferred to the capital account as a decrease in investment. Thus the capital account would be debited and the drawing account would be credited.

Step 6: Balancing and Ruling the Accounts

After the closing entries have been posted to the accounts, all the temporary accounts have zero balances. The remaining ledger accounts—showing assets, liabilities, and owner's investment—are

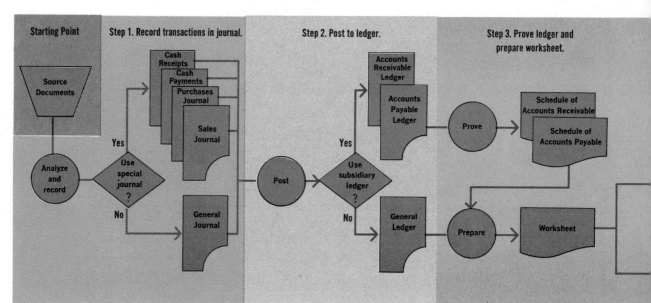

balanced to begin the new accounting period. All the accounts in the ledger with more than one entry are ruled to clearly separate the entries in one accounting period from those of the next period.

Step 7: Preparing a Postclosing Trial Balance

At the end of the accounting period, a trial balance was prepared to prove the equality of the debits and the credits in the general ledger. After the adjustments were prepared on the worksheet, an adjusted trial balance was prepared to verify the equality of the debits and credits in the adjustments. Now a postclosing trial balance is prepared to verify that the debits and credits in the ledger are equal after all the adjusting entries and closing entries have been posted and all accounts have been balanced and ruled.

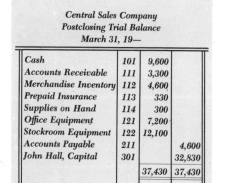

Central Sales Company Postclosing Trial Balance March 31, 19—			
Cash	101	9,600	
Accounts Receivable	111	3,300	
Merchandise Inventory	112	4,600	
Prepaid Insurance	113	330	
Supplies on Hand	114	300	
Office Equipment	121	7,200	
Stockroom Equipment	122	12,100	
Accounts Payable	211		4,600
John Hall, Capital	301		32,830
		37,430	37,430

Interpreting Financial Data

A major purpose for keeping accounting records is to provide data needed to make business decisions. Interpreting financial data is so important a function, it is often considered the final step in the accounting cycle. To facilitate interpretation, financial data is prepared in a number of ways by various employees. One way is to prepare a comparative income statement or a comparative balance sheet. The totals of the major parts of the income statement (Net Sales, Cost of Goods Sold, Gross Profit, Total Expenses, Net Income) can be compared with corresponding totals for previous years. Elements of the balance sheet can be compared to identify significant increases or decreases, so that any important trends can be observed. Management may also examine other areas, such as the details of accounts receivable, inventories, expenses, due dates for accounts payable, and capital needs for growth and expansion.

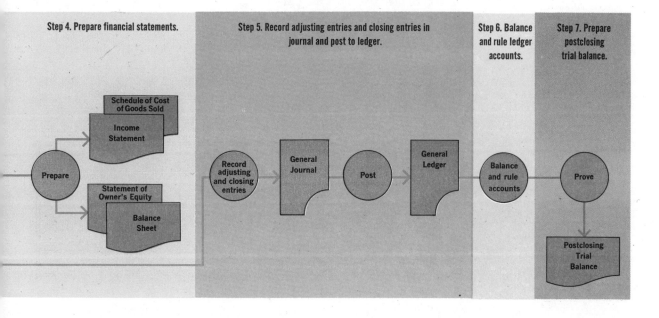

TOPIC 3 ■ PROBLEMS

50   Answer the following questions about the income statement shown on page 277 and the schedule of cost of goods sold shown on page 278.

a   Where is the data obtained for preparing the income statement?

b   What is the total amount of sales?

c   What is the net amount of sales?

d   Explain the difference between total sales and net sales.

e   How much is total purchases?

f   How much is the net purchases?

g   Explain the difference between total purchases and net purchases.

h   How much is the cost of goods available for sale? How was it obtained?

i   How much is the cost of goods sold?

j   Explain the difference between the cost of goods sold and the cost of goods available for sale.

k   How much is gross profit on sales?

l   How much is the net income?

m   Explain the difference between gross profit on sales and net income.

Answer these questions about the balance sheet shown on page 280.

n   Where is the information obtained for preparing the balance sheet?

o   Is the beginning or the ending merchandise inventory recorded on the balance sheet? Why?

p   Are there any prepaid expenses on the balance sheet? If so, what are the account titles and balances?

Answer these questions about the adjusting entries shown on page 282.

q   Where is the data obtained for making the adjusting entries?

r   Why was Prepaid Insurance credited for $30?

s   Was the ending inventory less than or more than the beginning inventory? by how much?

Answer these questions about the closing entries shown on pages 283 and 284.

t   Where was the data obtained for making the closing entries?

u   How was the $9,435 credit to the Income and Expense Summary account determined? What is the purpose of this entry?

v   How was the $7,805 debit to the Income and Expense Summary account obtained? What is the purpose of this entry?

51   Complete the following schedule of cost of goods sold.

J. A. Swanson Company
Schedule of Cost of Goods Sold
For the Quarter Ended March 31, 19—

Merchandise Inventory, January 1......................		8,400 00
Purchases..	6,375 00	
Less: Purchases Returns and Allowances.......... 85.00		
Purchases Discount...................... 120.00		
Net Purchases.......................................		
Cost of Goods Available for Sale......................		14,570 00
Less: Merchandise Inventory, March 31.................		9,100 00
Cost of Goods Sold...................................		

52 Supply the missing amounts in the following table.

	Beginning Inventory	Purchases	Purchases Returns	Purchases Discounts	Net Purchases	Cost of Goods Available for Sale	Ending Inventory	Cost of Goods Sold
a	2500	4000	?	400	3500	?	2000	?
b	3600	2400	50	150	?	?	3800	2000
c	?	3800	120	?	3100	7300	?	3300
d	3800	?	80	120	3000	?	4100	?
e	?	?	140	60	3400	8400	?	4300
f	6200	4100	120	80	?	?	6300	?

53 Complete these items using the data in the worksheet prepared for the Towne Men's Shop in Problem 48. (No additional investments were made during the month.)
  a Prepare an income statement with a schedule of cost of goods sold.
  b Prepare a statement of owner's equity and a balance sheet (account form).
  c Journalize the adjusting entries and the closing entries.

54 Complete these items using the data in the worksheet prepared for the Golden Record Store in Problem 49. (No additional investments were made during the month.)
  a Prepare a schedule of cost of goods sold and an income statement.
  b Prepare a statement of owner's equity and a balance sheet (in report form).
  c Journalize the adjusting and the closing entries.

The Language of Business

The following terms are important. Do you understand the meaning of each? Can you define each term and use it in an original sentence?

ending inventory	worksheet	gross profit on sales
beginning inventory	schedule of cost of goods sold	statement of owner's equity
prepaid expense	cost of goods available for sale	adjusting entry

Chapter Questions

1 An adjustment was not made to transfer $50 from the Prepaid Insurance account to the Insurance Expense account. What is the effect on net income? on total assets? on owner's equity?

2 Why does the total of the debits not equal the total of the credits in the Income Statement section of the worksheet? In the Balance Sheet section?

3 What procedure is followed to record the purchase of a prepaid expense? When and how is the expense recorded?

4 Describe the procedure followed to determine the cost of goods sold.

5 Describe the sequence that is followed in preparing the worksheet.

6 In what ways does the drawing account differ from the capital account?

Management Cases

Merchandise Turnover   The number of times each year that a business can convert its merchandise inventory into sales is known as merchandise turnover.

One way to compute the rate of merchandise turnover is to divide the number of units sold by the average number of units kept in inventory.

Units Sold ÷ Average Units in Stock = Rate of Merchandise Turnover

For example, the Great Fall Automobile Agency keeps on hand an average of 20 automobiles for customers to examine and test-drive. If it sells 200 automobiles during the year, the rate of merchandise turnover is 10 (200 ÷ 20 = 10).

This does not mean that each model on hand was sold and replaced 10 times. Some models may have been sold and replaced many more times than others. However, the *average* sale and replacement for all models was 10.

Another way to compute the rate of merchandise turnover is to divide the cost of goods sold by the average merchandise inventory.

Cost of Goods Sold ÷ Average Merchandise Inventory = Rate of Turnover

For example, the Walk-More Shoe Store had an average merchandise inventory of $20,000 during the year. The cost of goods sold during the year was $160,000. Thus the rate of merchandise turnover is 8. ($160,000 ÷ 20,000 = 8). This rate of turnover does not mean that each kind of shoes handled by the store was sold and repurchased 8 times. The rate is an average figure applicable to all merchandise in stock.

The merchandise turnover rate is important for two major reasons:

1   The more times a business can turn over its inventory, the more gross profit it may make. As a result, it may be able to lower its selling prices. Suppose a business purchases an item for $140 and sells it for $200. Each time this item is sold, the business makes a gross profit of $60. If the business can purchase and resell this item four times during the year (4 turnovers), it has a gross profit of $240 (4 × $60) on the item. If, however, the turnover rate is doubled (from 4 to 8 times), the business can sell the item for $180 and still have a larger gross profit.

$180 − $140 = $40 gross profit per item
  8 × $40 = $320 gross profit for year
$320 − $240 = $80 increase in gross profit.

2   The amount of capital that is required for a business depends in part upon its rate of merchandise turnover. For example, a business whose annual sales are twice its merchandise inventory must have a larger amount invested in its merchandise inventory than a business that converts its merchandise into sales 10 to 12 times yearly. With a merchandise turnover of 10, a merchandise inventory of $10,000 produces sales of $100,000. But if the turnover is only 2, an inventory of $50,000 is needed to produce sales of $100,000. To enable store owners and managers to compare their operations with those of similar businesses, the average rate of merchandise turnover for various types of businesses is compiled and published regularly.

Automotive accessories and parts stores	3.0	Shoe stores	1.8
Grocery and meat stores	13.5	Sports goods dealers	3.1
Hardware stores	2.1	Women's ready-to-wear shops	3.8

Case M-13

The Modern Dress Shop had an average merchandise inventory of $11,000 during the year. The cost of goods sold for the year was $32,000.

a What was the rate of merchandise turnover during the year?
b Was the turnover rate smaller or greater than that for similar stores?
c What would this information tell you about the store's operations?

Case M-14

This schedule of cost of goods sold was prepared for the N & N Sports Shop.

N & N Sports Shop
Schedule of Cost of Goods Sold
For the Year Ended December 31, 19—

Merchandise Inventory Jan. 1..........................	26,348 00	
Purchases..	105,405 00	
Cost of Goods Available for Sale.......................	131,753 00	
Less: Merchandise Inventory, Dec. 31....................	24,653 00	
Cost of Goods Sold................................		107,100 00

a What rate of merchandise turnover did the store have during the year? (The average merchandise inventory is obtained by adding the amounts of the January 1 inventory and the December 31 inventory and dividing by two.)
b Was the turnover rate smaller or greater than that for similar stores?
c The owner thinks the average inventory can be reduced 20 percent without affecting total sales by discontinuing some slow-moving items. If all other factors do not change, how many turnovers will occur next year?

Case M-15

Edward Malcolm plans to open an automotive accessories and parts store. He estimates that his sales for the year will total $225,600 and that his average gross profit will be 40 percent of sales.

If Mr. Malcolm is able to achieve the same rate of merchandise turnover as the average similar business, how large a merchandise inventory will he need to carry?

Working Hint

Using the Worksheet Efficiently

The worksheet is a timesaving device because the account titles need to be written only once; the amounts, not the titles, are extended to the appropriate columns. This arrangement can, however, present a problem in preparing the financial statements. The account titles appear at the extreme left side of the worksheet, and the balances of the accounts appear at the extreme right. Because of the distance between these columns, it is fairly easy to make an error by looking at the wrong line for the balance and then copying an incorrect amount.

This error can frequently be avoided by folding the worksheet so that the statement columns line up next to the account title column.

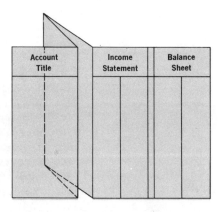

Project 3

Patrick Ryan, the owner of the Blue Ribbon Paint Store, has been keeping his own books. In addition to a petty cash book, he uses the following journals and ledgers:

cash receipts journal   sales journal   general ledger
cash payments journal   general journal   accounts payable ledger
purchases journal   accounts receivable ledger

The balance sheet he prepared on May 31 appears below.

Blue Ribbon Paint Store
Balance Sheet
May 31, 19—

Assets

Cash	$ 8,245
Merchandise Inventory	13,628
Store Supplies on Hand	20
Store Equipment	3,815
Total Assets	$25,708

Liabilities

Sales Tax Payable	$70

Owner's Equity

Patrick Ryan, Capital	25,638
Total Liabilities and Owner's Equity	$25,708

Mr. Ryan has asked you to assume responsibility for keeping his financial records. Therefore, perform the following activities for the month of June. The chart of accounts for the general ledger is listed below. (If you are not using the workbook, establish the accounts and record the balances shown on the balance sheet for May 31. Allow seven lines for Sales Tax Payable, six lines for Sales, and five lines for each of the other accounts.)

BLUE RIBBON PAINT STORE
CHART OF ACCOUNTS

101	Cash	399	Income and	503	Purchases Discount
102	Petty Cash		Expense Summary	504	Advertising Expense
103	Accounts Receivable	401	Sales	505	Cash Short and Over
104	Merchandise Inventory	402	Sales Returns	506	Donation Expense
105	Store Supplies on Hand		and Allowances	507	Miscellaneous Expense
106	Store Equipment	403	Sales Discount	508	Office Expense
201	Accounts Payable	501	Purchases	509	Rent Expense
202	Sales Tax Payable	502	Purchases Returns	510	Store Supplies Expense
301	Patrick Ryan, Capital		and Allowances	511	Telephone Expense
302	Patrick Ryan, Drawing				

The subsidiary ledgers have accounts for the following customers and creditors:

Accounts Receivable Ledger

Mason & Company
Wayne Decorators

Accounts Payable Ledger

Ford Brothers
Grove Mills

(If you are not using the workbook, establish accounts for the subsidiary ledger. Allow six lines for the account for Mason & Company and four lines for each of the other accounts.)

Journalizing the Transactions

1 Record the following transactions in the appropriate journal or petty cash book. On the dates indicated, prepare cash proofs to verify the checkbook balance; on the same dates, post from the special journals.

June 1 Enter memorandum entry in cash receipts journal for cash balance.

1 Received Invoice 4281, dated May 31, from Ford Brothers for merchandise purchased on credit for $640; terms 2/10, n/30.

1 Issued Check 305 for $110 to pay June rent.

2 Issued Invoice 843 to Mason & Company for merchandise sold on credit for $425, plus $4.25 sales tax; terms 2/10, n/30.

2 Issued Check 306 for $70 to remit sales tax collected during May.

3 Issued Check 307 for $30 to establish petty cash fund.

4 Received Invoice L15, dated June 2, from Grove Mills for merchandise purchased on credit for $875; terms 1/10, n/30.

5 Recorded $1,245.20 weekly cash sales and $12.45 sales tax.

5 Received Credit Memorandum C09 for $50 from Grove Mills for merchandise returned to them.

5 Deposited all cash in bank; checkbook balance is $9,292.65. Prepare cash proof to compare checkbook balance with Cash account balance. (Remember that the entries have not been posted to the Cash account.)

8 Issued Check 308 for $110 to Mr. Ryan, for personal use.

8 Paid $3.50 from petty cash for stamps.

June 9 Issued Invoice 844 to Wayne Decorators for merchandise sold on credit for $720; terms 2/10, n/30 (no sales tax, since company is out of state).

9 Issued Check 309 for $627.20 to Ford Brothers to pay Invoice 4281, less discount.

10 Paid $5 from petty cash for contribution to Boy Scouts.

10 Issued Check 310 for $26.80 to pay telephone bill.

11 Received Invoice 4405, dated June 10, from Ford Brothers for merchandise purchased on credit for $980; terms 2/10, n/30.

11 Received check for $420.75 from Mason & Company in payment of Invoice 843 of June 2, less discount (sales tax not included in computing discount).

12 Found that cash was short $5 when the cash proof was prepared for the cash register.

12 Recorded $1,580.10 weekly cash sales and $15.80 sales tax.

12 Deposited all cash in bank; checkbook balance is $10,540.30. Prepare a cash proof.

15 Paid $4 from petty cash for support of local fire company.

15 Issued Invoice 845 to Mason & Company for merchandise sold on credit for $480 plus $4.80 sales tax; terms 2/10, n/30.

June 15 Issued Check 311 for $32.60 to pay electric bill.

16 Issued Credit Memorandum CM41 for $30.30 to Mason & Company for returned merchandise of $30 plus $.30 sales tax.

16 Paid $4.60 from petty cash for stationery.

17 Received $2,000 check from Mr. Ryan as additional investment.

18 Issued Check 312 for $60 to M-R Supplies for store supplies.

19 Received $705.60 check from Wayne Decorators in payment of Invoice 844 of June 9, less discount.

19 Paid $4.75 from petty cash for advertising in newspaper.

19 Recorded $1,240.05 weekly cash sales and $12.40 sales tax.

19 Deposited all cash in bank; checkbook balance is $14,405.75. Prepare cash proof.

22 Paid $3.10 from petty cash for coffee (Miscellaneous Expense).

22 Received Invoice L371, dated June 20, from Grove Mills for merchandise purchased on credit for $635; terms 1/10, n/30.

June 23 Issued Check 313 for $180 to Mr. Ryan, for personal use.

24 Issued Invoice 846 to Wayne Decorators for merchandise sold on credit for $390; terms 2/10, n/30.

25 Issued Invoice 847 to Mason & Company for merchandise sold on credit for $720 plus $7.20 sales tax; terms 2/10, n/30.

26 Recorded $1,142.30 weekly cash sales and $11.42 sales tax.

26 Deposited all cash in bank; checkbook balance is $15,379.47. Prepare cash proof.

29 Issued Check 314 for $5,000 to Mr. Ryan, as a permanent withdrawal of part of his investment.

30 Issued Check 315 for $825 to Grove Mills to pay Invoice L15, less returns.

30 Issued Check 316 to replenish petty cash fund. Amount in petty cash box is $5.05. Prove the cash.

30 Checkbook balance is $9,529.52. Prepare a cash proof.

2 Foot, prove, and rule the journals.

Posting the Transactions
3 Post the entries from the journals to the appropriate accounts in the ledgers.

Proving the Accuracy of the Work
4 Prepare a schedule of accounts receivable; prove it with the controlling account.
5 Prepare a schedule of accounts payable and prove it with the controlling account.
6 Prepare a trial balance in the trial balance section of a worksheet.

Preparing the Statements
7 Complete the worksheet. A physical count of the merchandise showed an inventory of $10,930, and a count of the store supplies showed an inventory of $65.
8 Prepare a schedule of cost of goods sold and an income statement.
9 Prepare a statement of owner's equity and a balance sheet (account form).

Adjusting and Closing the Books
10 Journalize and post the adjusting entries.
11 Journalize and post the closing entries.

Preparing for the Next Accounting Period
12 Balance and rule the ledger accounts.

Proving the Accuracy of the Books
13 Prepare a postclosing trial balance.

Index